The Encyclopedia of Home Maintenance

The Encyclopedia of Home Maintenance

Edited by
Julian Worthington

ORBIS PUBLISHING
London

Printed in Hong Kong

Hard cover ISBN: 0 85613 320 5
Paperback ISBN: 0 85613 340 X

Acknowledgements *Advertising Arts* 142–144 (artwork),
148, 170–175 (artwork), 177–180) (artwork); *Arka Graph-
ics* 137–139 (artwork); *Don Bax* 129–130, 160; *Graham
Bingham* 108–111 (artwork); *Bissell Appliances* 83 (top);
Blue Hawk 128; *Click Systems Ltd* 146 (photos 3 and 4);
A Cheeseman/GBW Design 163; *Gordon Cramp Studio*
21, 103 (artwork); *Crown Copyright* (from Home Office
leaflet *Protect Your Home*) 168–169; *Crown Decorative
Products Ltd* 21 (photo); *Bill Easter* 61–64, 131–133
(artwork); *Esta Heating* 147 (photo 10); *Eugene Fleury*
112–115 (artwork), 150–151, 158–159, 185; *Harrison
Beacon Ltd* 104 (photo 3), 112–113 (photos), 115
(photo); *Hayward Art Group* 56–59, 84–85, 88–89 (artwork), 90–91, 121–123, 127, 154–155 (artwork); *Len
Huxter Associations/David Lewis* 19–21 (artwork); *ICI*
22 (inset), 107 (photo 10), 114 (right photo); *Jon
Isherwood* 77; *Archibald Kenrick & Sons Ltd* 146 (photos
6 & 7); *Dennis Mansell* (courtesy of *Crittall Warmlife*)
149, 154–156 (photos); *Ray Martin Art Services* 26–30;
Bill Mason 131 (photo); *Brian Mayor* 23–25;
Orbis/Langham Studios 9–14, 22, 33, 36–37, 38 (photo),
181, 182–184 (tools), 186–187; *Orbis/Peter Pugh-Cook* 8,
15–16, 39, 184 (workbench); *Orbis/Dudley Reed* 126;
Orbis/Terry Trott Cover, 1–7 (photos), 31, 42–45, 55,
65–69 (photos), 87, 88 (photo), 92 (photo), 94 (photo), 98
(photo), 104 (photo 5), 116, 120, 134, 140–144, 145,
152–153, 157, 161–162, 170–179 (photos); *Orbis Verlag*
78; *David Penney/Ed Stuart* 50–54, 124–125; *D St
Romaine* 137 (photo); *A Sanderson & Sons Ltd* 103
(photo), 106 (photos); *Studio Briggs* 40–41, 67–70 (artwork), 72–76, 80–82, 92–93 (artwork), 94–97 (artwork),
99–102, 135–136; *Tebrax Ltd* 146–147 (photos 5, 8 & 9);
Trewax Manufacturing Ltd 83 (bottom); *Velux Company
Ltd* 60; *Venner Artists* 32, 34–35, 38 (artwork), 117–119,
164–167; *Susan Weldon* 170 (logo), 176 (logo); *Peter
Weller* 48–49; *Elizabeth Whiting Agency* 46–47, 71 79, 104
(photo 4), 105 (photos 6 & 7), 107 (photo 11), 108–110
(photos), 114 (left photo).
We wish to thank the following for their co-operation in
the production of this book: Armitage Shanks Ltd,
Berger Paints, Boulton & Paul (Joinery Sales) Ltd,
Designers Guild, H & R Johnson Ltd, Latham Timber
Centres, Littner Hampton Ltd, MK Electric Ltd, Nairn
Floors and Osborne & Little Ltd.

Contents

Introduction

The home is a place every owner should be proud of and happy to live in. But getting it into that condition and keeping it that way can be an expensive business, particularly if it means using help from outside. Of course there are many things we would like to do with our home, but we are not always in a position to afford them. It is with thoughts such as these that we may be tempted to despair and wish on what might be. The good news to drive away the gloom is that there is a great deal we can do for ourselves to make the home look attractive and keep it running smoothly. The cost? Well, that comes down to the materials and equipment needed or chosen. The cost in terms of time – and patience – is down to the individual.

So where do you start? One very good place is our home encyclopedia. This carefully compiled, practical guide to jobs around the home gives a sound introduction to home improvement with instructions even the rawest beginner can follow and understand. Practical, stage-by-stage illustrations – in colour – and comprehensive but clear instructions will lead you successfully through all the routine jobs in the home and some which you may have thought about but decided against because they had always seemed too difficult.

To give the home a simple, immediate facelift, you will probably put decorating first on the list. But once a room has had a fresh coat of paint or new wallpaper, other aspects suddenly look horribly shabby – the flooring, for example, or the upholstery or curtains. Here, the encyclopedia tells you how to lay or repair the different types of flooring, how to restore worn furniture and how to make and hang new curtains.

Even when you have made the home look good, niggly little problems threaten to spoil the effect of your efforts. Perhaps it is that dripping tap or burst pipe, unsightly plumbing, floors and odd corners filled with piles of books and magazines through lack of shelves or a door that gets in the way because it opens the wrong way. Again the encyclopedia will come to your rescue.

And just as you sit down to admire your handywork and enjoy the fruits of your labours, a howling draught whistles round your legs, you notice a crack in the window you had not seen before or a brown envelope arrives through the letter-box carrying the latest gas or electricity bill. Again there is no need to despair, since ways of solving these problems are also contained in the many useful pages which follow.

So when the lights suddenly go out or you overstretch the vacuum cleaner and the cable comes out of the plug, you will know immediately what to do. Yes, even the elementary electrical jobs are included in this mine of useful information. And because you have spent so much of your time – and, of course, some money – on making your home a place to be proud of, you are certainly not going to want to entertain any unwelcome visitors. Yes, our home encyclopedia has not forgotten that you will want to lock up against intruders and protect your property.

However closely you follow the instructions, the jobs included in this publication will probably only be completely successful if you use the right tools. This need not involve you in an enormous expense, particularly if you choose carefully; but it is false economy to buy the cheapest without first inspecting the goods. As a general rule, always buy the best you can afford; you will be surprised how much easier it makes the job. A guide to basic tools and some accessories which will be useful in the home is included.

One of the secrets of successful work is careful and thorough planning. Often this may be quite a time-consuming job, particularly when it involves preparing walls or wood surfaces before decorating. But the end result will always justify the means and there is nothing more annoying or wasteful than finding faults when the work is finished and having to go back and do part or even all of it again. Time given to checking you have all you need in terms of equipment and quantity of materials is also well spent, especially when hanging wallpaper, for example; if you buy rolls from a different batch, the colours may not match and this will show up clearly when the wall is finished. Equally, when working on the plumbing system, it will be inconvenient enough to have to cut off the supply for the time the job would normally take. If you start it late in the day and discover you need something else after the shops have shut, no one is going to love you with no water in the home. All these points may seem very basic, but it is surprising how often they are overlooked.

One very valuable hint for those who may not feel immediately confident to tackle a particular job is to practise first. This may mean buying a little extra material or spending that much longer on the work, but it could mean the difference between success and failure – and the latter can prove very expensive in terms of both time and money, not to mention frustration. Confidence plays an important part whatever you are attempting; with it you should have no difficulty in handling all the jobs we describe.

It is inevitable that at some stage you are going to make a mess, whether you are working with paint or water or wood. However careful you set out to be, by the time you realise you should put down some protective covering it is usually too late. Whatever the job, it is always sound policy to protect everything in the immediate area of the work – and that includes yourself. Cover the floor and furniture with old sheets or newspapers, wear old clothes or overalls and keep plenty of rags handy for wiping up or cleaning off.

You may well be tempted to crack on and finish a particular job before the enthusiasm wears off. However admirable this attitude may seem, it will not always have the right effect on the quality of the work. Without realising it, you will find mistakes creeping in and maybe tempers fraying as you get tired. Make sure you have regular breaks – even if it is only for a cup of tea or coffee – if you know you are going to be spending several hours working. Not only will you eliminate those careless mistakes, but you will also keep in the right frame of mind until you have finished.

We hope this volume should prove one of the home's best friends. Refer to it whenever there is a maintenance or repair job to be done and follow stage-by-stage the right way to improve your valuable home.

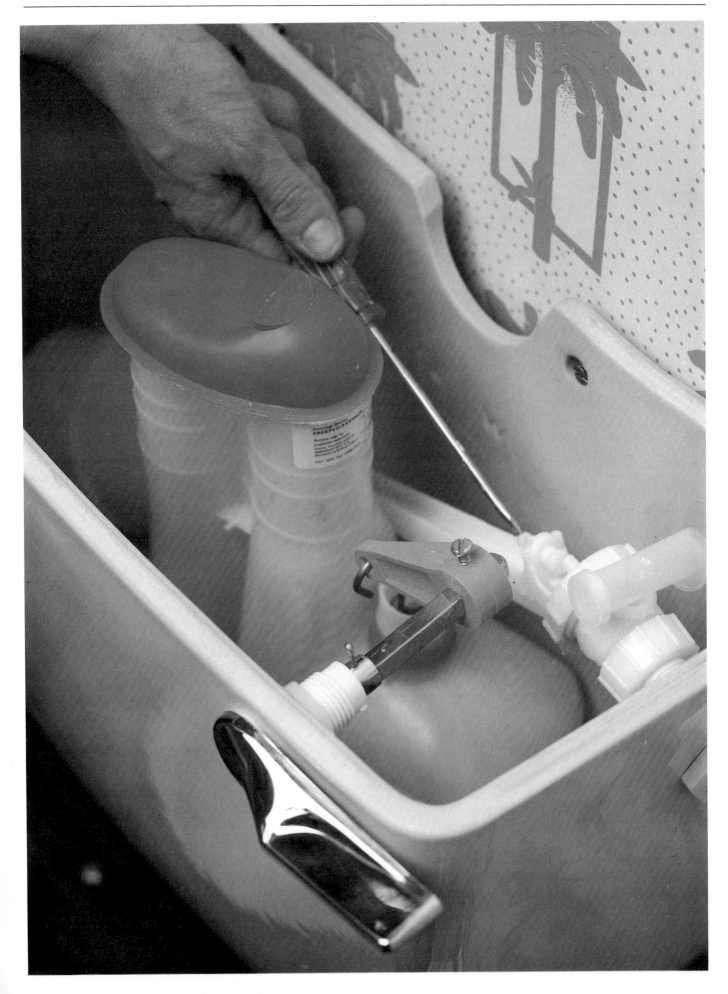

Decorating the home

Painting and wallpapering will transform any room in the home overnight. This section deals with the choice of equipment and materials, preparation and detailed instructions on application. Take care to prepare all surfaces to be decorated thoroughly and check on the correct order of work. Make sure you have the right equipment and enough materials to finish the job and always remember to clean up afterwards; paint brushes, for example, will soon be ruined if left full of paint. If you run into problems when painting, check the guide to faults to see why the job is going wrong.

Paints, brushes, rollers & pads

Until quite recently choosing paint for interior work was fairly straightforward – emulsion for walls and ceilings, gloss for woodwork – and the only real choice you had was on colours.

The real difference today is not in the paint groups themselves – still essentially emulsion and gloss – but in the manufacturing processes constantly being developed which have made it possible to produce several varieties of each type.

This enormous variety can be confusing at first, but once you have sorted out which type of paint is for which job you will find the choice of intermediate finishes they provide invaluable.

Thinning Any proprietary brand of paint is ready for use and should not require thinning. The one exception is with emulsion, where it might be necessary to thin slightly with water when applying the first coat on a porous surface such as raw plaster.

Range of types

Basically, paint is made up of pigment and either an oil or water-based binder. Water-based paint (emulsion, vinyl and latex) dries purely by evaporation, while oil-based paint has a chemical drying agent added. Paints with a water base are not as hard or durable as those with an oil base although they are improving all the time. The greatest advantage of water-based paint is that brushes and rollers can be washed in water; no special cleaning agent is needed.

The proportion of pigment to binder in any paint dictates the amount of gloss the finished product will have. The glossier the finish, the more hard-wearing it will be. There are three main categories of finish: matt, gloss and a range in between the two which varies according to the manufacturer and is designated in many different ways – silk, satin, semi-gloss, suede, eggshell etc.

The following brief description of types, uses and application should help you.

Gloss

This is oil-based and includes resin to give it a hard-wearing quality. The standard gloss that has been available for many years contains alkyd resin, but new manufacturing techniques have produced varying degrees of sheen, such as matt gloss and silk gloss.

Uses For woodwork and metal.

Application Prime and undercoat bare timber and key (rub down well with fine glasspaper) existing gloss finishes before repainting. If you are redecorating with a different colour gloss, obliterate the old colour with one or two layers of the appropriate undercoat.

The smell of the paint will linger for some time after application; allow several hours for drying.

Polyurethane gloss

Polyurethane resin added to oil-based paint makes it tougher, providing a really hard-wearing surface to withstand greater abrasion than standard gloss.

Uses For woodwork and metal.

Application Prime all bare surfaces; although undercoat is not always necessary, you might need to apply two top coats to get a really good finish.

Key existing gloss and then cover with one or two coats, depending on the previous colour.

Silthane

A combination of silicone and polyurethane, this paint is claimed by the manufacturers to be stronger than polyurethane as the silicone gives extra protection, especially during the drying period when paint is most vulnerable. Uses and application are as for polyurethane gloss.

Emulsion

Water-based, but with vinyl or acrylic resins incorporated to make it harder-wearing. This results in varying degrees of sheen in the finish, with a progressively durable surface as the shine increases. The range includes matt, eggshell, silk, satin and full gloss.

Uses Although normally intended for walls and ceilings, you can use it on woodwork, but be sure to use a water gloss type specially produced for woodwork and don't expect the same hard-wearing qualities as with oil-based paints.

Application Prime bare plaster with a plaster primer or a thinned coat of emulsion (water-diluted) before applying one or two top coats. For previously painted plaster use one or two neat (undiluted) coats of emulsion depending on the colour being covered. Existing gloss surfaces must be keyed with fine glasspaper.

If you have a distempered surface, such as a ceiling in an older house, scrape and wash away with sugar soap all traces of the distemper before attempting to paint. Seal with a special primer sealer and then apply one or two coats of emulsion.

This paint has a less pungent smell which does not linger after application and dries quickly, usually within two hours.

Thixotropic (non-drip)

An alternative type of gloss, this paint is non-drip and of a jelly-like consistency. It is ideal if you find difficulty in painting without drips falling from the brush, as its consistency allows a blob of paint to be picked up by the brush and then applied to the surface where it spreads out normally.

Uses For woodwork, metal and plaster.

Application Take all the normal preparatory precautions according to the surface before applying. Lightly brush out using random strokes and never overbrush as this will cause runs, thus defeating the object of using this particular type of paint.

Remember not to stir the paint before application, however much you are tempted to do so. It may look lumpy and unworkable, but that is the nature of the paint. Stirring will only break down the consistency and possibly ruin your finish. If you do stir the paint through force of habit, leave it for a while until it becomes jelly-like again. If you want to strain a thixotropic paint, stir first to a free-running liquid, strain and then leave to gel again.

Other types of paint

There are occasions when you will want to use a type other than the standard gloss or emulsion, according to the job in hand. These include certain paints with special properties for particular uses.

Primer This may be oil or water-based and is used to seal unpainted surfaces to prevent further coats of paint soaking in. It is vital to use the right type of primer for the surface being painted – wood, metal or plaster – although there is an all-purpose primer available.

Undercoat Usually oil-based, undercoat is applied between primer and top coats to build up the surface and provide the right colour base for the finish paint.

Enamel Term was used by manufacturers as synonymous with gloss; now commonly used to describe an alkyd modified paint.

Anti-condensation For use in steamy conditions, such as in kitchens and bathrooms, this paint is specially formulated to prevent the surface becoming cold to the touch and therefore less conducive to condensation. It is not a cure for condensation, only a way of reducing its effect on painted surfaces. (Normal emulsion paints are satisfactory here, provided the level of steam is not too high.)

Fire-retardant Containing an additive to provide a fire-resistant quality, this type will not resist fire completely, but has a greater resistance than ordinary paint and will reduce the spread of flames. Use it as an added safety measure on expanded polystyrene ceiling tiles or timber, hardboard and chipboard or any combustible surface which can be painted.

Anti-burglar Two types are available, both non-toxic. One remains slippery when dry and is used particularly to prevent people climbing walls. The other dries on the surface, but sticks to the hand when pressure is applied. White spirit will take off the paint, at the same time releasing a dye which cannot be removed.

Bituminous Thick and usually black, this is for areas where high water resistance is needed. Apply it with an old paint brush on the inside of your cast iron gutters and metal cold water tank.

Warning Never apply normal gloss or oil-based types over bituminous paint before applying a coat of aluminium sealer; otherwise the bitumen will bleed through and stain the fresh paint brown.

Paint brushes

Even with all the new additives and manufacturing processes now used to make painting easier, a first-class finish can often be ruined for want of a good paint brush. So don't waste your money on a cheap brush that will have a limited life but buy the best quality you can afford and look after it.

Pure hog's bristle This is the very best quality, with bristles set in rubber mastic which is then vulcanized to hold them firmly. The rough-textured bristles hold paint well and the natural taper at the tips enables you to apply a smooth, even coat.

1. 2 Radiator and crevice brushes. Long wire handles and shaped heads help painting in awkward areas
3 Cheap brush with short bristles gives acceptable finish, but top quality type with good bristle length produces best results
4 Side view shows the difference: go for well bulked springy bristles for a smooth finish

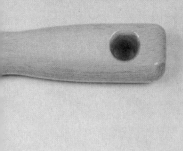

A good check for pure bristle is to bend the bristles back to 90 degrees to make sure they are well bulked and have a stiff, springy feel. A good length of bristle (known as the filling) is also important; so is price – the more you pay, the better the brush.

Artificial fibre bristle This is either cheap animal hair or nylon – the closest synthetic material to pure bristle. Although the bristles may be well bulked they will not have that all-important springy feel. And, being smoother, they will not hold the paint nearly so well or bind sufficiently at the tips. This will result in brush marks on the finished surface.

The worst of the cheap brushes contain the minimum of bristle, causing a 'mouth' through their centre. You can see this if you bend back the bristles and it becomes even more noticeable when dipped in the paint. This type of brush holds very little paint and the bristles are likely to work loose as you are painting. Even worse is when the ferrule (the metal band joined to the handle and covering the bristles) is loose and moves when in use.

Warning All brushes – even the best quality – will shed hairs at first; before you use one for the first time, dip it in clean water and brush it out on a rough surface such as an outside wall of your house. Wash it in soap and water to remove dust and any loose hairs, rinsing out thoroughly in clean, cold water. Finally, dry it out by first squeezing the bristles and then spinning the handle between your palms. Leave to dry.

Before using, ensure the brush is thoroughly dry, as moisture will affect your finish. This is particularly important with oil-based and gloss paint. With water-based and emulsion types, paint will trickle down the handle if the brush is damp, especially when working overhead.

Temporary storage

For short periods between painting you can wrap the bristles tightly in kitchen foil (which is preferable to putting the brush in water) as this will delay the paint from drying on the brush.

A brush to be used with oil-based paint frequently over several weeks is best stored by suspending the bristles in a container with a mixture of three parts white spirit (not paraffin) and one part linseed oil. Before using the brush again, wipe out the bulk of the liquid and brush off any surplus on a clean, dust-free piece of wood or hardboard. You can

keep the mixture topped up, but you will need to decant the liquid and remove the solid residue from time to time (**see Cleaning**).

Sizes and types

Brushes are available from 13mm ($\frac{1}{2}$in) bristle width to 150mm (6in). For a useful kit, start with a

5 Excellent quality, pure bristle brush for minimum effort and maximum coverage
6 Small straight brush for narrow areas
7 Smooth synthetic fibre brush does not hold paint so well as a pure bristle one and tends to leave brush marks on surface
8 Cutting-in brush for painting window frames without smudging onto glass

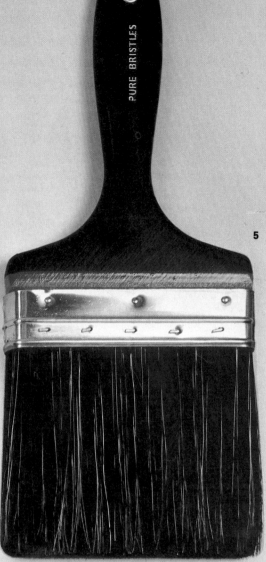

5

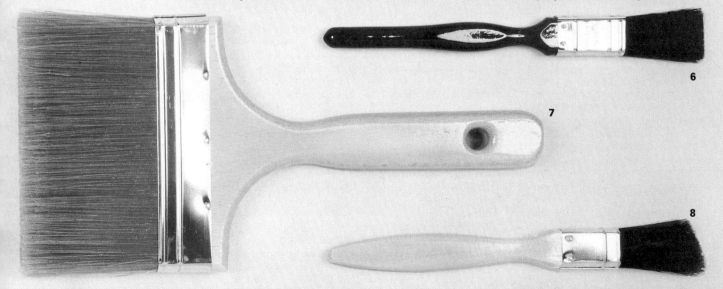

6

7

8

13mm and 25mm (1in) brush for narrow sections and a 50mm (2in) or 75mm (3in) one for larger flat surfaces, such as doors. Use the 75mm size on wet edges that have started to dry before they are joined up, as the larger brush will make for speedier work and eliminate the risk of runs appearing on the finished surface. For walls and ceilings a 100mm (4in) or 125mm (5in) brush will give a good quick finish with the maximum coverage and the minimum of effort, although the smaller size is less tiring to use – especially when there is a lot of overhead work to do.

With this range of brushes you will be able to apply most paints, interior and exterior. Don't throw away your old brushes, even if the bristles are worn down; they are ideal for painting inside gutters or dusting off glasspapered surfaces, so you can still make use of them.

In addition to orthodox brushes there are certain types intended to carry out a specific job. These you can buy as and when you need them.

Cutting-in brush Used for painting window frames, this 13mm ($\frac{1}{2}$in) wide brush has bristles cut at an angle to allow for the normal 3mm ($\frac{1}{8}$in) overlap onto the glass. (With an ordinary brush, even in the steadiest hand, you get smudges on the glass.) You can make one yourself by cutting to an angle the bristles of an old brush.

Crevice and radiator brushes The long wire handle can be bent to any shape and this, with the shaped head, allows you to paint awkward areas, such as behind radiators and pipes.

Paint rollers

These really come into their own on large areas of wall and ceiling. Provided you use the correct type for the job you will get as good a finish as with brushes or pads. Although better suited to emulsion and other water-based paints, rollers can be used to apply oil-based types, but the finish will be slightly stippled. Three basic types are available.

Foam The cheapest type and a good general purpose roller. It gives a reasonable finish and is best suited to the application of water-based paints. Don't overload it, as paint tends to drip easily from foam; if you press too hard paint will ooze out of the ends. If squashed while stored away, a roller will lose its shape. New sleeves can be fitted when necessary.

You can also use this type of roller for applying wallpaper paste – especially with wall coverings, where the paste is applied direct to the wall.

Mohair Here a short, fine pile sleeve is fixed to a rigid cylindrical frame which you can remove for cleaning. Suitable for use with all types of paint, it is ideal for the application of oil-based ones if you want a really smooth gloss finish.

Lamb's wool or nylon Available in a variety of pile lengths and thicknesses which will deal with many different types of surface, this is probably the most popular type of roller for applying water-based paints to walls and ceilings.

For the best results always match a roller to the surface you are painting. Follow the general rule of a smooth surface needing a short pile and a rough surface a longer one and you will not go far wrong. Pile lengths vary from 6mm ($\frac{1}{4}$in) to 31mm ($1\frac{1}{4}$in). Bearing in mind what type is best used where, choose either a foam, short pile mohair, lamb's wool or nylon roller for smooth or lightly textured surfaces. For highly textured surfaces pick

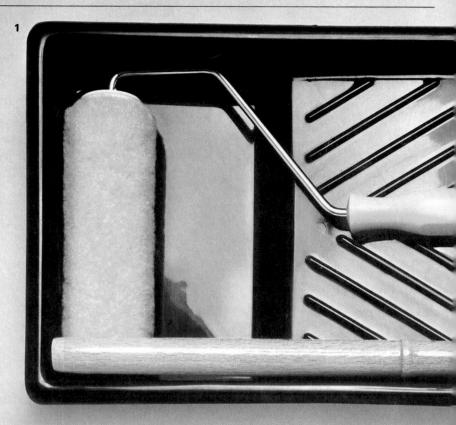

a long shaggy pile lamb's wool or nylon type. For outside walls buy a roller with a tougher pile specially designed for exterior use, as this will be more durable on rough surfaces such as stucco or pebbledash.

Warning Don't use a short pile roller on a heavily textured surface as the pile will not reach right into the indentations and the paint will not cover properly. Conversely a long, shaggy pile used on a smooth surface will coat too heavily.

Small rollers in a variety of pile types are available for reaching behind radiators and small pipes.

Other equipment

To load your roller ready for use you will need a special paint tray (sometimes supplied with it) which is sloped at one end. Pour the paint into the deep end and load the roller by rolling half the pile through the paint and moving up the slope to spread the paint evenly over the pile and remove any surplus.

To save cleaning the tray after use, line it with aluminium foil, which you can throw away when you have finished.

A step ladder with a top platform, on which to place the tray when painting ceilings, is essential unless your tray has special hooks that latch onto one of the top steps.

If you do not have a step ladder you can paint ceilings from ground level with a hollow-handled roller into which you insert a long pole.

For corners and edges you will need a 25mm (1in) paint brush. Paint these areas first, working round the perimeter of the ceiling.

Using a roller

To avoid splashes make sure the roller is not overloaded. Remove any excess while it is still in the tray. Take it carefully to the work surface to avoid 'spinning' and when it needs reloading never pull or push it sharply from the surface.

1 Synthetic pile roller with extension handle and plastic tray supplied
2 Plastic form roller – general purpose, but specially good if using emulsion
3 Medium pile sheepskin – for covering textured surfaces
4 Simulated sheepskin pile – for smooth walls and ceilings
5 Short, fine pile mohair type gives really smooth finish with gloss paint

however, you do want to roll on oil-based paints it is better to keep two rollers, one for each type. Store the roller, when cleaned and dry, in a polythene bag (**see Cleaning**).

Warning Avoid using a roller with water-based paints over long periods in excessively hot weather, because the paint tends to dry hard on the pile. If you are painting in these conditions, wash out the roller once or twice when you reach a natural breaking-off point, such as the end of a wall.

Paint pads

Pads are becoming increasingly popular, especially for use on walls and ceilings, because they are simpler, quicker and less tiring to use than brushes.

The basic pad is a foam rectangle fixed to a metal or plastic handle, with fine mohair pile 'bristles' on the surface of the foam. Sizes vary from 62×50mm ($2\frac{1}{2} \times 2$in) to 228×101mm (9×4in), the largest size being ideal for ceilings and walls and the smallest for doors, skirtings and narrow sections. There are special pads for window frames, mouldings and radiators.

As well as individual pads, you can also buy sets of various sizes, sometimes including a handy paint trough incorporating a plastic roller. This roller transfers paint from the trough to the pad, ensuring it is not overloaded.

The more usual loading method is direct from the can, paint kettle or an old metal tray. Remember when loading to cover only the mohair and wipe off the excess onto the container before painting. A thin, all-over coating of paint on the pile is all you need for successful application.

Some pads can be detached from the handle, making replacement easy. A hollow-handle type is available to take a broom handle which can act as an extension pole.

Pads will cope quickly with smooth walls and ceilings; they will also give a good covering to

Use the roller in random directions in a crisscross pattern (to ensure even distribution of the paint) and join up all these 'wet' patterns before the paint has started to dry. This will be no problem as rolling paint is far quicker than working with a brush.

Though oil-based paints can be cleaned off, it is a long, messy job and we recommend you keep your roller for use with water-based paints only. If,

lightly textured surfaces. Unfortunately the short pile will not cope with deeper textures without using excessive pressure, causing the paint to ooze out and drip from the foam backing.

Using a pad

You must first rub the pad over your hand to remove any loose pile. Load it carefully, use with random strokes and don't brush out too far before reloading. Clean cutting into corners is a big advantage with a pad, but if you are painting up to wallpaper which is not going to be changed it might be easier to finish off the edges with a 25mm (1in) paint brush. Provided you load and use a pad correctly, you can work quickly with far less danger of splashing than with a brush or roller.

Keep old pads, even when the pile has worn down, as they will be useful for odd jobs such as soaking wallpaper prior to stripping or applying size to walls.

Cleaning

This is always an unpopular job, but if you want to ensure a long life for your painting equipment you must clean it thoroughly after use.

Brushes Wipe off surplus oil-based paint by running the bristles across the back of a knife over the open paint can or newspaper. Then half-fill a container (a jam jar or old bowl will do) with white spirit (turpentine substitute) to clean off what is left. Press the bristles well into the liquid before removing and wiping dry with a rag. Cleaning off the final traces of paint is easier if you rub a little linseed oil well into the bristles before finally washing out with warm water and washing-up liquid or kitchen soap. Then rinse in cold water, shake well and hang up to dry. (If necessary make a hole in the handle to take a piece of wire or string for hanging.)

You can use this cleaning liquid again if you keep it in a screw-top jar, but decant it and leave behind the sediment. Proprietary brush cleaners in liquid form are effective, but costly, and usually have a pungent smell.

Follow the same procedure for water-based paints, but use only warm water and washing-up liquid and then rinse in cold water.

Rollers and pads Clean immediately after use or the pile will stiffen and clog and be ruined. Both rollers and pads are better used with water-based paints as they only require thorough washing under a running tap – hot or cold. If, however, you use them with oil-based paints you must go through the same method of cleaning as for brushes. Use the roller tray for cleaning so you wash the tray at the same time. If you previously kept the tray clean with a layer of kitchen foil, you may prefer to use your old bowl for cleaning off or line the tray with a clean piece of foil and clean the roller in that. Hang up rollers to dry since if you leave them lying around they will develop a flat edge.

Storing

Before storing away brushes, wrap them in newspaper or brown paper, folding carefully so as to keep a square end to the bristles, and secure around the ferrule with an elastic band or string. Don't leave them unwrapped or moths may get at the bristles. Once dry, rollers and pads can be stored flat and unwrapped in a paint tray.

1 Large general purpose paint pad with hollow handle to take extension pole
2 Crevice pad for painting behind pipes. **3** Wand type for painting mouldings

4 Small pad good for lightly textured surfaces
5 Shield pad with guard on one side to protect glass when painting window frames
6 Paint trough with roller to ensure you get right amount of paint on pad

Stripping paint

A new coat of paint can transform a room. But you'll be wasting your time if you don't make sure the surface is properly prepared.

A sound paint film, even if it is several layers thick, is a perfectly suitable base for repainting. Just give it a quick rub down with medium coarse glasspaper wrapped round a wood or cork block, dust well and the surface is keyed ready for its first coat.

A heavy build-up of paint on the closing edges of doors and windows can result in sticking and adding another coat of paint on top of the old layers will only accentuate this problem. There is no need to remove the old paint from the whole surface though; trimming away from the edges themselves is sufficient.

If the paint is peeling, pitted, badly chipped or crazed, however, then the only way you will achieve a satisfactory and long-lasting surface is to strip back to bare wood ready for filling and making smooth before starting to repaint.

There are three ways of stripping: by hand (or mechanical) sanding or applying chemicals or heat.

Hand sanding

This method is suitable only when a very thin film of paint has to be removed. Use a piece of medium coarse wet and dry glasspaper wrapped round a wood or cork block and be prepared to exert plenty of elbow grease when rubbing. Wetting this type of glasspaper reduces the spread of dust.

Mechanical sanding

There are various sanding attachments for electric drills, but circular ones are not easy to work with and there is a real danger of scoring the wood if the correct technique is not used. If the wood is scored, you will have to do a great deal of repair work before you can repaint it.

A drum sander is the best attachment to use. This comprises a foam drum onto which an abrasive belt is fixed. The belt action is along the grain so avoiding any circular scuffs to the surface of the wood. The action is efficient and quick, the only drawback being excessive dust.

Various grades of abrasive belts – from coarse to fine – should be used. When dealing with a really thick film start with a coarse grade and switch to a fine grade for the final sweep. After a quick dusting

Left Remove thick paint film evenly with drum sander which does not damage wood
Below Take off heavy coats of bad paintwork rapidly with paint and varnish remover attachment

Above Bad paintwork needs stripping before repainting
Below Remove thin film of paint with medium coarse glasspaper round block

down and a wipe with a cloth dampened with white spirit, you can begin repainting.

You can take off a heavy coat of paint more rapidly with a special power drill accessory known as a paint and varnish remover. This is a chuck-held metal disc with perforations punched through the surface to allow the loosened material to pass through the disc without clogging.

When sanding, take the work outside whenever possible to avoid too much mess indoors and, for personal safety, use a dust mask (or a handkerchief tied to cover up your nose and mouth) and protective spectacles or goggles.

Chemical stripping

Decorating shops stock chemical strippers under various brand names. Use a jelly type as it will adhere to the paint longer and will not run on vertical surfaces.

Chemical stripper can be expensive so it is not really suitable for large areas, nor where a thick film of paint has to be removed as two or even three applications may be needed before bare wood is reached. Pour a little of the stripper into a metal container and, using an old paint brush, apply liberally. After a few seconds the paint will start to shrivel and you can remove it with a flat paint scraper. Keep this as upright as possible to prevent digging into the wood and damaging the surface.

To strip paint from mouldings or other awkward crevices use a shave-hook. The best type is a heart-shaped scraper which has a series of intricate shapes around the workhead for dealing with all types of angles and curves.

When all the old paint has been removed, apply a thin layer of stripper and finish off by rubbing over the surface with medium steel wool. To make the wool last longer, tear off small amounts from the main ball and, as you work, turn the piece inside out until all the edges have been used. This final rub over will remove all small nibs of paint not obvious to the eye.

Chemical stripper will remain in small traces on the surface and must be neutralized before applying fresh paint. So, using a constant supply of clean rags, wipe down the surface thoroughly with white spirit or the solvent recommended by the brand manufacturer.

You must wear an old pair of leather or thick rubber gloves, protective spectacles or goggles and preferably a dust mask as well. And remember to protect the floor covering with newspapers.

Heat stripping

Blowtorches have come a long way since the days when they were filled with paraffin or methylated spirit and needed energetic pumping before igniting. Today they are much easier to use since the simple burner head unit fits onto a throw-away gas cartridge. When ignited you can adjust the power of the flame by turning a ridged screw. Before tackling your surface, it is worth getting the feel of the blowtorch by practising on a scrap piece of painted wood. Hold the blowtorch at a constant distance, about 150–200mm (6–8in) from the paintwork. Play it back and forth across a small area and when the paint starts to wrinkle and melt it is ready for scraping off. If the paint sticks, play the flame over the area again and resume scraping.

Warning Take care not to scorch the wood by concentrating the flame for too long on one spot. Switch to a chemical stripper if the paint is thick in

mouldings and around window frames, where a build-up of heat can easily crack the glass.

If you do scorch the wood, glasspaper or scrape back to bare wood before repainting.

As with chemical stripping, some paint particles will be left and these should be glasspapered down.

Be careful when using the flame under the house eaves as birds often build their nests here and these can be easily set alight. When you are working near open windows, tie back the curtains and place a metal sheet on the floor to catch the hot paint peelings. Wear an old pair of leather or rubber gloves and protective spectacles or goggles.

For hand sanding/finishing off
medium coarse wet and dry glasspaper
wood or cork block

For mechanical sanding
drum sander, abrasive belts, white spirit
protective spectacles or goggles
dust mask

For chemical or heat stripping
chemical stripper or blowtorch
paint scraper, shave-hook
leather or rubber gloves, protective
    spectacles or goggles, metal sheet
metal container, old paint brush, medium
    steel wool, white spirit (for chemical
    stripping)

equipment

Top left Apply chemical stripper liberally with old paint brush
Top right Use shave-hook to remove blistered paint from mouldings and crevices
Centre Make sure paint has shrivelled sufficiently before scraping it off
Above left Keep blowtorch moving at constant distance from paintwork. Scrape off paint as soon as it blisters
Above right Priming paint will not adhere to scorched timber so any charring must be scraped back to sound surface before repainting

Guide to painting faults

Cause	Prevention	Remedy
Pimples Particularly noticeable in shiny, gloss surfaces, these are caused by specks of dust which may have been on the surface, on the brush or in the paint itself. Or a very fine skin on the surface of the paint (especially non-drip gloss) may have got broken and worked into the paint on application.	Make sure the surface is clean and free of dust at each stage of the work: after burning off or rubbing down, and before applying primer, undercoat and top coat. Clean the surface with a tacky (resin-impregnated) rag or a clean, lint-free one dampened with methylated spirit. Pay particular attention to corners since pockets of dust here, though difficult to clean with a rag, will be picked up on the brush and spread across the surface. Use a pointed stick under the rag to ensure every particle of dust is removed from the corners. Paint brushes must be cleaned and even new brushes need rinsing before use as the bristles will contain some dust and loose hairs. Wipe the lid and rim of the paint can before removing the lid otherwise any dust will fall into the tin. It is a good idea to transfer a small amount of paint into a clean paint kettle or other container and work from this. If dust falls into the kettle only a small amount of paint will be affected. Clean the room thoroughly before starting work and allow time for dust to settle before using paint.	Don't try to remove specks while the paint is still wet as you will only add to the problem by smearing the paint. Allow the paint to harden for several days; even though it may seem dry after a few hours, only the surface will have dried. Rub down the affected areas with fine wet and dry glasspaper, wash with clean water, dry thoroughly and apply a new finishing coat. Skin often forms on old paint. If you spot it, carefully lift it away before stirring; if it is extremely thin you can stir it into the paint and then strain the paint through fine muslin or mesh.
Flaking Paint falling away from surface is due to poor preparation or bad use of primer. It can take weeks to show and will usually be confined to small areas on the surface.	Clean and prepare the surface thoroughly. If stripping back to bare wood apply a suitable primer. Emulsion flaking from walls or ceilings normally means you have applied the paint over distemper. Before painting, remove distemper by washing and scraping off the loose material, covering the remainder with a coat of primer sealer.	If flaking occurs in small patches, strip these areas back to the bare surface, fill depressions with fine surface filler and repaint. If flaking is extensive, however, you will have to strip off the whole lot and start again.
Slow drying Sometimes paint (particularly oil-based paint) will take a few weeks to dry or even remain permanently tacky. This indicates you applied the paint over a dirty or greasy surface, used an unsuitable thinner or did not stir the paint before applying.	Clean and prepare your surface thoroughly paying particular attention to skirtings which tend to collect a build-up of polish from the floor. Always stir the paint. You can add a small amount of proprietary dryer to stocks of old paint but never to new paint, which should be returned to the manufacturer for testing.	If the room is badly ventilated, open the windows for a few days to see if this accelerates drying. If not you will have to strip off all the paint with thinners and start again or refer to the manufacturer for advice.
Blisters Mostly affecting exterior woodwork, blisters can vary in size from pin heads to large areas. The cause is moisture in the wood or on the surface, trapped between coats of paint, or there may be resinous knots in the wood. Another less common cause is painting over a soft, thick coat. The action of very strong sunshine when any of these conditions exist is likely to cause blistering.	Try to paint external woodwork towards the end of the summer when, ideally, it should have dried out completely. If this is not possible, try to paint in dry, warm conditions. Don't paint immediately after rainfall or washing down, unless the surfaces are thoroughly dried off. Strip off any thick, soft paint and always apply knotting to all resinous areas after stripping back to bare wood.	Cut off the surface of the blister and with fine wet and dry glasspaper rub back to a sound surface – or bare wood if blistering is extensive. Apply knotting and primer as necessary, fill depressions with fine surface filler and apply undercoat and top coat.
Runs, sags and wrinkles Fine lines or drips on a painted surface result from bad application. Wrinkles are likely to occur on thick, sagging paint.	Do not overload the brush and always brush out each application before adding another. Look at the paint five minutes after application; it may still be possible to brush out any runs.	If you notice runs before the paint has started to dry, brush them out lightly; if paint is drying, you will smear the surface. Or treat as for **Pimples**.
Dull gloss Dull finish occurs if thinners used wrongly, surface not properly primed or undercoated, undercoat not given time to dry or finish over-brushed or painted in damp or frosty conditions.	Prepare thoroughly. Leave the undercoat to dry for the recommended time, avoid using a thinner in gloss paint and do not apply in damp or frosty weather conditions.	Allow the paint to dry, then rub down lightly with fine glasspaper, dust off and apply a new finishing coat.
Grinning The colour of the previous coat shows through the dry paint film indicating another coat is needed. Grinning may also occur if you use the wrong undercoat, do not stir paint sufficiently, thin it too much or overbrush finishing coat.	Use the correct undercoat and the recommended number of finishing coats. Make sure you stir the paint according to the manufacturer's instructions. Never brush out the finishing coat too far.	Apply extra finishing coats as needed.
Brush marks These can be seen in the finished paint. The cause is insufficient rubbing down of the old paint surface, faulty application (applying the paint too thickly and not brushing out correctly) or using poor quality brushes.	Carefully prepare the surface, making sure poor paint is rubbed right back. Apply the paint evenly and finish brushing out in the direction of the grain. Slightly thin excessively thick paint and always use good quality brushes.	As for **Pimples**.

Painting doors, walls & windows

General preparation

For general woodwork wash down the surface with sugar soap, washing soda or a proprietary paint cleaner, rinse off with plenty of clean water and allow to dry thoroughly. Fill in any cracks or holes in the wood with a proprietary wood filler. Make a key for the new paint by lightly rubbing down the old gloss to remove the shine with medium fine wet and dry glasspaper wrapped round a wood or cork block. Lightly wet the glasspaper to reduce the spread of dust and rub with the grain.

With painted walls wash down as for woodwork to remove all grease and dirt. If gloss paint has been used previously, key the surface with wet and dry glasspaper wrapped round a wood or cork block. Fill any cracks in the plaster with proprietary plaster filler, glasspapering smooth when dry. Make good any damaged plaster.

Painting techniques

When you apply free-flowing oil-based paints with a brush, spread and lay off the paint in the following way to avoid runs and sags. Spread a liberal coat using strong pressure on the bristles, finishing with long parallel strokes along the grain. Wiping any surplus paint on the sides of the can or paint kettle, apply lighter strokes across the surface to provide an even spread. Finally lay off with lighter strokes from the tips of the bristles along the original direction.

With emulsion paints, which are water-based and usually heavy bodied, or the gel type non-drip gloss paints (thixotropic), use the minimum of brushing out. Apply with even, random strokes to ensure a full application without paint running.

Keep the brushing of non-drip gloss to a minimum, as too much brushing or over-stirring will only make the paint too thin.

A second coat of gloss can be applied within 12–24 hours. Alternatively leave the paint at least four days to harden, then lightly rub down the surface with fine glasspaper and dust off before applying a second coat.

Always wipe the surface of the paint with a lint-free rag when dusting off before the second coat.

Painting walls

Paint a complete wall without a break to avoid edges showing through. If you have to stop, make sure you break off when you reach a corner, such as on a chimney-breast. Use a 100 or 130mm (4 or 5in) brush, paint pad or roller, working away from the natural light to see where you have painted. With emulsion paint work in 300mm (or 12in) deep horizontal strips across the wall in downward strokes, starting at the top. With oil-based paint work in 600mm (or 24in) squares (**see 1a and 1b**). If the paint is drying too quickly and the edges cannot be joined up in time to avoid unsightly marks, lower the temperature by turning off any heating to slow down drying. Reverse the procedure when work is complete to accelerate drying.

Painting over wallpaper

Some textured papers provide an ideal surface on which to paint, but thinner types can present problems. Make sure the paper is well stuck down

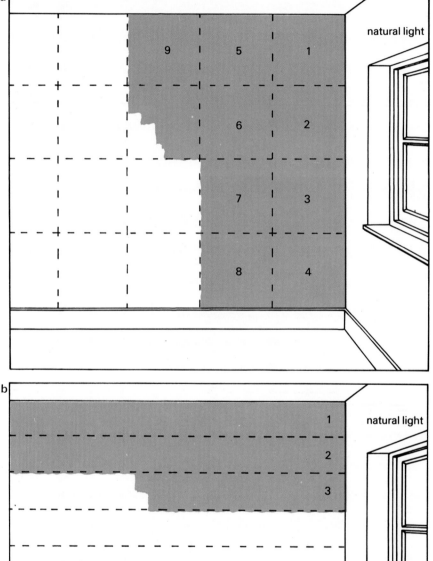

1a

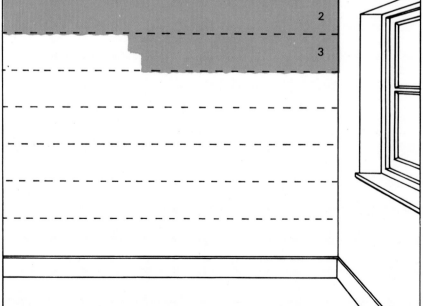

1b

Below left When applying oil-based paint to walls, work in 600mm (or 24in) squares and start at the top corner nearest the window. Complete the ceiling-to-floor area before starting the next strip and work away from the natural light

Bottom left When applying emulsion, work across the wall, again away from the natural light, with downward strokes in horizontal strips 300mm (or 12in) deep

Below Before painting window frames remove flaking paint and dirt right back to bare wood if necessary, with a paint scraper. Prime exposed wood before applying undercoat and top coat

Bottom centre Use a metal paint shield to prevent getting excess paint on the glass but allow for a 3mm ($\frac{1}{8}$in) strip of paint on the glass to keep moisture off putty

Bottom right Alternatively use masking tape, again allowing for a narrow strip of paint on the glass. Always remove the masking tape while the paint is still tacky

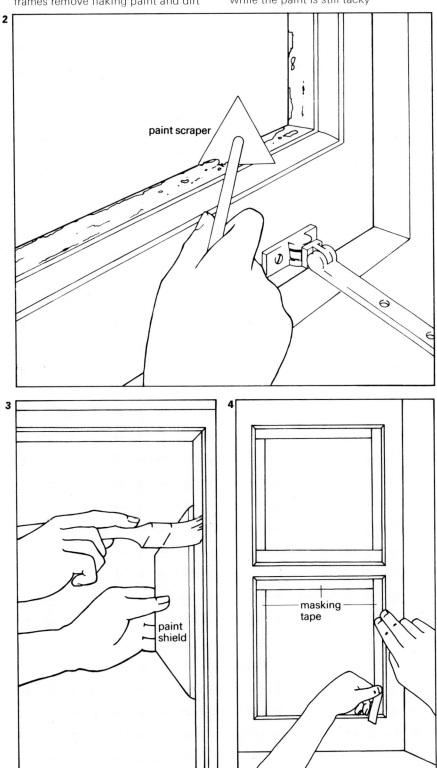

2

paint scraper

3

paint shield

4

masking tape

because the paint can soften the paper and cause it to bubble. The safest way to check the possible results is first to paint a small inconspicuous area, such as behind a piece of furniture permanently placed against the wall. If bubbles result you will either have to make minor repairs to the paper in the same way as for ceiling bubbles or strip off the paper completely.

You may find the texture or pattern of some papers will still show through, even after two or three coats of paint, and seams between lengths that were overlapped when hung will become more evident.

Painting doors
First remove handles, keyhole plates, finger plates and coat hooks to give yourself an uninterrupted surface. If you try to paint round these they will cause a build-up of paint, leading to unsightly runs. Clean out the keyholes to remove dirt and grease, which otherwise will be picked up on the brush and transferred to the rest of the work. It is a good idea to paint the top of the door as well, because although it is not normally visible it will make cleaning that much easier. Open the door and fix it in position with a wedge underneath, leaving both hands free for painting. This will also ensure the door stays where it is until the paint has dried.

Plan to finish painting each area in one session to avoid the edge line showing up where painting is restarted.

Panel doors Preferably use a 50mm (2in) brush, although you can use a 25mm (1in) one to make it easier to cut into mouldings. Don't overload the brush when painting the mouldings, as a build-up of paint will cause runs.

Flush doors A 60mm (2½in) or 75mm (3in) brush is best; if you prefer, a pad or suitable roller can be used. Any of these will enable you to complete the work quickly and join up all the edges before they start to dry.

When painting hinges, clean out the newly painted screw slots with a screwdriver before the paint has started to dry. Wipe the blade immediately after use. Clearing the slots is essential as you may want to remove the door at a later stage or adjust the hinges.

Painting window frames
Pay particular attention to preparing the bottom of the frame to ensure the finished surface is as good as the rest. Clear away all flaking paintwork and dirt, right back to bare wood if necessary **(see 2)**.

Flaking and general deterioration are caused by moisture from condensation running down the glass and mixing with the dust that collects on the frame. Prepare this part of the frame well or it will only deteriorate soon after being repainted. Prime bare wood before using undercoat and gloss.

Always brush about 3mm ($\frac{1}{8}$in) of paint onto the glass to prevent moisture getting into the putty and breaking it up. You may find it easier to use a cutting-in brush, specially angled for this job.

Alternatives are a metal paint shield **(see 3)**, which you rest on the glass at the correct distance from the frame, or masking tape **(see 4)**. If you use tape make sure to remove it while the paint is still tacky. If you leave it until the paint is dry you run the risk of pulling away the paint on the frame.

The general rule for painting frames is to paint any surfaces which show inside the room when the window is open in the interior colour.

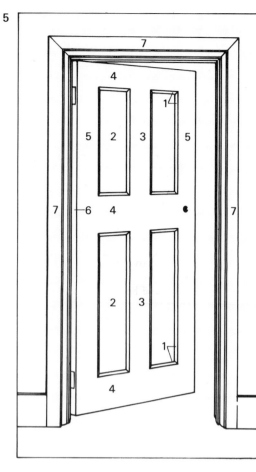

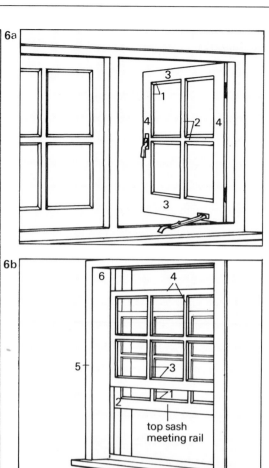

If you have to shut the door or window after painting, work first on the surfaces that come into contact when closed, to give them time to dry thoroughly

Left Always start with the panel or bead inside edge sections on panelled door (1)

Far left Follow same pattern for a casement window

Below left Paint a sash window in the same way, but first pull down the top sash and lift the bottom one to get at the top sash meeting rail. You need only paint those sections of the runners (5) that show when the window is open. Don't get paint on the cords or you will weaken them

Order of painting

The order shown for doors (**see 5**) and window frames (**see 6a and 6b**) is the one used by professionals and is very convenient. Complete the handle side last to make it easier to open and close during work, unless doors and windows have to be closed when painting has finished. In this case surfaces that come into contact when the door or window is closed must be painted first to allow for the longest possible drying time.

Warning If you touch a tacky surface with soft clothing, for example, that leaves bits on the paint don't rush in with a rag. Wait two or three weeks for the surface to harden thoroughly before gently rubbing down with fine wet and dry glasspaper, lightly wetted. Then dry off the surface and apply another top coat over the affected area.

Painting faults

Paint itself is rarely to blame for faults in the paintwork since reputable brands are subjected to careful quality control by the manufacturers. The following are the major causes of poor results.

- Poor surface preparation
- Getting dust in the paint
- Poor, incorrect or dirty equipment
- Faulty application technique
- Unsuitable paint for the job
- Adverse weather conditions

Causes of the common faults, their prevention and remedies are given with each section, but remember faults may arise through more than one factor.

Use colour to emphasize interior features – dark tones up to dado rail to contrast with walls, door and white mouldings (Crown scheme)

Wallpapering: what you need

As with all jobs around the home, if you have the right equipment you will make your task much easier. Although not all the items shown here are essential, you should use as many of them as you can to ensure the best possible results when papering a wall or ceiling.

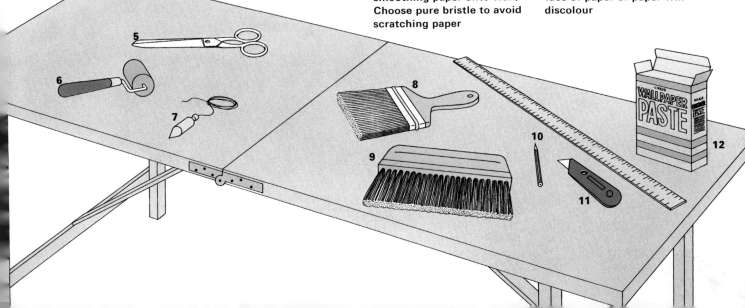

1 Working platform Essential to do a good job safely. Hire, buy or borrow two step ladders and a good scaffold board to give easy access to ceilings and top parts of walls

2 Paperhanger's apron Not essential, but has large pockets to carry brush and shears and so saves you time getting up and down step ladder fetching them. Could improvise by hanging plastic carrier bag at top of ladder

3 Paste bucket Must hold reasonable amount of paste. Line inside with polythene to save cleaning out. Tie piece of string across middle of bucket to rest brush on

4 Pasting table Can use kitchen table or board on trestles; but lightweight foldaway pasting table, about 1800 × 600mm (6 × 2ft), is convenient and inexpensive

5 Shears Paperhanger's shears, about 200–300mm (8–12in) long, ensure good, clean cuts

6 Wood seam roller Not essential, but handy for smoothing joins between lengths. Don't use on embossed paper as it will flatten pattern

7 Plumb bob To mark true verticals on walls as guide to hanging paper. You can make your own by tying string to balanced weight.

8 Paste brush Use old 125 or 150mm (5 or 6in) distemper brush

9 Paper-hanging brush For smoothing paper onto wall, Choose pure bristle to avoid scratching paper

10 Pencil and metal straight-edge For marking and measuring

11 Trimming knife For making intricate cuts round fittings and for trimming edges

12 Wallpaper paste Always use adhesive specified by wallpaper manufacturer and follow mixing instructions exactly. If you use wrong paste, paper might not stick properly or mould might develop behind paper. Don't get adhesive on decorative face of paper or paper will discolour

First steps to wallpapering

Once you know the advantages of special types of paper and pattern effects you will be able to choose the right wallpaper for your needs and get on with the surface preparation.

When it comes to choosing wallpaper, go for better quality, medium or heavyweight papers rather than thin, cheap ones which tear and stretch easily when pasted and need very careful handling. Cheaper wallpapers have the design printed directly onto the paper; better quality papers are usually given a protective coating before the pattern is printed. Top quality ones also have a clear coating over the pattern to protect the surface.

Basic types
The following run-down on the various types available will help you to select the right wallpaper for specific areas.

Washable The paper is covered with a clear water-resistant coating of matt or gloss PVA (polyvinyl acetate) making it ideal for use in the kitchen or bathroom.

Vinyl A layer of PVC (polyvinyl chloride) is fused onto a paper backing to produce a really tough vinyl-faced covering that is steam and water-resistant and can even be scrubbed clean.

Ready-pasted Dried fungicidal adhesive on the back does away with the traditional pasting operation. To activate the paste you draw each length of paper through a water-filled trough (usually supplied with the paper) immediately before hanging.

Polyethylene This type, such as Novamura, is lighter than ordinary wallpaper and warm to the touch. It is easier and quicker to hang than other wall coverings because you paste the wall rather than the paper and you do not have to cut the paper into lengths, but use it straight from the roll. Work with the special adhesive recommended for this type of wall covering.

Dry-strip Washable and ready-pasted papers already described are not easily removed using the conventional soak-and-strip method since the water cannot penetrate the water-resistant coating to act on the adhesive. But dry-strip papers and vinyls are available; you peel away the decorative face to leave a paper backing on the wall. If this backing is firmly fixed, use it as a base for re-papering or strip it off in the usual way.

Lining paper Thin paper used under the decorative wall covering to give a high quality finish. It is available in several weights: use light papers on smooth wall surfaces and heavier papers to help conceal uneven surfaces. Hang lining paper horizontally on the walls so the joins between lengths will not coincide with the vertical joins of the decorative wall covering.

Selecting a pattern
If you decide you would like a patterned paper, remember different types of pattern demand varying degrees of skill to apply. Complicated patterns are not easy to match and often mistakes only show when the lengths have been hung.

Free match paper The simplest type to apply since it has random motifs that do not require matching. It is also the most economical as there is no wastage.

Set patterns Demand more skill since you have to match the design horizontally across adjoining lengths. There will be some wastage (especially if the repeat does not fit in with your room height) but this can sometimes be minimized by cutting lengths from two or more rolls at a time.

Drop patterns Can be difficult to match as the design runs diagonally across adjacent lengths – the first length aligns with the third, the second with the fourth, the fifth with the seventh, and so on. Wastage is inevitable, but again this can be minimized by working from more than one roll.

Effects of patterns
Before choosing a design consider the size and shape of your room as the pattern on the wallpaper may appear to alter its dimensions. Vertical lines will seem to increase the room's height, while horizontal stripes will give the opposite effect. However attractive large motifs or bright colours look when you are flicking through a pattern book, remember these can be overbearing in small rooms.

Certain designs will show up faults in the structure of the room. If the ceiling slopes, the motifs in a set or drop pattern will gradually disappear along the ceiling line. This also applies to papering ceilings: if they are not perfect squares or rectangles the pattern will run out of true.

Unfortunately it is not easy to check ceiling line irregularities; they usually become apparent only when the wallpaper is hung. Vertical stripes will emphasize corners that are out of square, so you should always check these before buying this type of pattern. Suspend a plumb bob and string line from a small nail fixed as high up the wall as possible; the string line will hang down at a true vertical and you will be able to see if the corner is square.

Check the condition of your wall surface. If it is undulating or pitted, don't buy a striped paper as this will only emphasize the defects; go for a busy, colourful pattern that will hide the faults.

There is obviously a lot to recommend a free match paper. It is the simplest to hang, there is no wastage and it can disguise many structural defects.

Free match paper
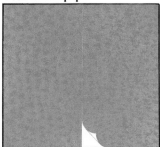

Set patterns

Drop patterns
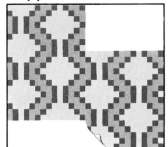

Below Consider the size and shape of your room before buying patterned wallpaper as the design may appear to alter the room's shape; height is increased by vertical stripes, while horizontal lines make the ceiling seem lower

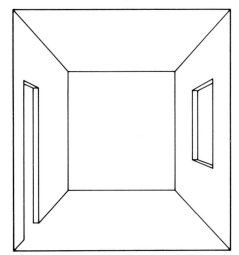
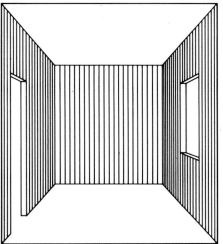
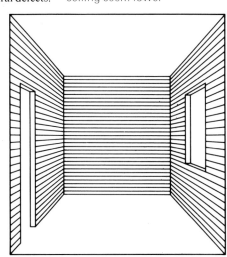

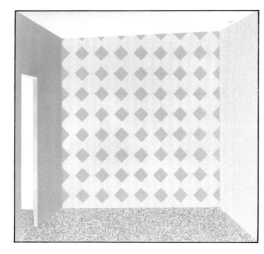

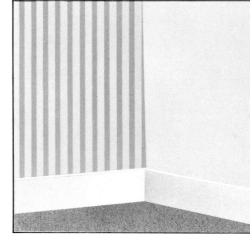

Right With washable papers score the surface with a wire brush to allow water to penetrate to the backing
Below right Remove ordinary paper with a stripping knife, taking care not to dig into the wall
Below left A steam stripper will take off a thick paper rapidly; the steam penetrates the paper and softens the old adhesive

Certain designs will emphasize structural faults in the room, so choose patterned paper carefully. **Above** If your ceiling slopes, don't go for a set pattern as the motifs will gradually disappear along the ceiling line. **Above right** Avoid using vertically striped paper on out-of-square corners

Estimating quantity

Measure the height of the room from the skirting to the picture rail or ceiling and also the distance around the walls, including doors and windows. Check with our calculating chart to see how many rolls of wallpaper you need. If your measurement for the distance around the room falls between two measurements on the chart, use the larger figure.

Basic measurements will be sufficient for plain or free match papers. Where you need to match the pattern you must allow for wastage at the foot of each length according to the depth of the repeat; usually an extra roll for every five is enough, although you may need to allow extra if the repeat pattern is very deep.

Extra paper will also be needed if the room has recesses or projections since the pattern should be centred on these to give a balanced look.

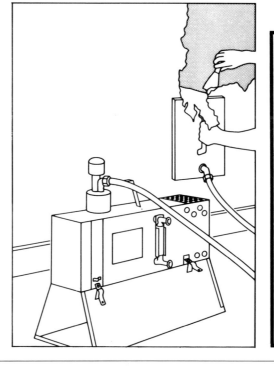

For preparing surface
wallpaper stripper or warm water and washing-up liquid
wallpaper paste (for soaking heavyweight paper)
wire brush or serrated scraper
steam stripper (if needed)
wallpaper stripping knife
medium wet and dry glasspaper
cellulose filler (if needed)
matchsticks (if needed)
glue size or wallpaper paste (for sizing walls)
fungicidal adhesive (for sizing if using vinyl paper)
old brush or paint pad

equipment

Distance in metres round walls incl. doors/ windows	NUMBER OF ROLLS REQUIRED – METRIC CHART							
	Height in metres from skirting							
	2 – 2.2	2.2 – 2.5	2.5 – 2.7	2.7 – 3	3 – 3.2	3.2 – 3.5	3.5 – 3.7	3.7 – 4
10	5	5	6	6	7	7	8	8
11	5	6	7	7	8	8	9	9
12	6	6	7	8	8	9	9	10
13	6	7	8	8	9	10	10	10
14	7	7	8	9	10	10	11	11
15	7	8	9	9	10	11	12	12
16	8	8	9	10	11	11	12	13
17	8	9	10	10	11	12	13	14
18	9	9	10	11	12	13	14	15
19	9	10	11	12	13	14	15	16
20	9	10	11	12	13	14	15	16
21	10	11	12	13	14	15	16	17
22	10	11	13	14	15	16	17	18
23	11	12	13	14	15	17	18	19
24	11	12	14	15	16	17	18	20
25	12	13	14	15	17	18	19	20
26	12	13	15	16	17	19	20	21
27	13	14	15	17	18	19	21	22
28	13	14	16	17	19	20	21	23
29	13	15	16	18	19	21	22	24
30	14	15	17	18	20	21	23	24

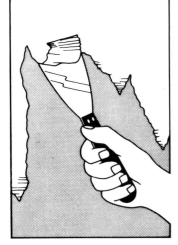

Buying the paper

Most wall coverings are sold in rolls 10m (11yd) long and 520mm (20½in) wide. They are normally supplied ready-trimmed, but if you do select a paper with selvedges (margins) ask your supplier to trim them for you – don't attempt it yourself.

Wallpaper is printed in batches and the colour may vary from batch to batch; make sure every roll you buy bears the same batch number. It is worth buying an extra roll at the outset since you may have trouble obtaining another roll of the same batch later on. Check if you can buy a spare roll on a sale-or-return basis.

If you realize halfway through a job that you will not have sufficient paper and you cannot buy another roll from the same batch, use the odd roll in an area where any colour variation will not be so noticeable, such as on a short wall or in a recess.

Unfortunately even corresponding batch numbers do not always guarantee an exact colour match. Before hanging the paper inspect the rolls in a good light; if you spot any shade differences, decide the best sequence for hanging.

Imperfections in the paper itself can be eliminated when you cut the paper into lengths. But if you find inconsistencies in the pattern take the roll back to your supplier, since you will have a lot of wastage if you try to eliminate 'repeat' defects.

If after hanging the paper you find the pattern on adjoining lengths will not align, it is probably the result of not soaking the rolls with paste for the same length of time or stretching the paper when putting it up.

Storing wallpaper

Always store rolls of wallpaper flat; never stand them on end or you will damage the edges and make it difficult to obtain neat joins between lengths when hanging.

Preparing the surface

To remove the existing paper you will have to soak it with a solution of warm water and washing-up liquid or proprietary wallpaper stripper. Allow extra soaking for heavyweight papers – add a handful of wallpaper paste to the water so the water stays on the wall long enough to soak through to the adhesive.

Stripping off Score the surface of washable wallpapers with a wire brush or serrated scraper to allow the water to soak through to the backing. If the paper is several layers thick or you cannot score it easily, it may be worth hiring a steam stripper to do the job quickly, but use it carefully since it can damage the plaster underneath.

Remove the paper with a wallpaper stripping knife; don't be too vigorous and try not to dig the knife into the plaster, as you will have to fill any holes you make.

Remember you can strip certain types of wall covering just by loosening a corner and pulling off each length, leaving the backing paper on the wall. If this is firmly fixed, use it as a base for repapering or soak and strip as already described.

Rub down the bare walls with wet and dry glasspaper to remove any final nibs of paper. Fill any cracks or holes with cellulose filler and, when hard, rub down any ridges with medium wet and dry glasspaper to form a flush finish.

If you have removed any fixtures, push matchsticks into the screw holes, allowing them to protrude about 6mm (¼in). When you hang the new wall covering ease it over the matchsticks so they poke through the paper and indicate the position for refitting the fixtures later.

Sizing the walls Before papering you will have to size sound, porous walls; this is to improve adhesion and ensure the water from the paste is not absorbed too quickly for you to position the paper correctly. You can buy a proprietary glue size or make your own by diluting wallpaper paste according to the manufacturer's instructions. When using vinyls, size with a diluted fungicidal adhesive since mould may develop on the wall if you use a diluted cellulose adhesive.

Apply the size liberally to all parts of the wall with an old brush or paint pad; take care to wipe off any that gets onto painted woodwork immediately as it will be difficult to remove later. Leave the size to dry thoroughly.

Distance in feet round walls incl. doors/ windows	NUMBER OF ROLLS REQUIRED – IMPERIAL CHART						
	Height in feet from skirting						
	7 – 7½	7½ – 8	8 – 8½	8½ – 9	9 – 9½	9½ – 10	10 – 10½
30	4	5	5	5	6	6	6
34	5	5	5	5	6	6	7
38	5	6	6	6	7	7	8
42	6	6	7	7	7	8	8
46	6	7	7	7	8	8	9
50	7	7	8	8	9	9	10
54	7	8	9	9	9	10	10
58	8	8	9	9	10	10	11
62	8	9	10	10	10	11	12
66	9	9	10	10	11	12	13
70	9	10	11	11	12	12	13
74	10	10	12	12	12	13	14
78	10	11	12	12	13	14	15
82	11	11	13	13	14	14	16
86	12	12	14	14	14	15	16
90	12	13	14	14	15	16	17
94	13	13	15	15	15	16	18
98	13	14	15	15	16	17	19

How to hang wallpaper

Hanging wallpaper the correct way is all important, since the final effect will be ruined
if you make awkward turns in the wrong places or don't hang the paper straight. And
always remember to prepare the surface properly.

Putting up lining paper

If using lining paper, hang it on the walls horizontally to avoid the joins coinciding with the
vertical joins of the decorative paper. Cut the
paper into lengths 25mm (1in) longer than the
width of the wall to allow for 12mm ($\frac{1}{2}$in) turns onto
the adjacent walls.

Lay one end of the length on the pasting table,
leaving the rest to hang to the floor, and paste this
piece carefully. Fold over, with pasted sides
together, about 380mm (15in) of paper. Then fold
over 760mm (30in) and turn back the first folded
piece to make pleats. Continue pasting and con-
certina pleating in this way until you near the end of
the length, then paste this end and fold it over to
meet the pleats.

Start hanging the paper from a top corner of the
wall, releasing one fold at a time and smoothing
out with a roller or brush. Work right round and
down the wall with subsequent lengths in the same
way, butting adjoining strips together.

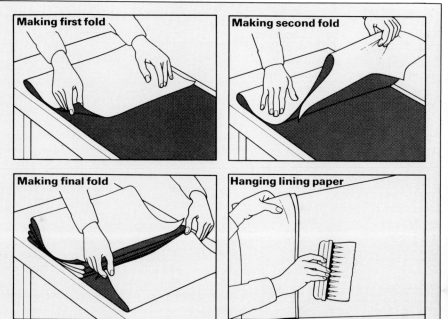

Marking the starting point

The usual starting point for vertical hanging is on a
wall adjacent to a window so any overlap between
adjoining lengths will not cast a shadow. When
using paper with a large pattern, centre the pattern
on the chimney-breast and on other main features
of the room, if desirable, to give an overall balanced
look when the room is finished.

On plain wall You must establish a true vertical to
align the edge of the first length. Measure out from
the corner of the starting wall a distance 12mm
($\frac{1}{2}$in) less than the width of the paper (this extra
12mm will be turned onto the window wall). At
this point suspend a plumb bob from a small nail
as high up the wall as possible. Mark the wall at
several points behind the line and use a straight-
edge and pencil to join the points together.

On chimney-breast Measure from the pattern
centre to the left-hand edge of the paper. Measure
this distance to the left of the centre line on the
chimney-breast, suspend a plumb bob at this
point, mark the vertical line and hang the first
length to one side of it. Hang the second length to
the other side of the line, butting up to the first
length.

Alternatively, you can hang two widths so the
motifs at the edges to be butted match up in
adjacent lengths at the centre of your chimney-
breast or projection. Suspend a plumb bob at the
centre of the projection, mark the line as before
and hang the first length against this. Hang the
second length on the other side of the centre line.

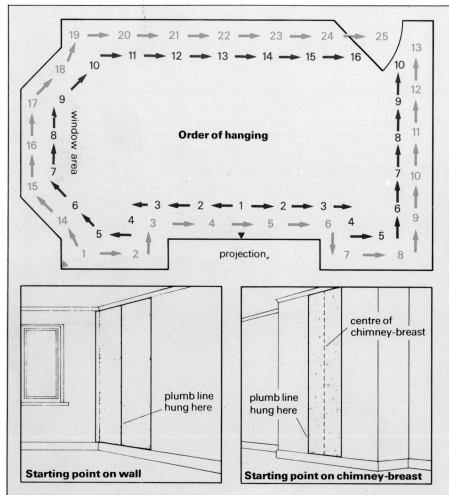

Cutting lengths and pasting

Cut the paper into lengths, each about 200mm (8in) longer than the height of the wall to allow for trimming later. If the paper has a set or drop pattern, match the lengths on the pasting table; remember to work from two or even three rolls at once to reduce wastage. As you cut the lengths number them on the back so you can tell at a glance the order in which to hang them. Also indicate which end is to be hung at the top of the wall to avoid hanging the paper upside down.

Lay the lengths, decorative side down, on the pasting table. Line up the end and far edge of the first sheet of paper with the end and far edge of the table, allowing it to overhang by 6mm ($\frac{1}{4}$in). At the other end let the rest of the paper fall onto the floor. Imagine the width of the paper is divided into three strips; paste the centre strip, then paste the section farthest away from you, working towards the edge (never work from the edges towards the centre as the paste will seep under the paper and spoil the decorative face). Pull the paper towards you so the near edge overhangs the table by about 6mm ($\frac{1}{4}$in) and paste this final strip, remembering to work from the centre towards the edge. Fold over the pasted end to the centre of the length, pull the unpasted paper onto the table and paste and fold as before.

You do not need to leave the paste to soak in with thin papers, which you can hang immediately. Heavier papers have to soak for about ten minutes. To save time lay the pasted length (with the ends still folded back onto the centre) on a clean surface and paste the next length. It is a good idea to write the time of pasting on the back of each length to ensure each piece soaks for the same time.

Matching lengths

cut roll   second roll   cut length

Pasting paper

2   2
1   1
3   3

Folding paper

Hanging the paper

Drape the pasted length over your arm, making sure you remember which end is to go at the top of the wall. Unfold the top half of the length, keeping a firm hold on the lower half so it does not stretch. The positioning of the first length is critical. Align the edge of the paper with the line you marked on wall and position the top with the ceiling line, allowing a 75–100mm (3–4in) overlap at the top for trimming and folding. Fold this top edge overlap back onto the pasted side to prevent paste getting on the ceiling; if paste runs onto plaster or wood-work, remove at once with dampened sponge.

Smooth down the centre of the paper with the hanging brush then work towards the edges to expel any air bubbles beneath the paper. Open out the lower half of the paper and repeat the procedure, folding the bottom edge overlap in the same way.

Run the back of your scissors along the edges at the ceiling and skirting board to mark the trimming line. Peel back the paper and cut carefully along the crease before brushing the edges back into place and smoothing down.

Hang subsequent lengths in the same way, matching the pattern (if any) at the top with the length already hung and position the edge of the new length as close as possible to the first. Slide the length along to form a neat butt join. After hanging each length go over the joins with a seam roller, unless the paper is embossed.

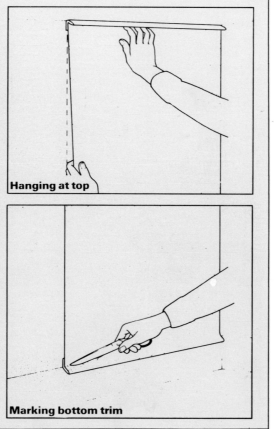

Hanging at top

Marking bottom trim

Vinyl wall covering Always use a latex adhesive when overlapping edges in corners or they will not stick firmly. Use a sharp trimming knife and a straight-edge rather than scissors for the best results and hold the knife at an angle to the wall so you do not dig into the plaster.

Ready-pasted wall covering Roll up each cut length with the pattern facing outwards. Immerse the roll in the trough of water for the time recommended by the manufacturer, usually about a minute. Take hold of the top corners of the paper and gradually pull the roll upwards, leaving the tail of the paper in the trough as long as possible so water will run back into it. Hang as ordinary wallpaper and smooth out each length with a brush or sponge, wiping off any excess adhesive.

Place plenty of newspapers under the trough to avoid splashing the floor covering. The paste at the edges may start to dry before you can brush out the paper so have ready a batch of suitable paste and a small brush to retouch the edges if necessary.

If overlapping edges lift on drying, stick them down with a latex adhesive. If the walls are lined with expanded polystyrene and you wish to use ready-pasted vinyl covering, hang lining paper over the polystyrene first to prevent the vinyl bubbling.

Polyethylene paper For this type of paper, such as Novamura, paste the wall with either the adhesive supplied with the paper or a vinyl adhesive. Since the material is so light to handle there is no need to cut it to length first, so you can hang it straight from the roll. Smooth down with a sponge.

Chimney-breast

Hang your first length of wallpaper in the centre of the projection (as already described when finding the starting point) and hang lengths either side until a gap of less than a full width of paper remains on both sides. Cut a strip wide enough to turn the corner by about 25mm (1in). Paste and hang the top half as usual, leaving the extra 25mm free. This you can brush round the corner after you have fixed the paper round the mantel piece.

Cut off as much surplus paper as possible around

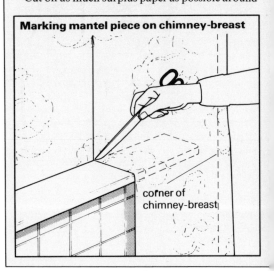

Marking mantel piece on chimney-breast

corner of chimney-breast

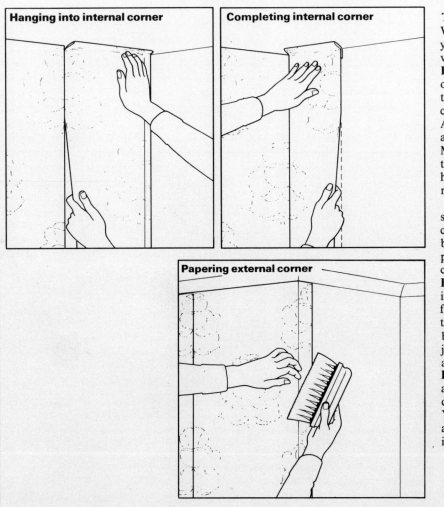

Hanging into internal corner

Completing internal corner

Papering external corner

Turning corners

Whenever you have to paper round a corner, use your plumb line on the new wall to establish a true vertical.

Internal corner Never turn more than 12 mm ($\frac{1}{2}$in) of paper round a corner or it will crease. Measure the distance from the edge of the last length to the corner in three places – top, middle and bottom. Add 12mm ($\frac{1}{2}$in) to the largest measurement and cut a strip of paper this width from the next length. Make sure this strip is cut from the correct side of the length or the pattern will not match. Paste and hang this piece with the extra 12mm extending round the corner.

Measure the width of the remaining strip and suspend a plumb bob at this distance from the corner on the new wall, marking pencil lines as before. Hang the strip with its edge aligned with the pencil line. There will be a slight overlap in the corner but this will not be too noticeable.

External corner Follow the same procedure as for internal corners, but when you measure the distance from the last length to the corner add 25mm (1in) to take round. Cut the paper and hang the strip as before. When you hang the remaining piece butt-join the lengths. If the corner is badly out of square, allow for a slight overlap.

Pattern clashes You must decide whether to have any pattern clash nearest to the external or internal corner, according to which would be less noticeable. You may find it easier to check this by using artificial light, when the discrepancy in the pattern is likely to show up more.

the mantle piece, leaving between 25–50mm (1–2in) for final trimming. Starting at the top of the mantel, press the paper into the contours of the fireplace surround and trim off along the crease lines, using small scissors if preferred.

Brush in the paper, including the 25mm turn allowance. Repeat for the other side of the surround, then continue papering on the side wall of the chimney-breast where your original papering was discontinued. There will be a pattern overlap here, but it should not be noticeable in the corner.

Cutting off surplus paper

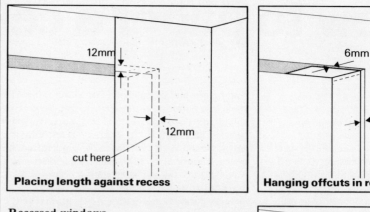

Placing length against recess

Hanging offcuts in recess

Recessed windows

Place a length of paper against the recess and mark the right-angle, adding 12mm (½in) where the top and side of the recess fall. Cut the length to shape. Measure inside the top and side of the recess, deduct 6mm (½in) from the depth of each and cut pieces of paper to size, matching the pattern as near as possible. Paste and hang these offcuts, butting them up to the back of the recess. Paste and hang the prepared length for the front wall, turning the extra 12mm (½in) into the recess so it overlaps the pieces already hung. If necessary, make a small diagonal snip in the paper where it turns into the corner of the recess for a tidy finish. Repeat for the other side.

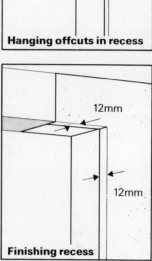

Finishing recess

Doorway

Paste and hang a full length of paper so it overlaps the door. Cut off most of the surplus paper to within 25mm (1in) of the door frame. Make a diagonal cut at the top corner and brush the paper into the angle between the wall and the frame. Turn back the extra paper and trim, then press the paper into place along the top and sides of the frame. Repeat for the other side of the frame. Cut and hang a piece of paper to fit the wall above the door.

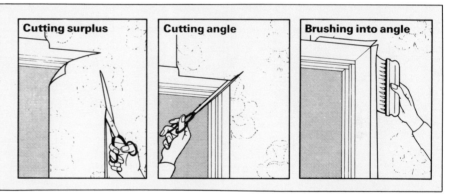

Cutting surplus

Cutting angle

Brushing into angle

Light switch

When dealing with a projecting light switch hang the top half of the length then press the paper against the knob of the switch. Make several cuts in the shape of a star from the centre of the knob to about 12mm (½in) past the mounting block. Press the paper over the block and crease it round the base before trimming off and brushing in.

With a flush switch always turn off the electricity at the mains before papering. Remove the fixing screws and pull the cover plate 12mm (½in) away from the wall. Hang the top half of the length and press the paper gently against the switch. Make a square cut in the paper to leave a 6mm (½in) margin inside the area covered by the plate. Hang and trim the rest of the length and refit the cover plate.

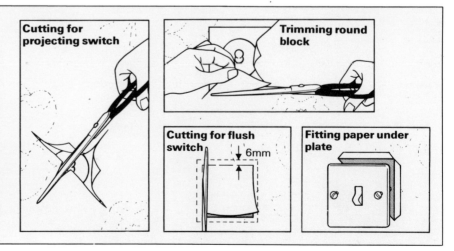

Cutting for projecting switch

Trimming round block

Cutting for flush switch

Fitting paper under plate

Stairwell

Paste and fold the paper concertina-fashion or the weight of the paste will stretch the long lengths of paper. Measure the width of the paper and subtract 12mm (½in). Suspend a plumb bob, on the side wall, at this distance from the side and end wall corner and hang the first length of paper to this, turning 12mm (½in) onto the end wall. Continue papering the side wall, butt-joining each length, then paper the end wall.

How to paper a ceiling

If the ceiling is in good condition, size the surface and leave it to dry before papering. If the plaster is uneven, line the ceiling first for the best result. As with walls, always hang lining paper at right-angles to the decorative covering so the joins do not coincide.

Hang ceiling paper parallel to the main window in the room so the joins are not too noticeable (**see 1**).
Measure the width of the paper, deduct 6mm ($\frac{1}{4}$in) for turning onto the end wall and mark this distance in pencil at both sides of the ceiling. Chalk a length of string and fix it at one side with a drawing pin. Stretch the string between the two pencil marks and pluck it so the chalk is transferred to the ceiling (**see 2**).

Cut the number of lengths required, allowing for the pattern to match and for trimming at both ends. Paste and fold each length concertina-fashion as for lining paper (**see page 26**). Hang the first length flush against the chalk line. Unfold the last pleat and smooth it onto the ceiling. Release the paper one pleat at a time, supporting the rest of the paper with a spare roll. Brush out each section onto the ceiling.

Turn 6mm ($\frac{1}{4}$in) onto the end and side walls then trim and sponge away any surplus paste (**see 3**).
Hang the other lengths in the same way, butt-joining the edges and turning 6mm ($\frac{1}{4}$in) onto both side walls. Remember to allow 6mm in the width of the last length for turning onto the end wall. At a ceiling light, make star-shaped cuts as for projecting light switches. Smooth paper round fitting and trim flaps (**see 4**).

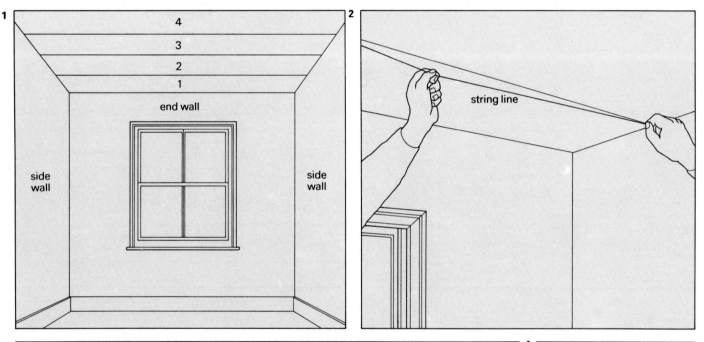

1

4
3
2
1

end wall

side wall

side wall

string line

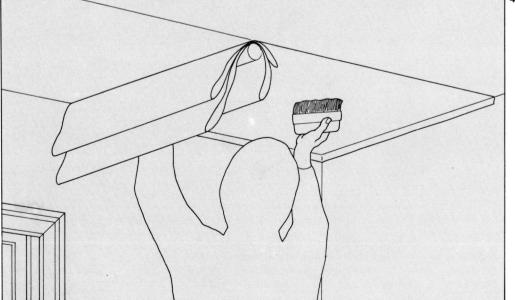

3

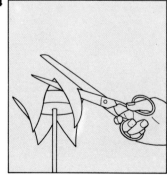

4

Covering the home

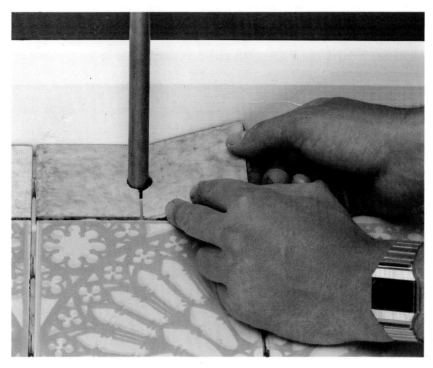

Floor and wall coverings can be a major expense in any home improvement budget, so it is vital they are laid correctly and materials are not wasted. This section deals with fitting, cleaning and repairing the range of coverings and shows you how to tackle those awkward areas such as the staircase, in doorways and around pipes. There is also a guide to the equipment needed, which will help ensure you get the best results. Careful planning is again important, particularly when buying material; you certainly do not want to buy more than you really need.

Renovating ceramic tiles

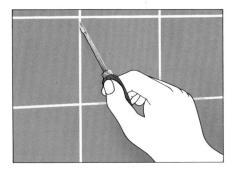

One of the quickest ways to give a face-lift to sound old tiling is to replace grout – filling material round each tile. Rake out old grout with worn screwdriver or old pair of scissors. Take care not to scratch surface of tiles while raking out

Spread new grout over tiles with dampened sponge. Remove any surplus material as you work, leaving just enough to fill gaps between tiles. When grout is almost dry, clean tiles with dampened sponge. Finish off with clean, dry soft cloth

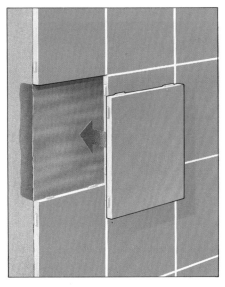

Far left Refix loose tiles before regrouting, chipping away any old cement from tiles with cold chisel. Spread impact (contact) or similar thin-coat adhesive (thicker adhesive will leave replaced tiles proud of surrounding surface) on wall and backs of tiles with small-toothed notched spreader. Refix tiles
Left Mortar may come away with loose tiles. If it does, try to glue back tiles with mortar still in place or chip it away. (If you have replacement tiles, throw away old ones.) Chop away any mortar from wall to form clean surface. Fix tiles with mixture of three parts builders' sand to one part cement. Apply just enough mortar behind each tile to bring its face level with surrounding ones to ensure flush finish over tiled surface

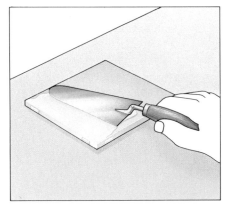

Remove broken tiles and old adhesive with small sharp cold chisel and club hammer. Work from centre outwards and take care as you get near surrounding tiles; protect any fittings from being scratched by broken pieces of tile. Always wear protective spectacles or goggles

Using flexible filling knife or round-ended (gauging) trowel, butter thin layer of adhesive on back of replacement tiles and push them into place. Make sure new surface is flush with old, building up adhesive if necessary. Complete repair by applying new grout

As temporary measure you can easily renovate old crazed tiles with self-adhesive transfers. Decorating entire wall may prove uneconomic so only use them to cover worst of tiles. Remove backing from transfers and smooth them out onto tiles with soft cloth, working from centre outwards

Fixing ceramic tiles

Ceramic tiles provide not only a practical but also a decorative solution to those problem areas in the bathroom and kitchen, where water splashes will ruin the ordinary wall decorations.

Consider first what sort or combination of tiles – plain, patterned or textured, or a mixture of the two – will best suit your colour scheme.

Plain tiles Produced to match the standard colours of bathroom and kitchen ware, this type is the cheapest and plain colours allow greater flexibility when changing other patterns in your rooms.

Patterned tiles Usually based on standard plain tile colours, these feature either a complete pattern or are used in groups of four to form a single motif. They are seen to their best advantage when used as a contrast to plain tiles and can also look attractive when concentrated on small areas.

Textured tiles In similar colours to plain, these are most striking when highlighting one particular area or covering an end wall between two plain walls. There is a limited range of 'feature' tiles with either a special motif or a rural scene. And you can even make up a mural to be hung on the wall like a picture or set into a plain-tiled area.

Heat-resistant tiles For fireplace surrounds and other areas likely to be subjected to extreme heat.

Types of tile

The two basic sizes are 108mm sq × 4mm ($4\frac{1}{4}$in sq × $\frac{5}{32}$in) and 152mm sq × 6mm (6in sq × $\frac{1}{4}$in), but larger sizes are available such as 200mm (8in) sq and 200 × 100mm (8 × 4in). Interesting shapes, some interlocking, are usually more costly and not so easy to work with as rectangular ones.

Certain areas of the room, such as corners and the top edge of a half-tiled wall, need specially shaped tiles to make your job easier and the overall look neater. And you must take these into account when calculating the number of tiles you will need. You should also add 5–10 tiles to your total to allow for breakages.

Spacer (or field) Designed for the main areas of your wall these are square-edged and have small projections – spacer lugs – jutting out from each edge. As each tile is positioned these lugs butt against one another, ensuring equal joints.

RE One edge is rounded off to give a neat finish to the perimeter of a tiled area. Use at the top of a half-tiled wall and at external corners. The three square edges of these tiles do not have spacer lugs.

REX These come with two adjacent rounded edges. Very few are needed in the average job as their use is restricted to external corners in the top row of a half-tiled wall. Like RE tiles the square edges do not have spacer lugs.

Border Square-cut alternative to RE and REX tiles, without spacer lugs. Used for finishing external angles on areas such as window recesses and corners. Two adjacent edges are glazed.

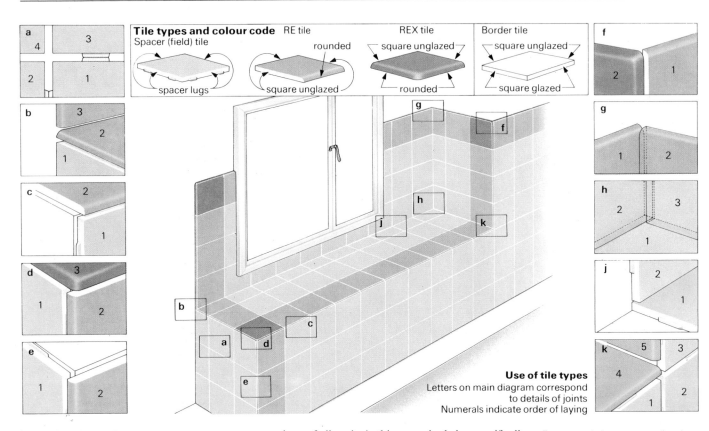

Tile types and colour code
Spacer (field) tile — spacer lugs — square unglazed
RE tile — rounded — square unglazed
REX tile — square unglazed — rounded
Border tile — square unglazed — square glazed

Use of tile types
Letters on main diagram correspond
to details of joints
Numerals indicate order of laying

Preparing the surface

As with nearly all decorative covering jobs it is the preparation that makes or breaks the finish. And this applies particularly with ceramic tiles as, like wallpaper or paint, they have to be fixed to a really smooth, flat surface, which must also be dry and firm.

A good way of finding out just how smooth your walls are is by using a timber straight-edge, about 1m (or 36in) long. Place this at different points across the surface, checking vertically, horizontally and diagonally. If you are getting a noticeable see-saw action a certain amount of levelling will be necessary.

Plaster Where only minor areas are affected, use a proprietary plaster filler. Follow the manufacturer's mixing instructions and then apply with a filling knife to the low areas of the surface. Two or three applications may be necessary to build up to the correct level.

As you become more expert this will not be necessary since you will be able to level shallow depressions accurately when applying the wet mix, using a straight-edge or filling knife.

Bad irregularities over large areas must be completely replastered, a job best left to the professional plasterer. New plaster must be allowed to dry out for at least a month before tiling and, as the surface is porous, sealed with a coat of plaster primer. This sealing is also necessary where a plaster filler has been used.

Wallpaper This must be completely stripped first and the plaster underneath raked out where loose and levelled as above.

Painted Glasspaper down to remove any flaking areas and provide a key for the tile adhesive. Where the paint is direct onto plaster, uneven patches must be levelled as above.

Timber Plane level and give the bare wood a coat of wood primer before tiling.

Ceramic tiles Existing tiles are probably the best

base of all, today's thin ceramics being specifically designed to suit tile-on-tile fixing. But as with all other surfaces the base must be sound. So make sure the existing tiles are clean, flat and firmly fixed. Remove any loose ones and refix with tile adhesive so they are level with adjacent tiles.

Half-tiled wall If you intend retiling here and taking the new tiles to ceiling height, you will need to build out the untiled part of the wall level with the existing area to avoid being left with a recess. This levelling up of the wall section can be done with plaster, plasterboard or other suitable building board.

Lining the wall

Where the surface of your wall is so uneven that refilling is impossible and replastering would be too costly, you can create a 'new' wall by lining with plywood, chipboard or plasterboard.

First construct a timber framework on the wall from horizontal and vertical 50 × 25mm (2 × 1in) battens. Drill countersunk holes in the battens at about 400mm (or 16in) spacing. Drill corresponding holes in the wall to take masonry plugs and screw the battens loosely to these using 50mm (2in) long No 8 countersunk screws. Start with the top and bottom horizontal battens. Follow these by the vertical battens spaced at 400mm (or 16in) intervals, working from left to right. Finally fill in with short horizontal battens spaced at 610mm (24in) intervals. Using a straight-edge horizontally, vertically and diagonally, level up the battens using pieces of scrap hardboard, laminate etc. as packing between the battens and 'low' areas of wall before tightening up the screws. Take care with this stage of the job as the final accuracy of the lining could otherwise be affected.

Apply a coat of primer or sealer to all board surfaces and edges, then screw to the battens with 32mm (1¼in) long No 8 countersunk screws through countersunk holes drilled in the boards.

For most jobs you need only four types of tile as shown above

Opposite page

1 If surface is too uneven to provide suitable base for tiling, screw batten framework to wall. Pack low areas behind battens with pieces of scrap hardboard to ensure framework sits flush against wall. **2** Screw plywood or chipboard panels to battens, butt joining edges
3 To find starting point nail batten to wall, one tile width above floor. Mark off batten in tile widths, leaving equal spaces at each end. At last full tile width nail upright batten to wall at true vertical. Lay first tile at corner formed by two battens. **4** Spread adhesive with small round-ended trowel over one square metre of wall. **5** Comb adhesive horizontally to leave series of ridges. **6** Press tiles into place, butting each squarely against its neighbour with spacer lugs touching. Complete each horizontal row before starting next one

Previous page

With Caladium you can make up your own pattern from two related designs, 216sq mm/8½sq in (Cedit from Arnull)

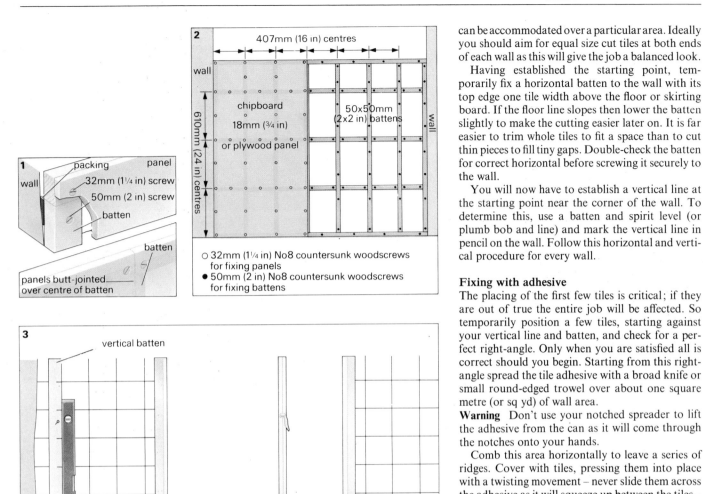

2
407mm (16 in) centres

wall

chipboard
18mm (¾ in)
or plywood panel

50x50mm
(2x2 in) battens

wall

610mm (24 in) centres

○ 32mm (1¼ in) No8 countersunk woodscrews
   for fixing panels
● 50mm (2 in) No8 countersunk woodscrews
   for fixing battens

1
packing   panel
wall
32mm (1¼ in) screw
50mm (2 in) screw
batten

batten

panels butt-jointed
over centre of batten

3
vertical batten

measuring staff

starting point   one tile width

adjoining wall   horizontal batten   floor

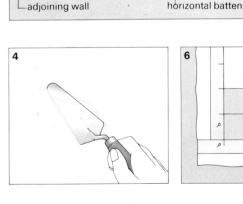

4

6

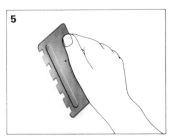

5

Planning

Very few houses have true vertical and horizontal corners so you must never begin tiling in a corner or at floor level. As you reach the end of each row cut to shape the tiles for these areas.

The first step then is to decide the best starting point by making a measuring staff from a long batten (if your room has several alcoves, you will need a shorter one as well) marked with tile widths. This will enable you to see how many whole tiles

can be accommodated over a particular area. Ideally you should aim for equal size cut tiles at both ends of each wall as this will give the job a balanced look.

Having established the starting point, temporarily fix a horizontal batten to the wall with its top edge one tile width above the floor or skirting board. If the floor line slopes then lower the batten slightly to make the cutting easier later on. It is far easier to trim whole tiles to fit a space than to cut thin pieces to fill tiny gaps. Double-check the batten for correct horizontal before screwing it securely to the wall.

You will now have to establish a vertical line at the starting point near the corner of the wall. To determine this, use a batten and spirit level (or plumb bob and line) and mark the vertical line in pencil on the wall. Follow this horizontal and vertical procedure for every wall.

Fixing with adhesive

The placing of the first few tiles is critical; if they are out of true the entire job will be affected. So temporarily position a few tiles, starting against your vertical line and batten, and check for a perfect right-angle. Only when you are satisfied all is correct should you begin. Starting from this right-angle spread the tile adhesive with a broad knife or small round-edged trowel over about one square metre (or sq yd) of wall area.

Warning Don't use your notched spreader to lift the adhesive from the can as it will come through the notches onto your hands.

Comb this area horizontally to leave a series of ridges. Cover with tiles, pressing them into place with a twisting movement – never slide them across the adhesive as it will squeeze up between the tiles – completing each horizontal row before starting the one above. Make sure each tile is butted squarely against its neighbours with spacer lugs touching. With RE and REX tiles, neither of which has spacer lugs, use matchsticks or pieces of cardboard to ensure equal spacing and remove after 24 hours.

As you complete each square metre of tiling be sure to check the tiles are correctly positioned vertically and horizontally by using your spirit level. Complete as many whole tiles as possible before tackling any cutting. When the area above the horizontal batten is complete, allow at least 12 hours' drying time before removing the batten and tiling the bottom course (row). Allow another 24 hours before starting to grout.

There are special water-resistant adhesives for tiled areas likely to be subjected to excessive splashing or heat, such as shower cubicles. You will need a trowel to spread this type in a thin layer and should allow at least 14 days before grouting or allowing the tiles to come into contact with water.

There is a 'fix and grout' product that enables you to stick down your tiles and then grout them in a matter of hours.

Grouting between the tiles

Carefully mix your chosen grouting powder with water to a creamy consistency and rub well into the joints with a dampened sponge. Remove any surplus with a dampened cloth before the grouting is dry. Any remaining traces can be polished off later with a soft dry cloth.

For extra colour you can add a dye solution to a ready-mix grout, or dye powder to a dry grout. Colours available include red, yellow, blue, green, brown and black.

A few of the many shapes, sizes, colours and designs of modern ceramic tiles. **1** Honfleur hand-printed all-over pattern, 108sq mm/4¼sq in (Rye Tiles)
2,3 Tuscan KT5 embossed design and matching mottle, 152sq mm/6sq in. **4** Mayfair Carnival motif (harmonizing solid colour available). 108sq mm/4¼sq in. **5** With Pattern Series Brasilia four tiles make up a motif to feature with matching solid colour ones, 108sq mm/4¼sq in
6 Dorchester elegant long tile, 216×108mm/8½×4¼in ·
7 Kontract Saxon Arena design, good over large areas or to feature with plain background colour, 152sq mm/6sq in. (All in the Cristal range by H. & R. Johnson)
8 Viscount stylized floral motif to feature singly or all over the wall, 152sq mm/6sq on (H. & R. Johnson for UBM)

Variations on provencale, circular and hexagonal shapes
9 Bordo Marron, 152 × 203mm/6 × 8in (Tile Mart)
10 Algier unglazed, about 73 × 98mm/3 × 4in (Langley)
11 Small Provencale, about 125 × 140mm/5 × 5½in (Verity)
12 Rouge Flamme and Cremona glazed about 65 × 65mm/2½ × 2½in (Tile Mart)
13 Biscarosse unglazed, 60 × 65mm/2⅜ × 2½in (Langley)
14, 15 Briare Ducats and hexagonal Gemmes in textured vitrified glass, 42mm/1⅝in and 25mm/1in diameter. Standard half piece fittings available (Langley)
16 Hexagon hand-printed tile, 100mm/4in diameter overall (Rye Tiles)

1 Scoring with tile cutter

2 Breaking over matchstick

3 Cutting with pincers

4 Oporto tile cutter

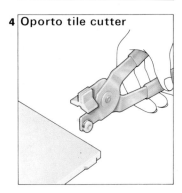

1 To cut tiles to fit, mark required width and score glaze
2 Place tile on flat surface with matchstick under scored line. Press down edges so tile snaps cleanly along line
3 Use pincers to cut thin sections or awkward shapes from tiles
4 With Oporto tile cutter score glaze with cutting wheel and squeeze handles together to cut tile cleanly

Cutting tiles

The most common tile cutter looks like a pencil and has a tungsten carbide tip to score the tile. To snap cleanly, place a matchstick under the scored line and press down evenly on both sides of the tile. A neat break should result. The Oporto tile cutter scores with a cutting wheel. Place the tile in the jaws of the tool and gently squeeze the handles, pincer-fashion, to make a clean break.

To mark an end tile for cutting to size, place it in position (front surface against wall) making sure one edge of the tile butts into the wall. Measure the distance from the end of the wall to the preceding tile in the row. Mark the width required in pencil, first on the reverse, continuing round the edges to the front face when you have turned the tile round. To join up these lines correctly place the tile face up on a firm, flat surface and using a metal straight-edge (your try square is ideal) align the two pencil marks and score through the glaze with your cutter. Use one of the two cutting methods described.

If really thin sections, less than 10mm ($\frac{3}{8}$in) thick, have to be cut, score deeply along the marked line and with pincers nibble away gradually at the waste portion. Never be tempted to take off a huge chunk in this way as the tile will break. Use this method, too, when cutting out L-shaped or curved sections. Make a card template (pattern) of the shape required and transfer it onto the tile.

Projecting pipes are tricky to tile around so use a template again. The safest way to tackle the job is to cut the tile in two, removing from each portion an arc to suit the shape of the pipe. When the two portions are positioned together round the pipe, the joint will not be obvious.

Tiling round fitments

Treat the top edges of sinks, baths and cupboard units as the floor level and nail or screw a horizontal batten above them. This will support the tiles above it while the rest of the wall is being completed. After the adhesive has set, remove the batten and apply the bottom course of tiles, trimming where necessary.

Tiling round windows

The window is very often the focal point of any room so it is important to try to arrange the tiles to achieve a good visual balance, with equal size tiles on either side of the window.

On horizontal sill surfaces fix whole tiles at the front, with any cut ones at the back nearest the window where they are not so obvious.

Above Tiara long tiles add height to small rooms and colours match bathroom equipment ranges, 216 × 108mm/$8\frac{1}{2}$ × $4\frac{1}{4}$in
Below left Florence is a strong design and needs to be used over a large enough area to show off its pattern. It looks well with adjacent walls in matching solid colour tiles (All in Cristal range by H. & R. Johnson)

Basic items
hand or electric drill
wood and masonry bits
countersink bit, screwdriver

For surface preparation
timber straight-edge
medium coarse glasspaper
filler, knife, primer (for plaster)
stripping knife (for wallpaper)
block plane, primer, paint brush
   (for wood)

For lining walls
50 × 25mm (2 × 1in) battens
No 8 countersunk screws, 50mm (2in)
   and 32mm (1$\frac{1}{4}$in) long, wall plugs
plywood or chipboard, sealer
hardboard or plywood pieces

For tiling
measuring staff and pencil
batten (for horizontal line)
spirit level, plumb bob and line
tile adhesive and notched spreader
broad knife, small round-ended trowel
grouting powder and water
sponge and two soft cloths

For cutting tiles
tile cutter, matchsticks and pencil
metal straight-edge or try square
pincers (for thin sections)
card and scissors (if template needed)

equipment

Fixing mirrors & mirror tiles

Mirrors play an important part in interior decoration; if they are carefully placed, a small room can be made to look larger and a dark room appear lighter. In every home there is a place where a mirror can be used to great effect – in an alcove, behind display shelving, in a recess or covering a door. But remember a mirrored surface will reflect everything which stands in front of it; so avoid overdoing it by placing mirrors on an adjacent or facing wall since the effect might be confusing and not what you expected.

Mirrors

A wide range of mirrors is available, either drilled for screw fixing or undrilled for other methods of fixing. Your glass merchant will be able to supply you with a mirror of almost any shape or size. Any top quality glass, free of imperfections, is suitable

for silvering; 6mm ($\frac{1}{4}$in) float glass is used for most of the larger mirrors. It might be necessary to use a thicker glass for mirror table tops, depending on the size requirements; your glass merchant should be able to advise you.

Decide when placing a special order for a mirror whether you will require a screw fixing. If you do, it is worthwhile getting the supplier to do the drilling for you. Large mirrors are expensive and, since the additional charge for drilling is very reasonable considering the overall cost of the mirror, it is best not to risk drilling the holes yourself.

All mirrors should have polished edges, unless they are to be set into a heavy rebated frame, when a clean cut edge will do. Take care when handling cut mirrors with unpolished edges; wear leather gloves since the edges of the glass are razor sharp.
Screw fixing A drilled mirror can easily be fixed in

Above Large slabs of mirror give an impression of increased light and space to any part of your home, as well as adding a touch of luxury for a relatively low cost

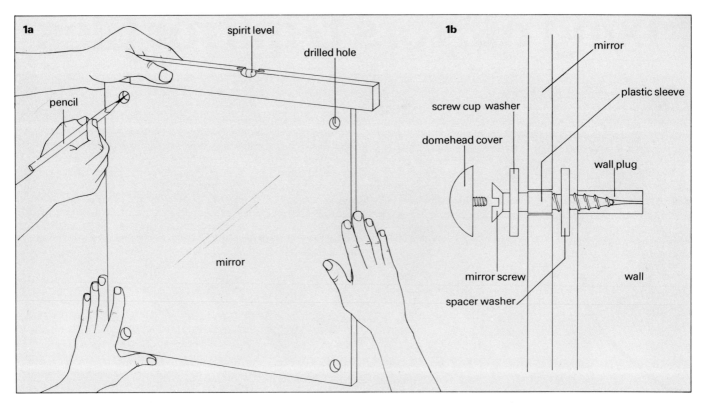

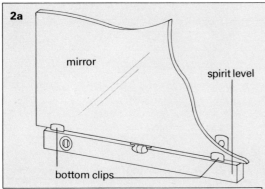

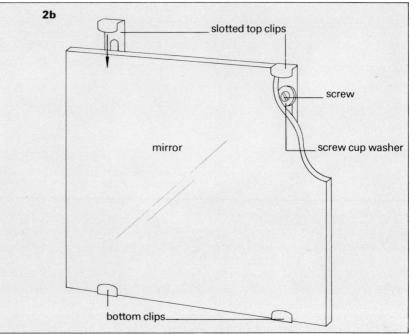

place, unless the wall surface is uneven; a really badly undulating surface should be covered with a base board of plywood or chipboard, although it is seldom necessary to go to this trouble.

First support the base of the mirror flat against the wall in its final fixing position. It is wise to get help at this stage, if only to check the mirror is set at a true vertical on the wall. Once you have established the right position, mark with a pencil through the drilled holes onto the wall behind. Remove the mirror and drill the wall at these points, using the correct size masonry bit and wall plugs for the mirror screws.

The screws used have rubber or soft plastic spacers and collars. Various types are available, although the principle is the same with each. The screw passes through a sleeve, which is centred in the hole of the mirror. At the back a spacer washer fits between the mirror and the wall, while a cup washer is placed between the face of the mirror and the countersunk head of the mirror screw. Great care must be taken when tightening the screws; work round them in turn, gradually tightening each one until its head gently squeezes the soft cup washer on the face of the mirror. Check at this stage the mirror is firmly held against the wall. If it is not, don't tighten the screws further since this will cause

the mirror to break. Remove whichever screw is not gripping the mirror firmly, insert packing behind the spacer washer to fill the remaining gap and screw through the packing into the wall. The decorative heads of the screws can then be fitted into the fixing screws to conceal the screw heads and the washers beneath.

Mirror clip fixing Undrilled mirrors can be mounted on a wall using mirror clips. Several types are available, including corner clips, plastic spring clips and hook-on clips. With the hook-on type the bottom clips are screwed to the wall in accurate alignment, so the bottom of the mirror rests on the upward facing jaws. Check your levels carefully before finally fixing these clips.

The upper clips have a long slot in the back plate

1a Hold a drilled mirror in the required position on the wall and mark through the holes; check the mirror is horizontal with a spirit level
1b Secure the mirror with the relevant fixings
2a Make sure the bottom clips are level when fixing an undrilled mirror with clips
2b Fix the top clips, place the mirror in position and slide the top clips down; you can fit additional slotted clips on each side for extra stability

3a Before fixing mirror tiles, remove the protective paper from the tabs on the back
3b To mark the position of the tiles, number each one and write the numbers in order on the board
3c Press the tiles in place, applying light pressure over each tab in turn; don't apply pressure between the tabs since you might break the tile

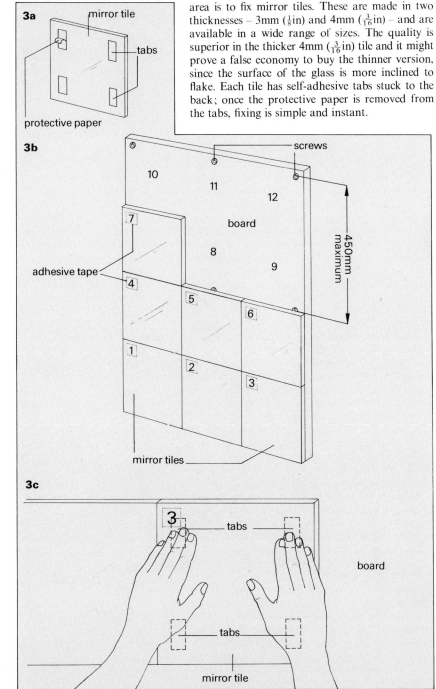

3a
mirror tile
tabs
protective paper

3b
screws
10
11
12
board
450mm maximum
7
8
9
adhesive tape
4
5
6
1
2
3
mirror tiles

3c
3
tabs
tabs
board
tabs
mirror tile

through which they are screwed to the wall, tightly enough to allow the clip to slide up and down behind the screw head. The mirror is then placed in the bottom clips and pushed flat against the wall, while the downward facing jaws of the upper clips remain in the open position. The upper clips are then slid down so the jaws hold the top edge of the mirror. The mirror can be easily taken down by opening the upper clips and lifting the mirror out of the bottom ones.

Frame fixing Small mirrors can be framed and backed and hung in position using mirror plates or chains. Larger mirrors can be built into wall fitments and held with facing mouldings and beading. A mirror can also be placed in a sliding frame to provide a mirrored door for a unit.

Mirror tiles

The simplest method of providing a large mirrored area is to fix mirror tiles. These are made in two thicknesses – 3mm ($\frac{1}{8}$in) and 4mm ($\frac{3}{16}$in) – and are available in a wide range of sizes. The quality is superior in the thicker 4mm ($\frac{3}{16}$in) tile and it might prove a false economy to buy the thinner version, since the surface of the glass is more inclined to flake. Each tile has self-adhesive tabs stuck to the back; once the protective paper is removed from the tabs, fixing is simple and instant.

Before you start fixing, you must prepare the surface onto which the tiles are to be stuck. Any surface which is not perfectly flat will cause the tiles to lie in an uneven plane, which will result in a distorted reflection. Plaster surfaces are particularly bad since they are seldom perfectly flat. Although the tabs will stick effectively to painted or untreated plaster – unless the paint is badly flaking – it is advisable not to try it if a perfect surface is required.

Fixing to board Mirror tiles are best stuck down to a suitable board such as plywood or chipboard. The thicker the board the better, since there is more chance of achieving the perfect flatness you require. For a really uneven wall surface use an 18mm ($\frac{3}{4}$in) thick board; don't use board less than 12mm ($\frac{1}{2}$in) thick, even on a wall which looks true.

Screw the board in place using the appropriate wall plugs and countersink the heads of the screws slightly below the surface of the board. The screws should be about 450mm (18in) apart around the edge and across the surface of the board. Don't drive the screws in tight, but stop just as the screw begins to bite into the board; an overtightened screw in a depressed part of the wall will cause the board to follow the depression and lose its flatness. This is more likely to occur with thinner board.

Setting out tiles This is an important stage and should be done with care. Individual tiles are seldom cut with perfect accuracy and can vary slightly. Over a large area this variation can be cumulative and result in a poor finish. Wherever possible set out the tiles loosely on the fixing board before it is screwed to the wall; you will finally fix them into place starting at the bottom and working upwards.

When the tiles are set out squarely to your liking, number each tile, using a small piece of adhesive tape on the face of each, and write these numbers in the same order on the board. Fix the tiles in place so the numbers correspond. Fix them into place in the same order and you will be sure of a perfect run of joints.

Fixing tiles When fixing take care to note the exact position of each tab on the back of the tile. Remove the protective paper and place the tile in position on the board, applying light pressure to each tab in turn. Avoid applying pressure to the tile between the tab positions – especially when using thinner tiles – since this might break them. If you make a mistake and have to remove a tile, use a thin broad bladed knife and try to slide it beneath each pad in turn. Don't try to lever the tile away or you will break it.

New adhesive tabs can be stuck into place on the back of a mirror tile if the original one has to be removed. These tabs have strong adhesive and work effectively the first time on most surfaces. As a safeguard on porous boards, brush away any dust and apply a thin coat of impact adhesive to correspond with the tab positions. Allow this to dry thoroughly before bringing tabs into contact.

Warning Care must be taken in areas where there is excessive moisture; bathrooms are particularly prone to heavy condensation. Never use a porous-type chipboard as a backing for mirrors or mirror tiles in these conditions, since rot will set into the chipboard, causing mould and damaging the silvering of the mirror. Use a resin-bonded plywood and check edges are thoroughly sealed with primer.

An air space of at least 3mm ($\frac{1}{8}$in) should be left between the fixing surface and the back of the mirror; with tiles the tabs determine the space.

Laying ceramic floor tiles

Traditionally ceramic tiles have been used to cover areas around basins, baths and sinks, where splashing is likely to occur. But they are also very practical for covering floors.

Now that central heating has taken the chill from ceramic floor tiles, people are beginning to appreciate their hard-wearing qualities and easy maintenance. Provided it is correctly laid on a properly prepared sub-floor, ceramic flooring has good resistance to impact and general wear and high resistance to crazing. It only needs to be swept regularly and washed from time to time with water and detergent. Stubborn stains can be removed from this type of tile with a household abrasive – or paint brush cleaner.

Types of tiles
It is essential to use only flooring grade tiles – wall tiles are much thinner and would break under pressure. Flooring tiles are available glazed or unglazed. Glazed tiles come in a wide range of colours and patterns and some have a roughened glaze to make them slip-resistant. Unglazed tiles are produced only in plain or mottled colours; but they are the most durable form of tile and are available in a range of anti-slip surfaces and also coving tiles to provide a clean curve from floor to wall. They are more difficult to cut than glazed tiles, but you can hire or buy a special tool for cutting them.

Tiles are made in a variety of shapes, square ones being the easiest to lay. The most common size is 152mm (6in) square, which means you will need 43 tiles to cover 1sq m (36 for 1sq yd). Always buy six or so extra ones for cutting in or in case of breakages.

Mosaic tiles are small squares of glazed or unglazed ceramic covered with peel-off sheets 305mm (12in) square which you remove after laying.

Preparing the surface
It is essential to lay ceramic tiles on a clean, dry, level surface; any distortions may cause the tiles to move and crack under pressure. They can be laid on a solid floor of concrete or existing hard flooring such as terrazzo or quarry tiles or on a suspended timber floor. But in each case the floor needs some preparation before the tiles are laid.

Concrete The concrete must be dry, clean and flat. Tiling will not cure damp, so if the concrete is letting moisture through, lay a damp proof membrane and screed.

Fill any small depressions in the concrete with sand and cement, using a mixture of three parts washed sharp sand and one part cement – and make sure you level off after filling. If there is a slight fall-away in the surface in any direction, correct it with a concrete levelling compound. A badly depressed surface should be levelled with a waterproof screed. Chip away any small nibs of concrete and sweep the surface thoroughly.

Hard flooring Tiled or terrazzo floors should be flat and firmly fixed. Remove any traces of grease

or polish and make sure it is dry before you start tiling. Any loose sections, such as a loose quarry tile, should be securely glued back in place.

Timber floor Make sure there is adequate ventilation below the floorboards to prevent rot forming after tiling. Don't lay tiles directly onto a suspended timber floor made of tongued and grooved boards since the movement of the floor would cause the tiles to shift and crack. Make the floor more stable by covering it with sheets of plywood at least 12mm ($\frac{1}{2}$in) thick, fixed at 300mm (or 12in) intervals with countersunk screws. If the floor is likely to be splashed with water, such as in a shower area, use exterior grade plywood.

When all existing floorboards have to be removed, due to rot for example, you can screw flooring grade chipboard directly to the joists and lay tiles on this. Use screws for fixing sheet flooring since nails cannot be relied on to hold the material securely in place once the tiles have been bonded to them. Make sure the panels butt closely together; if any small gaps do appear, pack them tightly with a filler or the floor tiles may crack along the joint lines due to movement on the sub-floor.

Before laying tiles over plywood or chipboard, always brush the surface with a priming coat; most manufacturers recommend a water-based polymer for this purpose. The primer must be properly dry before you begin tiling, so leave it overnight.

Working with adhesive
Manufacturers recommend a cement-based powder adhesive which can be used as a thin or thick-bed adhesive. Use a thin bed of about 3mm ($\frac{1}{8}$in) for flat-backed tiles; if the tiles have studs on the back or there is a slight unevenness in the floor (test with a straight-edge), use a thick bed of about 6mm ($\frac{1}{4}$in). For thin-bed fixing, you will need about 3.5kg (or 8lb) of adhesive per square metre (or

1 Apply adhesive to the floor with a notched spreader; only cover 1sq m (or sq yd) at a time
2 Lay the first tile in the right-angle formed by your marked lines
3 Position the next few tiles with spacer lugs touching, matching any pattern carefully
4 If using studded tiles on a thick bed of adhesive, lightly coat the back of the tiles to ensure they sit firmly on the floor

2

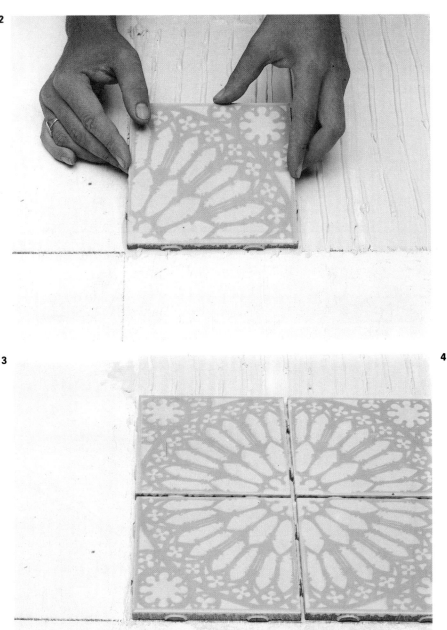

3

4

from the point where the strings cross. If the space remaining at the end of a row is less than half a tile, adjust the string lines half a tile off centre to give a bigger space for the perimeter tiles. This will give a balanced border and avoids having to cut narrow pieces of tile. Check the door will open over the laid tiles; if not, remove the door and trim the bottom edge with a block plane.

Fixing the tiles

Tile one quarter of the room at a time, starting with the section furthest from the door and finishing at the door. Starting from the centre, spread the adhesive evenly over the floor with a notched spreader, which is often supplied with the adhesive. Don't cover more than 1sq m (or 1sq yd) at a time. Place the tiles in position, starting in the angle of the chalked lines. Don't slide them into place or adhesive will build up against the front edge of the tile. When laying studded tiles on thick-bed adhesive, spread a thin layer of adhesive on the back of the tile to ensure a solid bed when it comes into contact with the adhesive on the floor.

Most tiles have spacer lugs to ensure the distance between each one is correct; if yours do not have

these, place pieces of card or matchsticks between the tiles to give a space of 3mm ($\frac{1}{8}$in). Remove any adhesive that oozes up between the joints (to leave space for grouting) and clean off any adhesive on the tiles before it sets.

Tile each section of the room in turn, leaving the border until last. If you need to kneel on the tiled area while working, place a board across it to avoid damaging or disturbing the tiles.

Cutting border tiles To cut a tile for the border, lay it face down on top of the last whole tile and slide it forward so the front edge butts against the wall. Mark the back of the tile at each side where the edge of the last tile finishes. Place it on a firm, flat surface and join up the two marks, using a straight-edge as a guide. Score and cut the tile along this line with a tile cutter. The front section of the cut tile will fit neatly in the gap.

Cutting corner tiles Place a new tile face down over the last whole one near the corner. Place a second tile on it, slide it flush to the wall and mark its edge on the tile below. Then move the marked tile to the last whole tile round the corner without

---

11sq ft); allow double this quantity for a thick bed. There is also a bitumen-based adhesive which can be used for thin-bed fixing.

Cement-based adhesive can be used on concrete or timber floors, but it is not suitable on concrete which has not fully dried out or on ground floors which are affected by damp. In these cases, and for areas subjected to prolonged soaking with water (such as shower floors) use a waterproof adhesive. Always mix the adhesive according to the manufacturer's instructions.

Setting out the tiles

The best way to set out tiles is from the centre of the room so you have an even border all round the edge. To find the centre, mark the halfway point on the two pairs of opposite walls and stretch a piece of string (preferably chalked) between each set of marks. Ensure the strings cross at right-angles and secure the ends with nails or pins. If the strings are chalked, pluck them to leave marks on the floor.

Before fixing down any tiles, try out the layout with dry tiles. Lay one row of tiles in each direction

turning it. Place the second tile over it, butt it against the wall and mark as before. Score and cut along these lines and nibble the corner away with pincers or tile nippers to give an L-shaped tile which will fit round the corner. Take away only very small pieces at a time; if you try to cut too much at once, you may break the tile. When you have cut the shape you want, smooth the rough edge with a carborundum stone.

Cutting shapes To cut curved shapes, use a contour tracer or make a template and scribe the outline onto the tile. Then nibble away the tile with pincers or tile nippers as before.

To fit a tile round a pipe, cut the tile in two where the pipe falls, cut out a semi-circle from each piece and fit them round the pipe.

When tiling round a WC or wash-basin pedestal, lay full tiles as far as possible round the pedestal. To avoid having to cut very narrow sections, you may have to adjust the layout when setting out the loose tiles. Cut a template for each tile, using a contour tracer to mark the curve – and with this cut the tile; lay it in place before making a template for the adjacent tile. When all the tiles are cut and smoothed, fix them in position. Remember to leave enough space between tiles and pedestal for grouting.

Mosaic tiles Lay mosaic tiles in the same way as ordinary tiles, leaving on the paper. When the adhesive has set, soak the paper with cold water and peel it off. Where possible, use whole mosaic squares, rather than cut ones, to fill in the gaps round the perimeter of the room.

Grouting

When all the tiles have been fixed, leave them for at least 12 hours before grouting. Don't walk on them during this time since any disturbance may affect the bonding of the adhesive. If you used card or matchsticks for spacing, remove them after 24 hours. It is a good idea to wait for 24–48 hours before grouting.

Most tile manufacturers recommend a powder grout which has to be mixed with water to a creamy consistency. Mix only enough to last for about 40 minutes since it becomes unworkable after that time. Cover a small area at a time and rub the grout into the joints with a sponge or the straight side of a notched spreader, making sure all joints are filled. Leave the grout to harden in the joints for about 30 minutes before wiping off the surplus with a dampened cloth. Wipe away all traces of grout from the tiles, rinsing frequently with clean water. You can blend the grout with the tiles by colouring it: mix grout colour mix with the grout powder before adding water.

Warning Try to avoid washing the floor for a week or two, since water may dilute the adhesive and affect the strength of the bond.

Replacing a damaged tile

Chip the damaged tile away with a club hammer and cold chisel, working from the centre, taking care not to damage surrounding tiles. Remove the old adhesive with the chisel and stick down a new tile.

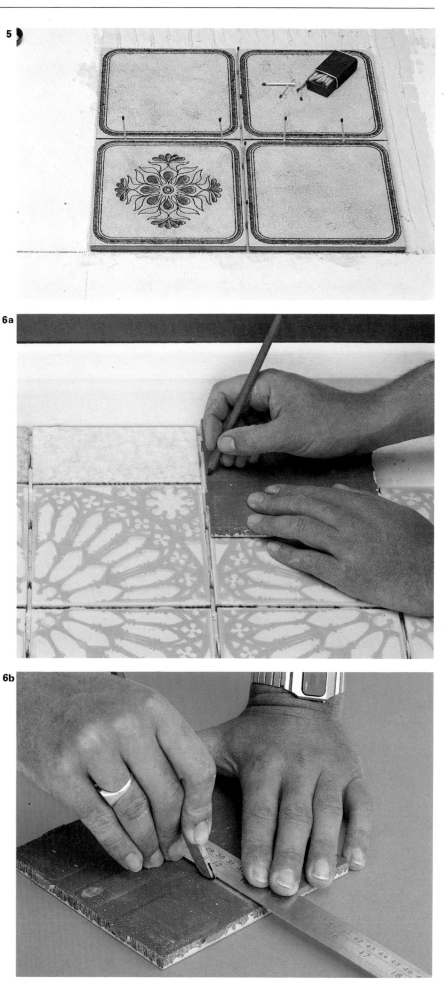

5

6a

6b

7a
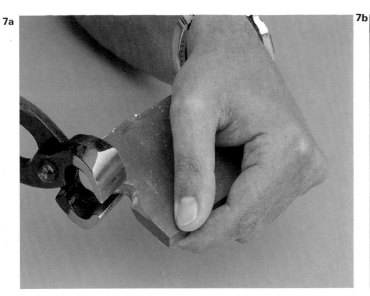

7b
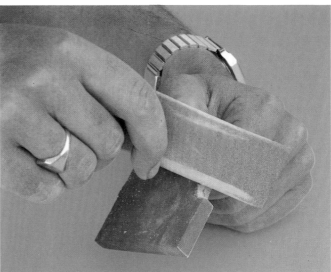

5 If your tiles do not have spacer lugs, use matchsticks to keep a 3mm ($\frac{1}{8}$in) gap

6a To cut border tiles, mark the back of the tile at each side where the last tile finishes

6b Join up the marks and score along the line using a straight-edge as a guide

7a Cut shapes by nibbling small pieces from the tile with pincers

7b Smooth the rough edges with a carborundum stone

8 To fit tiles round piping, cut the tile in two, remove a semi-circle from each piece and position the pieces round the pipe

9a Apply grouting between the tiles with the straight side of a notched spreader

9b Leave the grout to harden and wipe off any excess with a dampened cloth

8
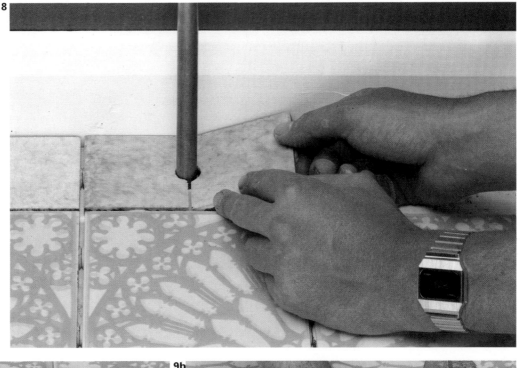

9a

9b
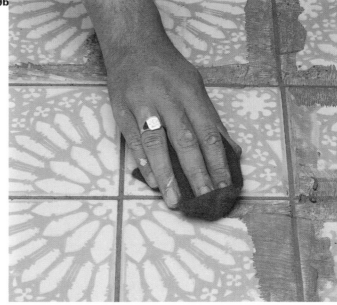

Laying cork & vinyl tiles

Cork and vinyl tiles are ideal as floor coverings in different areas of the home and offer a wide range of colours and designs. Using the correct methods, these tiles are quite straightforward to put down, as long as you ensure the surface on which they are laid is dry, firm and level.

Above The pale, smooth colours and textures in this modern kitchen are set off effectively by the warmth of a natural cork floor

One of the real advantages of tiles rather than sheet flooring material is that, when laying, you can deal with awkward shapes one by one and any mistakes in cutting will be confined to individual tiles; you may even be able to reshape those cut in error and put them elsewhere. A mistake in cutting sheet material could involve much greater wastage. Both vinyl and cork flooring come in tile form: vinyl is waterproof, resistant to oil, grease and most domestic chemicals; cork is non-slip, has good thermal insulation and reduces noise.

Vinyl tiles
These offer a wide choice of designs, from alternate rows in two or more colours and chess board effects to more complicated diamond patterns or squares-within-squares using a variety of colours. If you choose a complicated pattern, draw the design on paper to make laying easier – some manufacturers provide blank squared paper for this purpose.

Vinyl tiles are sold in packs sufficient to cover a square metre (or square yard) and the most common size tile is 300mm (or 12in) square. Always buy a few extra tiles since, apart from cutting mistakes, spares can be useful later on when worn tiles need replacing.

Pure vinyl tiles are supple and easy to lay. They have a smooth gloss finish and come in a wide variety of patterns and colours. Vinyl asbestos tiles are cheaper but more rigid and tend to crack if not stuck to a solid, level surface. They are not as easy to lay as the pure vinyl type and the choice of designs is limited, although sculptured and embossed designs are available. Some vinyl tiles are self-adhesive; if wrongly placed, these can be removed immediately and repositioned but, if you move them more than once, the adhesive tends to become less effective. Self-adhesive tiles are protected by a paper backing and you should always cut the tiles to shape before you remove this. If the tiles you choose are not self-adhesive, fix them with special vinyl flooring adhesive.

Cork tiles
Cork tiles come in a range of textures and shades. The choice of finishes is wide, too, and you should consider carefully which is best suited to your needs.
Unsealed Good where a non-slip but not particularly hard-wearing surface is required. This type is supplied with a sanded finish, but you can sand the surface again once the tiles have been laid to conceal any joint irregularities. To make unsealed tiles more durable, you can apply a polyurethane sealer but, before doing this, leave the laid floor for about 12 hours to allow the adhesive to dry thoroughly.
Hard wax These tiles provide a scuff-resistant semi-sheen surface which is particularly suitable for use in the bathroom and living areas, especially where elderly people and children are concerned. After laying the tiles, apply a coat of wax polish to conceal the joins but don't apply a sealer as the wax will prevent a good bond.
Polyurethane Suited to areas likely to be subjected to very heavy wear such as kitchens or playrooms, since the polyurethane coating makes this type particularly tough and long-lasting.
Vinyl-faced Perhaps the most popular cork surface, this consists of a thin layer of cork sandwiched between two layers of vinyl. It is particularly suitable for kitchens where heavy appliances are likely to be moved about, since any indentations recover rapidly and the easily cleaned vinyl surface protects the cork against spilt liquids.

Various adhesives are available for use with cork flooring, but it is important you use the one recommended by the manufacturer for the type of

Above Vinyl tiles make a very practical kitchen floor and are available in a wide range of colours and patterns

making sure the screw heads lie flush with or slightly below the surface.

If the fixing surface is very uneven, cover it with 12 or 18mm ($\frac{1}{2}$ or $\frac{3}{4}$in) chipboard or plywood screwed into position. Use flooring grade chipboard when fixing to timber, and resin-bonded plywood for concrete. On an old, worn, uneven concrete floor you may need to use a levelling compound. When mixed with water the compound finds its own level and provides a smooth, even surface.

Cork Level off any uneven surfaces in the same way as for vinyl tiles. Where timber boards are laid at ground level or on joists or battens on ground level concrete, protect the cork from moisture penetration by fixing bituminous felt paper with bituminous adhesive before overlaying with hardboard or plywood. Ideally you should remove any existing floor covering before laying cork; if this is too difficult, you can lay cork over vinyl tiles and other similar non-porous floor surfaces, provided the existing surface is level. Wash with detergent to remove any grease and use wire wool to remove polish and to provide a key for the adhesive.

It is not advisable to lay cork directly onto asphalt surfaces since these are very non-porous. With natural cork, the solvent in the fixing adhesive is likely to be absorbed into the underside, which may cause the centres of the tiles to sink slightly before the adhesive has fully set. So, before laying cork, use a latex levelling compound on top of the asphalt.

When laying vinyl-faced cork over flagstones and other paved interior finishes laid direct to the earth, first cover the sub-floor with a layer of rock asphalt at least 16mm (or $\frac{5}{8}$in) thick, then use a levelling compound. Before laying cork tiles on concrete screeds or solid floors, make sure the floor incorporates an effective damp proof membrane and that it is completely dry. Porous floors such as concrete screed, plywood and chipboard should be primed before the tiles are fixed.

Some kinds of cork tile can be used over underfloor heating although, because of cork's good thermal insulating quality, this could be an unnecessary expense. If you do decide to use cork in this way, make sure the surface heat does not exceed 27°C (80°F). The heating system should have been working for at least two weeks before the cork is laid and should be switched off for at least 48 hours before and after laying. It is better not to use vinyl-faced cork in this situation since the heat will eventually give the tiles a pebbly effect. Also make sure any underfloor hot water pipes are adequately insulated.

Warning Before laying vinyl or cork tiles, make sure timber floors have adequate ventilation underneath. Poor ventilation can cause condensation which could lead to rotting of both floorboards and floor covering.

cork you have chosen. Some tiles are self-adhesive, but if you choose ones which are not, follow the manufacturer's instructions on where to put the adhesive – on both tiles and floor, or floor only.

Preparing the surface
Thorough preparation of the fixing surface is essential for good results. Make sure it is clean, dry and level so the tiles lie perfectly flat.
Vinyl If your fixing surface is slightly uneven, first cover it with plywood or tempered hardboard, smooth side up. You can use hardboard nails if fixing to a timber floor, but with concrete you will have to drill holes, insert suitable plugs and fix the hardboard into position with countersunk screws,

Laying the tiles
Start laying tiles from the centre of the room, which can be located by stretching two lengths of string (preferably chalked) from the mid-point of each pair of opposite walls across the floor so they cross at the centre (**see 1a**). Make sure the pieces of string cross at right-angles and secure the ends with nails or pins.

Position two rows of dry tiles, working from the mid-point to the skirting boards (**see 1b**). This will give you the width of the tiles around the perimeter. If only a very narrow strip is left, the floor will have an unbalanced look, especially if you are using vinyl tiles in a dual colour or chess board design. To prevent this, adjust the string line half a tile width off centre to leave wider perimeter tiles (**see 1c**). If using chalked string, pluck it and the chalk will leave an accurate impression on the floor. Alternatively, use a straight-edge and a pencil to trace the string lines accurately.

Vinyl Lay the tiles in the order shown (**see 2**). Complete each section of the room with as many full tiles as possible, leaving all cutting jobs until later. If using tiles that are not self-adhesive, spread a thin layer of adhesive on the floor (not on the back of the tile) about a square metre (or square yard) at a time. Don't spread more than this because the adhesive sets quickly and the tiles must be laid while it is still tacky. Start laying the tiles, pressing each one firmly into position from the centre of the tile outwards to prevent air being trapped underneath.

Cork Lay cork tiles in the same order as for vinyl tiles, but fit the cut border tiles at the same time as the adjacent full tile. You can ease the tiles slightly for the final positioning, but don't slide them into position. To ensure a good bond, roll the tiles or, using a hammer and a block of wood, bang firmly over the surface. Remove any excess adhesive from the surface of vinyl-faced cork with a clean cloth dampened in white spirit.

Cutting tiles

Use either a strong, sharp pair of scissors or a stiff, sharp knife held against a metal straight-edge to ensure clean cuts.

Edge tiles Place a whole tile A on top of the last tile in the row and another whole tile B over A with its far edge flush to the skirting board. Draw a line across A, using the near edge of tile B as a guide, and cut off and fit the near section of tile A (**see 3**).

Shaped tiles These can be cut by making a card template of the shape required and tracing it on to the tile to be cut. Alternatively, lay tile A on top of the last whole tile in the row nearest the corner and another whole tile B over A with its far edge flush to the skirting board. Draw a line across A, using the near edge of B as a guide (**see 4a**). Slide A on top of the last whole tile in the row around the corner, but don't twist it; the line marked on it must remain parallel with the first skirting marked out. Place tile B over A with its far edge pressed up against the skirting and draw a second line across tile A using the near edge of B as a guide (**see 4b**). Cut out the L-shaped portion, which will fit neatly around the corner (**see 4c**).

Cutting around pipes The easiest way to cut a tile to fit around a pipe is to make a card template of the required shape and trace the shape on to the tile. Cut a slit directly from the hole made for the pipe to the skirting board (**see 5**). When the tile is fixed and pressed into position this line will hardly be visible – especially with a patterned tile.

Awkward shapes Tiles can be cut using either a card template or a special tool called a shape-tracer or contour gauge (**see 6**). This houses a series of tightly packed wires which, when pressed against a shape, forms its outline. The outline can then be transferred to the tile to be cut.

Doorway Floor coverings get the greatest amount of wear in doorways; if the joins between the coverings are not secure the edges curl up. This

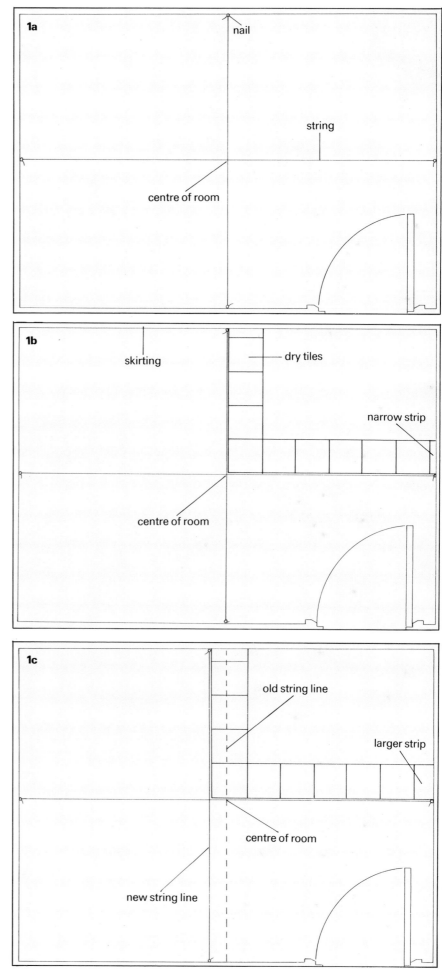

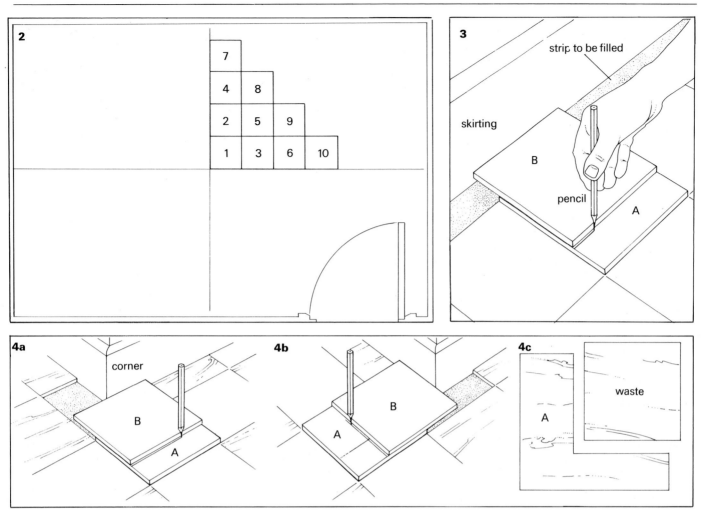

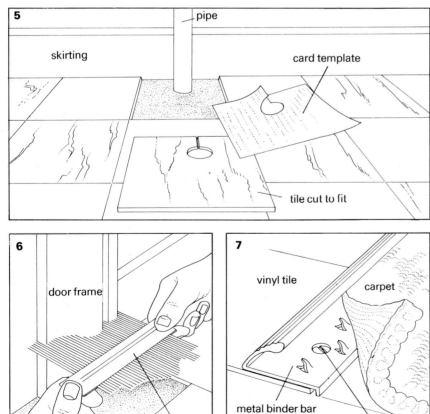

increases wear and tear and can become a hazard. Metal binder bars will solve this problem. Available in various finishes and with different clamping edges that take all kinds of materials, they will join vinyl to vinyl, or vinyl to other floor coverings (see 7).

Door clearance One of the most common mistakes when laying floor coverings is failure to allow for door clearance. The floor level has probably been raised sufficiently to obstruct free movement of the door, especially if using a hardboard base. Vinyl needs a clearance gap or the door's constant rubbing will wear it down very quickly. If the door touches the vinyl, remove the door and trim the bottom edge with a block plane.

Looking after tiles

To maintain the surface of vinyl or vinyl-faced cork tiles, clean them periodically with a mop or sponge and a little mild, liquid detergent. Never use excessive water, strong cleaning agents or abrasives which might damage the finish. Use white spirit to remove stubborn marks from rubber-soled shoes and, should the vinyl become scratched, apply an emulsion wax polish. Prevent spirit-based polishes, rubber compounds and nail varnish remover coming into contact with the surface since these could cause permanent damage to the vinyl.

Laying sheet vinyl

Sheet vinyl is a practical, hard-wearing flooring material which only needs to be swept, washed and occasionally polished to keep it in condition. It is therefore suitable for rooms where there are likely to be spills and water splashes.

Buying vinyl

Vinyl is available in a variety of colours, patterns and effects such as ceramic tiles, cork, natural stone and timber and surfaces are both smooth and textured. Cushioned vinyl, which has a layer of foam material between the vinyl and the backing, is quieter, warmer and more comfortable than un-cushioned vinyl and is particularly suitable in the kitchen, where you may spend time standing.

Estimating quantity Most vinyl flooring comes in 2m (or 6ft 7in) widths; it is also available in 4m (or 13ft 1in) widths, which may eliminate the need for joins. If the room is wider than that, you will have to cut the vinyl into suitable lengths and join them. Remember to allow an extra 75mm (3in) for each length. Manufacturers will normally state pattern repeats for the material, so when you are matching patterns you will be able to estimate how much extra is needed. Usually you should allow for an extra pattern repeat on each length except the first. Most suppliers will give you a free estimate on the quantity needed if you submit a floor plan before ordering the material.

Preparing the sub-floor

Vinyl can be laid on almost any floor provided the surface is smooth, level, dry, clean and free from polish or grease – and of sound construction. All types of floor should be covered with flooring grade plywood – at least 4mm ($\frac{5}{32}$in) thick – or tempered hardboard – not less than 3mm ($\frac{1}{8}$in) thick.

Solid floor A solid floor should incorporate a damp proof membrane; if it does not, this is a good opportunity to have one installed and thus save problems later on. Fill any cracks or holes in the floor with a levelling compound which should also be used to level off a slightly sloping floor. To fix sheets of plywood or hardboard you must drill and plug holes and secure with countersunk screws.

Timber floor Check there is adequate ventilation below the floorboards; installation of airbricks will solve problems in this area. Secure any loose boards and punch down protruding nail heads. If the floor is uneven, plane down any projections.

Always lay hardboard sheets rough side up and fix them to the floor with ring shank or serrated nails at 100mm (4in) intervals. The rough surface enables the nail heads to be well bedded in and provides a better key for the adhesive. Hardboard has a low moisture content and if it absorbs any moisture it will expand; when it dries out, it will then shrink. You should wet the hardboard with water, using a dampened sponge, at least 48 hours before laying it. When it dries out, it will grip tightly around the nail heads.

For a very uneven floor, screw down 12 or 18mm ($\frac{1}{2}$ or $\frac{3}{4}$in) flooring grade chipboard at 300mm (12in) intervals, using countersunk screws, to provide a level surface. Alternatively, if the boards are severely warped, rotten or otherwise damaged, it is worth removing them and laying a new floor to avoid trouble later.

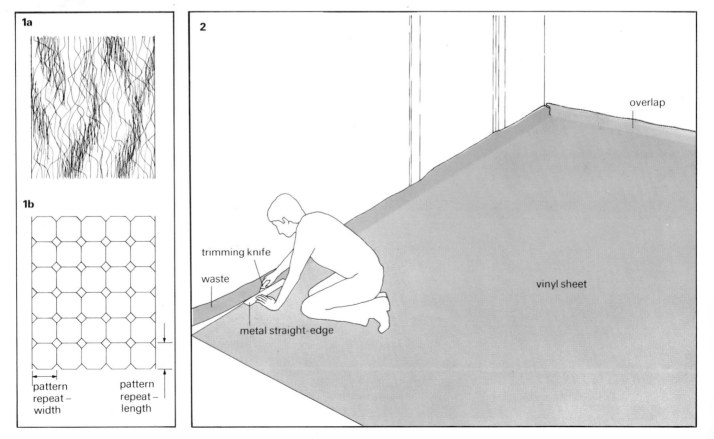

1a

1b
pattern repeat – width
pattern repeat – length

2
overlap
trimming knife
waste
metal straight-edge
vinyl sheet

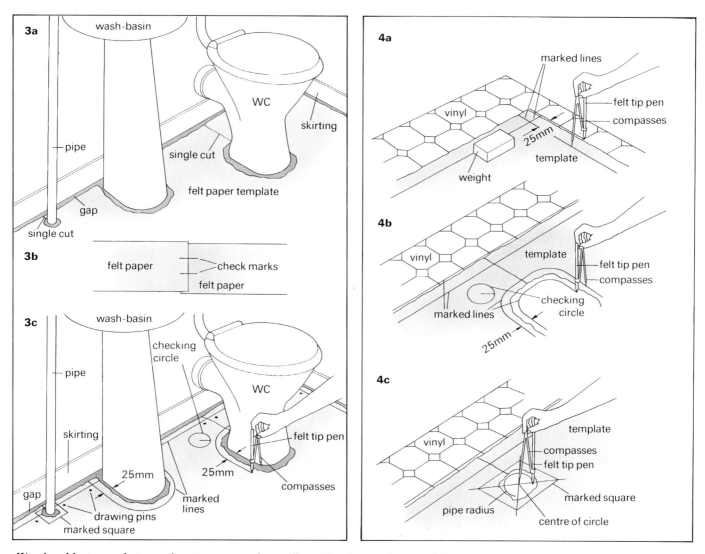

3a wash-basin
pipe
WC
skirting
single cut
felt paper template
gap
single cut

3b felt paper
check marks
felt paper

3c wash-basin
checking circle
pipe
WC
skirting
25mm
25mm
felt tip pen
gap
drawing pins
marked lines
compasses
marked square

4a marked lines
vinyl
felt tip pen
compasses
25mm
template
weight

4b vinyl
template
felt tip pen
compasses
checking circle
marked lines
25mm

4c vinyl
template
compasses
felt tip pen
pipe radius
marked square
centre of circle

Warning Most manufacturers do not recommend laying vinyl over a timber floor which has been treated with wood preservative, although you can lay Kraft paper with an aluminium facing onto the timber, aluminium side down. If a preservative has been applied, leave it for a month before laying Kraft paper and fixing plywood or hardboard on top. If you have underfloor heating, make sure the temperature does not exceed 27°C (or 80°F).

Preparing vinyl
Before laying vinyl, slacken the roll and leave it in a warm room overnight so it will soften, relax any strain in the sheet and be easier to work. Some manufacturers suggest reverse-rolling the vinyl or laying it flat.

Fitting a single sheet
Since walls are rarely straight, you must cut the vinyl to fit the contour of the walls. If you are working in a small room which can be covered with a single width and the vinyl is very flexible, you can lay it out so it overlaps all round and cut it into the edges of the wall with a trimming knife. Use a metal straight-edge to push the vinyl into the angle between the floor and the wall. If the vinyl is not flexible enough to do this or if you feel more confident having a cutting guide, you should make a template. This is particularly useful when laying vinyl in a bathroom, where you will have to fit the flooring around a wash-basin or WC pedestal. Use

stiff card for the template – or felt paper, which is thick, lies flat and does not slide about; this is the paper used under carpets and you can buy it from a carpet supplier. Make sure any curls are face down.
Making a template Lay a sheet of felt paper – or any stiff card – on the floor to be covered. Rough-trim the paper to fit the required area, leaving a gap of about 16mm ($\frac{5}{8}$in) around the wall and the fittings. When fitting the template – and later the vinyl – on the floor, you will have to make a single cut from the back of the fitting cut-out to the nearest edge; as long as you follow lines on the pattern, this will not show once the vinyl is laid.

If you have to use more than one sheet, overlap the sheets and draw two check marks across the overlap to ensure the sheets can be repositioned accurately later. Once the paper is lying flat and has been roughly fitted, secure it with drawing pins (if working on a timber floor) or heavy weights (on a concrete floor) to prevent any movement.

Use a pair of compasses with a locking device, set at about a 25mm (1in) radius, and with the pointer vertical against the wall or fitting trace the outline of each in turn onto the template with a felt tip pen. Pipes and supports which are true circles can be squared off using a straight-edge on three or four sides. Draw a check circle on the template so you can check the compasses are correctly set when marking the vinyl.
Transferring template to vinyl Lay out the sheet of vinyl to be fitted in a convenient area (face up) and

1a Random pattern with no repeat needs no matching
1b Tile design vinyl has repeat pattern that must be matched when laying lengths
2 When laying single sheet, cut waste with trimming knife held against straight-edge pushed into angle between wall and floor
3a When covering awkward areas, make template to fit roughly around fittings
3b If you need more than one sheet of felt paper, draw check marks on each to help accurate alignment later
3c Secure template to floor; set compasses to 25mm radius and trace fittings outline onto felt paper; for pipes, mark sides of square on paper
4a Hold template on vinyl; with compasses at same radius transfer wall outline
4b Use same procedure to transfer fittings outline
4c Mark diagonals of square to find pipe centre and draw circle of pipe radius on vinyl

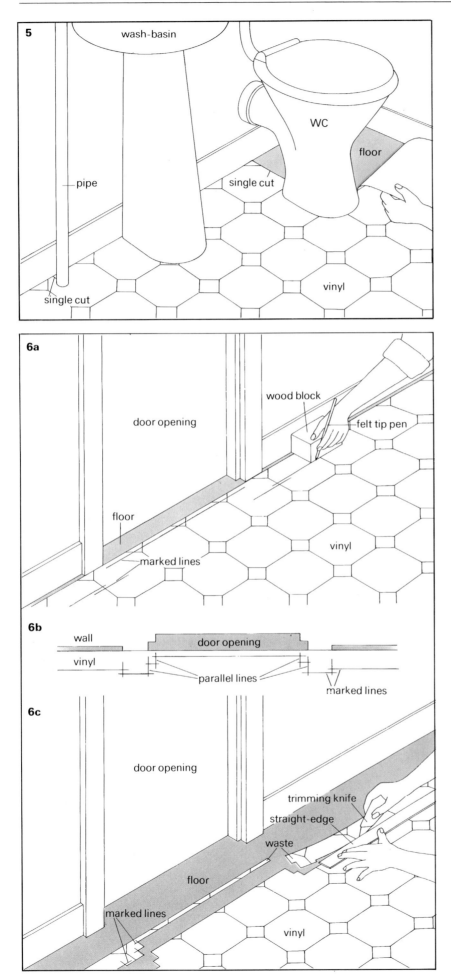

position the template accurately on top of it, using pins or heavy weights to prevent any movement. When working with a patterned vinyl, you may have to adjust the template to make sure the pattern runs correctly in relation to the fittings. If using more than one sheet of felt paper, make sure the check marks align.

Check the compasses are still at the same radius and, keeping the point always on and at right-angles to the marked outline, follow the outline so the felt tip pen marks the flooring. Any squared-off pipes can now be traced back, using a straight-edge, the centre of the square located and an accurate circle (the diameter of the pipe) drawn on the vinyl. Before removing the template, check again the compass setting has not altered and that the paper has not moved. Take off the template and cut out or trim the marked areas on the vinyl, which should then fit neatly around the fittings.

Fitting lengths

If the room is too large to be covered by a single sheet, you will have to adopt a different procedure. Measure the width of the room and cut a length of vinyl from the roll, allowing an extra 75mm (3in). Tackle the area by the door first, since this is going to have the most wear and you should always allow a full width of vinyl around it. Lay the vinyl square to the door opening.

Using a square-cut wood block 125 × 75 × 25mm (5 × 3 × 1in), with a felt tip pen on the side furthest from the wall, follow the contour of the wall on either side of the door and across the door opening to mark the outline on the vinyl. Mark on lines parallel to the door opening from the edge of the wall outlines already marked to ensure the vinyl fits snugly in the door opening and the edge is not visible when the door is closed. A shape-tracer is ideal for marking out the outline of an architrave to achieve a really neat finish. You can now cut along the marked lines on each side of the door. Place a straight-edge on the vinyl to be laid and cut along the outline with a trimming knife, with the waste on the outside of the knife. You will find it easier to work if you pull the vinyl away from the wall.

Reposition the first length against the wall with the door and mark a guide line on the floor along the opposite edge. Place your block of wood centrally on this edge and mark lines at either end of the block on both the vinyl and the floor. It is important the length of the block is more than the surplus to be removed from that length of vinyl. Slide the vinyl the length of the block along the edge guide line so the marks transferred from either end of the block coincide. With the block positioned

5 Having cut fittings outline, make single cut from cut-out to nearest edge, following pattern line where necessary, and lay vinyl
6a When laying lengths, trace wall contour and door opening on vinyl with block guide
6b Mark exact position of door opening
6c Cut waste with knife against straight-edge
7a Fit to wall and mark other edge on floor
7b Mark each end of block on vinyl and floor
7c Pull vinyl, length of block, away from wall
7d Trace wall contour on end of vinyl
7e Cut waste with knife against straight-edge
7f Push back to wall; block marks will align
8a Match next length and overlap trim edge
8b Mark pattern repeat on straight-edge
8c Trace wall contour on end of vinyl

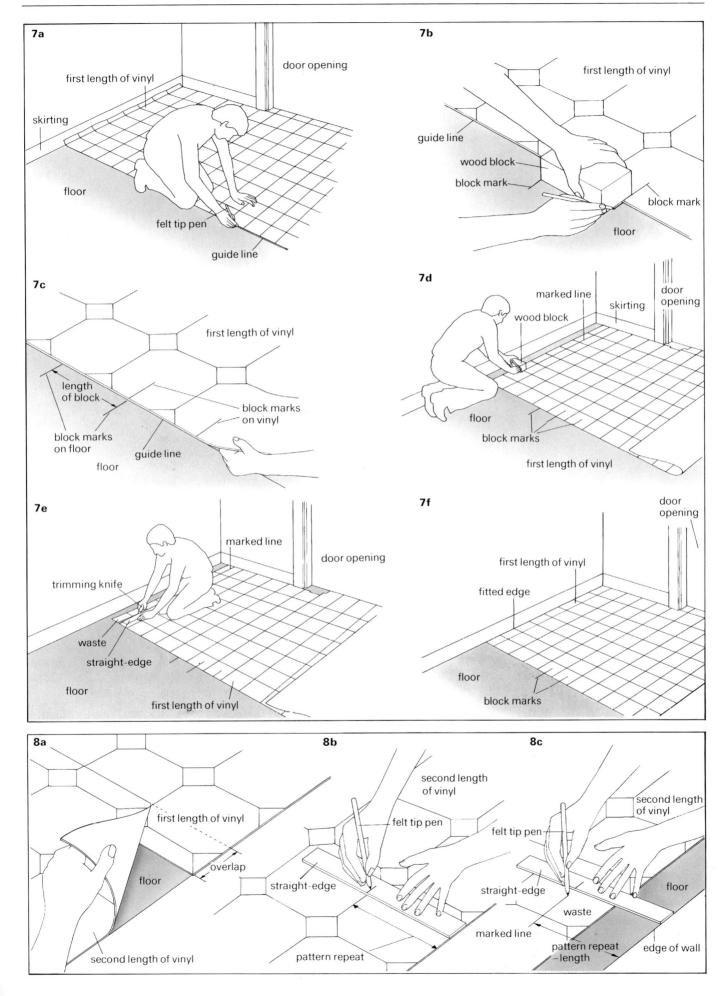

7a
door opening
first length of vinyl
skirting
floor
felt tip pen
guide line

7b
first length of vinyl
guide line
wood block
block mark
block mark
floor

7c
first length of vinyl
length of block
block marks on vinyl
block marks on floor
guide line
floor

7d
marked line
door opening
wood block
skirting
floor
block marks
first length of vinyl

7e
marked line
door opening
trimming knife
waste
straight-edge
floor
first length of vinyl

7f
door opening
first length of vinyl
fitted edge
floor
block marks

8a
first length of vinyl
overlap
floor
second length of vinyl

8b
second length of vinyl
felt tip pen
straight-edge
pattern repeat

8c
felt tip pen
second length of vinyl
straight-edge
waste
floor
marked line
pattern repeat – length
edge of wall

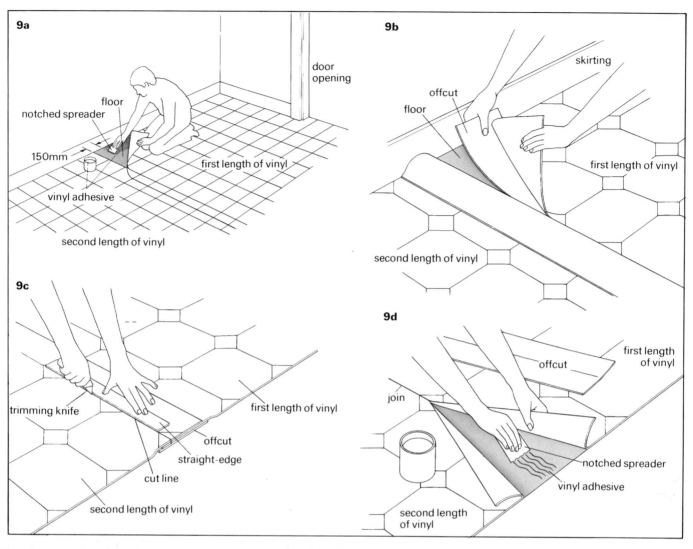

9a Spread adhesive on floor to hold vinyl
9b Lay offcut under overlap of lengths
9c Cut through both overlapping lengths
9d Remove offcut and put adhesive under join

lengthways against the wall, mark a line onto the vinyl as you move the block along the wall. Trim off the surplus with a straight-edge on the marked line. Reposition the vinyl along the guide line and check for fit.

This method ensures a perfect fit, since any irregularities or projections on the wall will be transferred onto the vinyl. Repeat for the opposite wall, sliding the vinyl the length of the block in the opposite direction.

To lay the second length of vinyl, overlap the trimming edges on both lengths and check the pattern aligns and matches exactly. Measure the size of one pattern repeat; the repeat dimension is marked from the wall to the edge of the vinyl to be cut, following the contour of the wall along the width of the vinyl. The surplus, which is never more than the measured dimension of the repeat, can then be trimmed off in the usual way.

Before cutting along the overlapping lengths, spread a 50mm (2in) strip of vinyl adhesive at the ends of the vinyl sheets, stopping within 150mm (6in) of the join, to prevent the lengths of vinyl slipping out of position. Place an offcut of vinyl under the overlapping lengths to protect the blade of the knife as it cuts. Make a vertical cut along the overlap as near to the centre as possible – along the border if you have a tile pattern – through both sheets of vinyl. Remove the surplus vinyl and the lengths will lie neatly together.

When laying the final length of vinyl, position it

against the wall opposite the door and then draw it away until the pattern matches the previous length on the overlap. Measure the width of one pattern repeat and mark a line the same measurement as the pattern width onto the edge of the vinyl, following the contours of the wall; trim off the excess as before. Slide the last length against the wall and trim the overlap as before. Where you cut the overlap will depend on whether you want to save any waste for use elsewhere.

Sticking down vinyl
Vinyl can be loose-laid when just one sheet is used to cover a small area, although you should still stick down the area around a door. When laying more than one length, you should always stick down the vinyl at the ends and along each seam with adhesive or double-sided adhesive tape – as recommended by the manufacturer. Some recommend sticking down the whole floor covering – and certainly the centre sheet if laying more than two sheets of vinyl – particularly when laying cushioned vinyl. Any shrinkage will be in the length of the vinyl. If you make sure you stick down the sheets at each end, you will overcome this problem since each length will be held securely.

When using adhesive, apply it to the floor with a notched spreader. Press the vinyl onto the adhesive and rub with a clean dampened cloth. Always wipe off excess adhesive immediately with a clean, dampened cloth.

Repairing floor coverings

Over the years most floor coverings – such as sheet vinyl, parquet blocks, cork, ceramic and vinyl tiles – will lose their finish or become damaged. Fortunately you can repair minor damage and renovate floor surfaces without going to any great expense.

Cork tiles

You can renovate the surface of a cork floor with one or two coats of sealer, but you must first remove all traces of polish. Scrub the floor with fine wire wool, dipped in white spirit, and sand with medium abrasive paper before wiping over again with a cloth dipped in white spirit. Allow the floor to dry before applying polyurethane sealer, available in matt, silk or gloss finish.

Damaged tiles Holes or cracks in cork tiles may be filled with plastic wood or wood coloured stopping; when this has dried, rub the surface smooth and treat with sealer so the repair matches the surrounding tiles. If the tiles are worn over a large area, it is advisable to hire a floor sanding machine; but if the tiles are only worn in places, such as around a doorway or in front of a sink, you can replace them with new ones.

Make a clean break between the damaged tile and the surrounding tiles, using a sharp knife held against a metal straight-edge to cut along the join. Use an old chisel to remove the tile; work from the centre to the edge, holding the chisel bevel side down so it cuts between the old tile and the surface without cutting into the sub-floor. Scrape away the old adhesive from the sub-floor so the new tile will lie flush with the old tiles and check the sub-floor is sound and free from movement.

New tiles should be fixed as recommended by the manufacturer. Apply adhesive with a notched spreader to give a good key, press the tile into place from the centre towards the edges and wipe away excess adhesive. Weight the new tile with books until the adhesive has dried, then apply sealer or finish to match the old tiles. If you cannot obtain replacement tiles, you can use different tiles at random intervals or in a pattern to make a feature of the replacement tiles.

Vinyl tiles

You can replace individual vinyl tiles as for cork tiles; thicker tiles will be easier to lay if they are first gently heated with a blowtorch. Some types of tile are self-adhesive and you can lay these after cleaning the sub-floor; otherwise you will have to apply adhesive to the sub-floor. You may be able to patch thick vinyl tiles with glass fibre filler, which can be painted to match the tiles, if the area is small or unlikely to receive heavy wear.

Repairing sheet vinyl This floor covering is prone to curling at the edges and seams, usually a result of failure to stick down the edges sufficiently. Lift up a curled edge and clean the sub-floor by scraping and vacuum cleaning 75–100mm (3–4in) strips. Wash the sub-floor and the back of the vinyl with hot water and detergent, allow it to dry and apply tile adhesive with a notched spreader. When this becomes tacky, press the edge back into place.

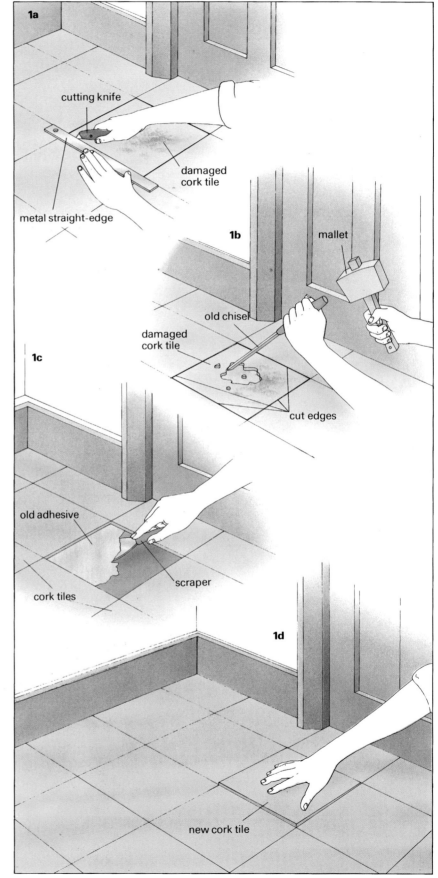

1a cutting knife — damaged cork tile — metal straight-edge

1b mallet — old chisel — damaged cork tile — cut edges

1c old adhesive — scraper — cork tiles

1d new cork tile

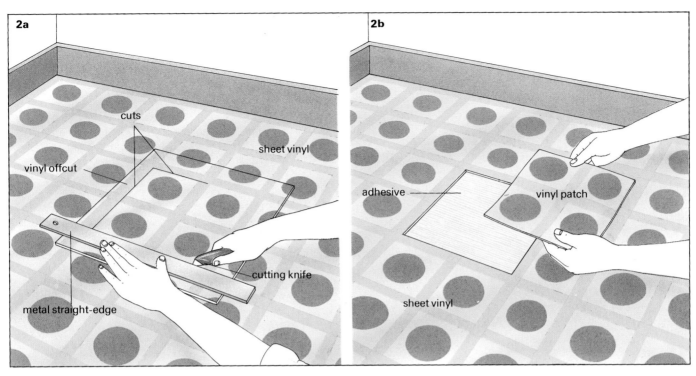

2a cuts
vinyl offcut
sheet vinyl
cutting knife
metal straight-edge

2b adhesive
vinyl patch
sheet vinyl

1a To replace damaged cork tile, cut round tile with sharp knife held against metal straight-edge
1b Use old chisel, bevel side down, to remove tile; work from centre outwards
1c Scrape off old adhesive
1d Check fit of new tile and apply adhesive with notched spreader; fit tile, pressing from centre towards edges, and wipe off excess adhesive
2a When repairing damaged sheet vinyl, position offcut slightly larger than area of damage — making sure to match pattern; cut through both pieces, following line in pattern
2b Check fit and pattern match; apply adhesive to floor with notched spreader and fit patch, placing weights on it until adhesive has dried

Splits in sheet vinyl are usually caused by movement of the sub-floor; pull back the vinyl and nail or screw down the floor to prevent further movement. Apply adhesive to the cleaned floor surface and press the vinyl back into place when the adhesive becomes tacky; place weights on the vinyl until the adhesive is dry.

A hole worn into sheet vinyl can be patched with offcuts you have saved or vinyl cut from an area normally hidden under furniture. Cut the patch slightly larger than the damaged area and lay it over the damage to match the pattern. Cut through both pieces with a sharp knife held against a straight-edge; if possible, cut against a line in the pattern so the patch will be less noticeable. Remove the worn area and fit the new piece into position with adhesive; hold it in place with weights until the adhesive is dry.

Ceramic or quarry tiles

If the floor tiles are very uneven, you may decide to replace them or re-cover the floor; a self-smoothing floor screeding compound is applied directly over the tiles to form an ideal sub-floor.

Cracked or crazed tiles cannot be repaired; they must be replaced with new ones. You can, however, make a temporary repair on slightly pitted tiles with cementwork or glass fibre filler. Move a damaged tile carefully so you do not damage adjacent tiles. You should wear protective spectacles when breaking up the tile with a hammer and small cold chisel; start at the centre of the tile and work outwards. When the tile has been removed piece by piece, chip away the bedding mortar so the new tile will lie just below the surface of the existing tiles. Coat the back of the new tile with a thin layer of floor tile adhesive, using a notched spreader. Press the tile into place so it is level with adjacent tiles and move it so there is an equal gap around all its edges. After 24 hours you can fill the joints around the tile with grout or a mortar mix consisting of four parts fine, sharp sand to one part Portland cement.

Timber floors

Ways of repairing damaged timber floors are covered separately in this book; but, if the floor is in good condition, you can improve its appearance – and provide a durable, non-porous surface – by applying a polyurethane sealer. Wash the floor thoroughly with household detergent and water to remove dust and grease, then rinse with clean water and leave the floor to dry. To remove polish and stubborn stains, you can use white spirit; but afterwards always wash with detergent and rinse with clean water to ensure there are no traces of spirit left on the floor. If the floor is painted, you should hire a floor sanding machine and use it to strip the paint back to bare wood; then wash and rinse the floor as before. Apply the sealer, following the manufacturer's instructions, and leave each coat to dry before applying the next (three coats should be sufficient); on the penultimate coat, use abrasive paper or wire wool to give a perfectly smooth surface for the final coat.

Repairing hardwood floors Minor damage to parquet blocks and wood strips, such as deep scratches and cigarette burns, may be repaired by sanding the damaged area or the whole floor if necessary. If the damage is more extensive, you will have to replace the blocks; chop out the first block with a chisel and prise up subsequent blocks with a lever. When chiselling out parquet blocks, you should start from the centre and work towards each end, taking care the chisel does not cut into adjacent blocks. Replacement blocks should be the same thickness as the original ones; slightly thicker ones can be planed down after laying, but do not buy blocks which are too thin. It is quite difficult to place packing pieces to bring them up to the correct height.

Clean and scrape the sub-floor leaving it dust-free. Use a notched spreader to apply adhesive, either to the floor or to the back of the block. Some bitumen-based damp proofing liquids are suitable for fixing wood blocks. The blocks should be tapped into place with a hammer after the adhesive has

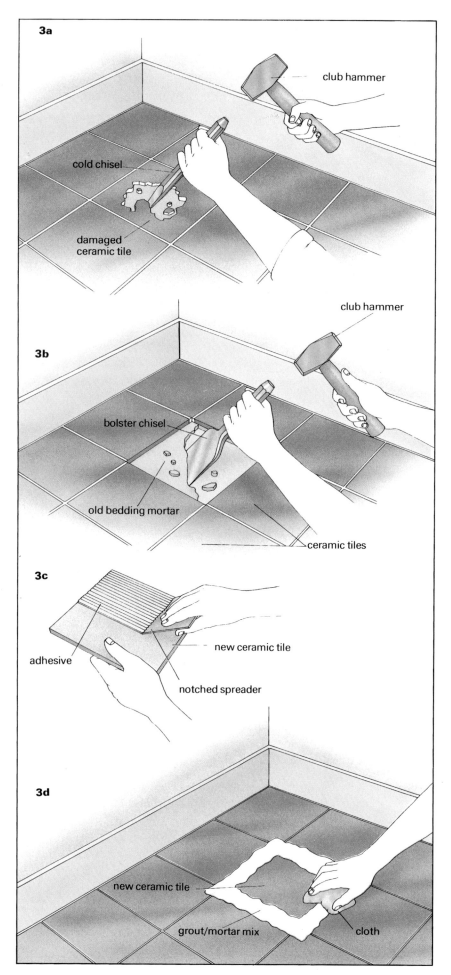

been applied; use a piece of scrap wood to protect the surface of the block.

Wood strips are repaired in the same way as blocks, but lifting them from the sub-floor may prove more difficult. Often the strips are tongued and grooved along their length and they may be fixed with hidden nails (secret nailing), which are inserted at an angle through the tongues as the wood strips are laid. The best lifting method is to free one end of the strip in the manner described to chisel out parquet blocks. It may now be possible to lever up the strip along its length. If this is not so, you can use a circular power saw, set to cut three-quarters of the distance through the strip, running down the centre of the strip. By levering the strip in the middle at the chiselled end you should now be able to split the board into two and pull out each half.

Fitting new strips is similar to fitting blocks; taper the sides of the strip inwards, so when it is hammered down it wedges into place along its length. If the strip is slightly proud of the surface after fixing, you can plane or sand it level.

Concrete floors

Greasy or oily patches on a solid floor in a garage, shed, cellar or kitchen, must be removed before you lay floor coverings. Grease can build up to such a level that it becomes a hazard and you should apply a concrete paint or a proprietary grease removing solution, which you can buy from motor accessory shops. Scrape the floor to remove as much grease and dirt as possible and brush on grease remover solution until the surface appears thoroughly wet. Leave for up to 15 minutes for the grease to soften and agitate it with a stiff brush from time to time. If necessary, apply more solution until the grease stain takes on a soap-like appearance. Wash with water and brush the floor; repeat the treatment if the stain remains after the floor has dried out.

Dusty concrete This can be cured with a concrete hardening and dustproofing liquid. Sweep the floor – or vacuum it clean if possible – and apply the liquid with a brush, according to manufacturer's instructions (two coats may be required). You can use a PVA bonding agent diluted with water, but allow the treatment to dry before subjecting it to normal traffic. According to the wear the floor receives, the treatment may have to be repeated every one or two years. If you need a more durable coloured finish for a garage, store or outside WC, you can apply a brush-on floor sealing compound to give a tough, dustproof coating which is impervious to water and oil.

3a To replace damaged ceramic tile, break up tile from centre outwards
3b Chip away old bedding mortar
3c Apply adhesive to back of new tile
3d Use dampened cloth to apply grout
4a To replace damaged parquet block, chop out first block with chisel and mallet
4b Lever up adjacent damaged blocks
4c Apply adhesive to floor or block
4d Tap new block in place
5a To replace damaged wood strip, chip away end of first strip with chisel
5b If strip will not lift, saw along length
5c Prise up strip with crowbar
5d Remove tongue and taper sides of new strip before tapping it in place

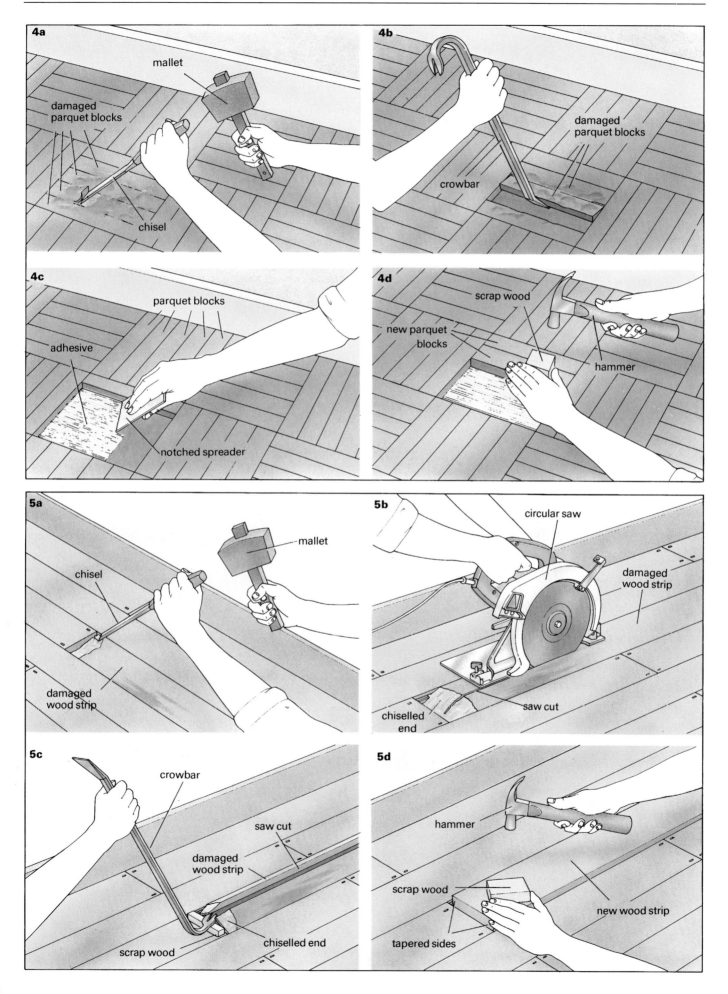

Repairing timber floors

Most homes have timber floors in upstairs rooms, but in houses built in Britain since 1945 – and in recent extensions to older houses – you will often find that the ground floor rooms have solid floors. As both timber and solid floors can be covered with wood blocks or plastic tiles it may not be immediately obvious which type you are dealing with. So always check first what sort of floor you have.

Timber floors downstairs consist of boards or sheets of chipboard nailed over sturdy timber joists, which are often supported on low walls (called sleeper walls). Upstairs the joists may be built into opposite walls or supported in galvanized steel brackets (joist hangers).

As they are supported on joists, timber floors are also called suspended floors. Unlike solid floors, they make a hollow sound when stamped on and also have a certain amount of bounce. Another means of recognizing a timber floor downstairs is the presence of airbricks on the outside walls just above soil level. These bricks allow air to circulate beneath the floor to keep it dry and free of rot. Solid floors at ground level do not have airbricks.

Fixing loose and squeaky boards

Loose boards move when you walk on them and will increase wear on any floor coverings laid over them. They may also develop annoying squeaks and creaks as two faces of timber rub together. To cure this, refix the boards by nailing them down properly. Possibly not all the nails were replaced the last time the boards were lifted; more likely the nails are loose. Renailing with cut floor brads or round head nails slightly to one side may solve the problem, but there is a danger this will cause the end of the board to split. It is better to drill small pilot holes and refix the boards, using No 10 countersunk screws 38mm (1½in) long. The screws must pass into the joists, the position of which can be seen by the line of nail heads on the surface of the boards.

If the boards are properly fixed but still squeak because they are flexing, the problem can be temporarily overcome by dusting the crack between the boards with French chalk or talcum powder. If the squeak returns, one of the boards must be lifted and the edge planed to give slight clearance.

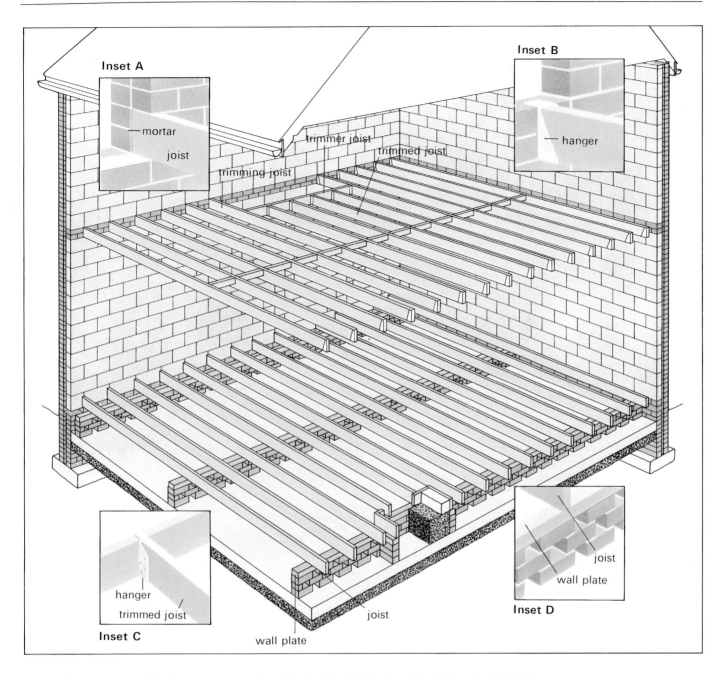

Inset A
mortar
joist

trimmer joist
trimmed joist
trimming joist

Inset B
hanger

hanger
trimmed joist

Inset C

wall plate

joist

joist
wall plate

Inset D

Sometimes boards which have been properly fixed to the joists still spring up and down, usually because the joists themselves are not properly secured. The only way to check this is to lift some boards in the affected area and examine the joists.

Lifting floorboards
Because of the way floors are made, lifting a floorboard is not always as straightforward as it may appear. Older houses usually have square-edged boards (**see 1**). These are not too difficult to lift, although some force may be needed.
Square-edged floorboards To lift these, check the surface of the board to see if it is secured with nails or screws; the screw slots may be filled with dirt, so look carefully. If it is held with screws, the board will come up easily once the screws are removed; if nailed, it must be levered up.

Start near the end of a conveniently placed board and insert a strong lever, such as a long cold chisel, car tyre lever or flooring chisel, into the gap between the boards (**see 2a**). Hammer the chisel to prise up the end until another lever, for example a

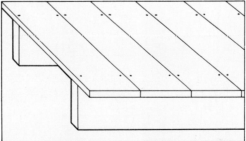

claw hammer, can be inserted under the board (**see 2b**). Work the two levers along the board until it is free. Alternatively, put a batten under the board, resting on boards either side, and hammer it along to avoid splitting the board or marking the next.

Another method is to slip a length of steel pipe or rod under the end which has been lifted. Stand on the loose end and the leverage of the rod will force up the board further along its length. Keep moving the rod forward until the entire board comes up (**see 2c**).

Above Example of timber floor construction in two-storey house, with joists and struts exposed
Inset A End of joist embedded into wall with mortar
Inset B End of joist supported by hanger in wall
Inset C Trimmed joist supported on trimmer joist by hanger
Inset D Joist supported by wall plate on sleeper wall
1 Square-edged floorboards

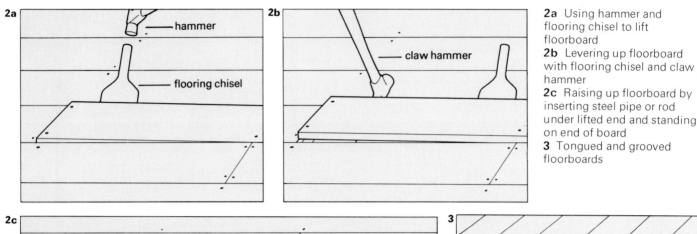

2a Using hammer and flooring chisel to lift floorboard
2b Levering up floorboard with flooring chisel and claw hammer
2c Raising up floorboard by inserting steel pipe or rod under lifted end and standing on end of board
3 Tongued and grooved floorboards

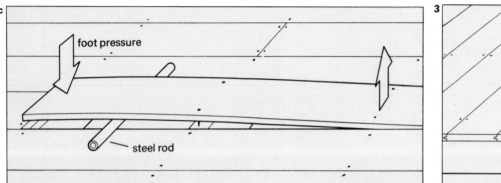

Tongued and grooved floorboards The tricky part of lifting these boards (**see 3**) is getting the first one up. Once this is out of the way the others can be lifted quite easily.

To test for a tongued and grooved floor. take a thin-bladed tool, such as a screwdriver, and try to push it between the boards in several places. If the floor is tongued, you will not be able to insert the blade more than about 6mm ($\frac{1}{4}$in).

The best way to cut through the tongue (to release the board) is with a flooring saw, which looks like a tenon saw with a convex curved cutting edge (**see 4**). Cut right along the join on one side and lever up the board as before. A circular power saw will cut through the tongue, but it makes a wide cut which may not be acceptable if the surface of the floor is to be left exposed.

You can use a small pad saw, but take great care not to cut through electric cables and water pipes under the floor. To be on the safe side, turn off the electricity and the water. Cut with the blade at a shallow angle (**see 5**) and use the tip to feel for cables and joists (which should be evident by the lines of nail heads).

Chipboard panels Modern homes may have floors of tongued and grooved chipboard panels, which are very difficult to lift. The best way to remove an entire panel is to saw round the joints on all four sides using a powered circular saw with the blade set to cut 19mm ($\frac{3}{4}$in) deep. If this does not allow the panel to be lifted, increase the depth of cut to 22mm ($\frac{7}{8}$in) in case thicker panels have been used.

Cutting across boards If there is not a convenient cut end at which to start lifting the board, make a cut across the board close to a joist. Look for the nail heads and use a thin blade to feel for the side of the joist. If you cannot get a blade between the boards, estimate the joist will extend 25–38mm (1–1$\frac{1}{2}$in) on either side of the nails. Mark with a pencil a line across the board to one side of the joist.

Drill three or four small holes at an angle away

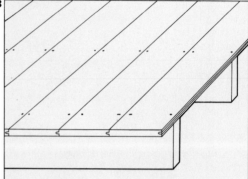

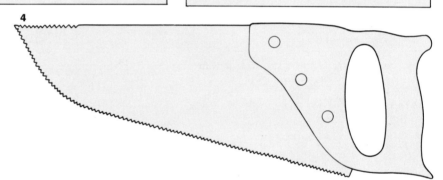

4 Flooring saw
5 Using pad saw at shallow angle to cut through tongue of tongued and grooved floorboard
6a Cutting across floorboard near joist with pad saw held at shallow angle

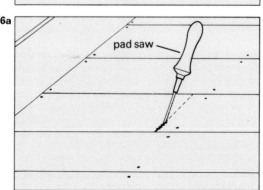

from the joist, just inside the pencil line, to enable you to insert a saw blade. Using a pad saw or powered jig saw cut across the board (see **6a**), keeping the handle of the saw tilted towards the middle of the joist so the board will be supported when it is replaced. Give the board some additional support when you replace it by gluing and nailing a piece of scrap wood (50 × 25mm/2 × 1in) to the side of the joist with clout nails 38mm (1¾in) long so its top is flush with the top of the joist (see **6b**).

Securing loose joists
When floorboards have been lifted, the exposed joists can be tested for movement. If the ends have rotted, it is best to check with a flooring expert to remedy the problem. Dampness in the supporting walls is the usual cause – or blocked or insufficient airbricks.

If the joists and floorboards show signs of woodworm attack (neat round holes surrounded by fine sawdust), brush them free of dust and cobwebs and spray with woodworm killer applied with a garden-type insecticide sprayer. If the attack is widespread, you should get professional advice.

The joists may be loose because the mortar which holds them firmly in place in the wall has dropped out (see **floor construction diagrams**). In this case the joist should be repacked with new mortar.

If the joist end is supported on a wall plate or in a metal joist hanger (see **floor construction diagrams**), you may be able to secure it by wedging it in place with a piece of scrap wood or by packing pieces of slate under it.

If the joists bounce, it is because they are fitted across too wide a span. They can be stabilized with timber struts fitted between them midway from the support points. Lengths of floorboard about 125 × 25mm (5 × 1in) nailed into the joists are the easiest to fit (see **7**).

Levelling boards
Uneven surfaces of old floors result in extra wear on floor coverings and could be a hazard, causing people to trip over raised sections.
Correcting surface levels If the floor surface is uneven in only a few places and is to be covered, lift the offending boards and pack them with pieces of scrap hardboard or plastic laminate to the correct level.

When the boards are high, the securing nails should be punched well below the surface, tacks should be pulled out and the surface of the boards levelled with either a plane or a coarse sanding disc attached to an electric drill.

Alternatively you can cut a rebate in the underside of the offending floorboard where it sits on the joists. Measure the depth of board to be trimmed, lift and hold it at right-angles to the floor. Mark on the underside the exact position of the joists, allowing 12mm (½in) on either side of each joist (see **8a**). With a try square complete your marks across the width of the board and shade in the rebate area. Measure and mark the depth of the rebate on both edges of the board (see **8b**) and tenon saw along the pencil lines to the depth marked on the edges (**8c**). Clamp the board and chisel out the rebate area, taking care not to chisel below the required depth (see **8d**). Replace the floorboard, check it is the same level as the other boards (see **8e**) and nail it to the joists with 63mm (2½in) cut floor brads or round head nails.
Warning Floorboards are usually 22mm (⅞in)

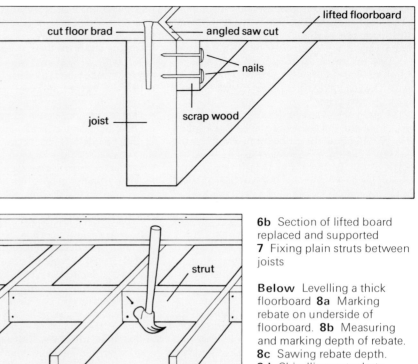

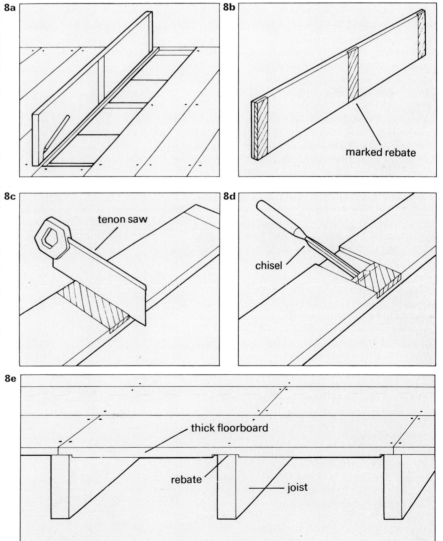

6b Section of lifted board replaced and supported
7 Fixing plain struts between joists

Below Levelling a thick floorboard **8a** Marking rebate on underside of floorboard. **8b** Measuring and marking depth of rebate. **8c** Sawing rebate depth. **8d** Chiselling out rebate. **8e** Thicker board now lies at correct level

thick. It is dangerous to remove more than 3mm ($\frac{1}{8}$in) from the thickness of the board. Pay special attention to this when making the saw cuts.

Resurfacing Where a number of boards are uneven, resurface the entire floor by sanding it with an industrial-type electric floor sander, which can be hired. This has a large drum covered with a belt of tough abrasive paper.

The machine will remove about 3mm ($\frac{1}{8}$in) of the surface without difficulty, but nail heads must first be sunk well below the surface or they will tear the abrasive paper. Move the sander up and down the length of the floorboards or slightly at an angle. Most of the dust is collected in a bag, but some will escape into the air so you must wear a mask when sanding.

The alternative to sanding is to lay sheets of hardboard on the floor surface. If there are any serious undulations, these should first be corrected by lifting and relaying the offending boards.

Usually 3mm ($\frac{1}{8}$in) standard hardboard is suitable for resurfacing, but use 5mm ($\frac{3}{16}$in) board if the floor is in a very poor state and there are gaps of more than 6mm ($\frac{1}{4}$in) between the boards. If the hardboard is to be laid in a kitchen, bathroom or where it could be subjected to damp, tempered hardboard should be used since it is resistant to moisture.

Conditioning hardboard To avoid buckling, hardboard must be conditioned before it is laid. Separate the boards and stand them on edge in the room where they will be fixed for up to 72 hours before laying. In new houses, and in kitchens and bathrooms, where there is likely to be more moisture, sprinkle the rough side with water – about 1 litre per 2440 × 1200mm sheet (2 pints per 8 × 4ft sheet). Stack the boards flat, back to back, and leave for 48 hours (standard hardboard) or 72 hours (tempered).

Laying hardboard sheets The boards should be laid as soon as they have been conditioned. If working with full 2440 × 1200mm (8 × 4ft) sheets, cut each one in half or quarters with a fine tooth saw since smaller sheets are much easier to handle. Either get someone to help hold the sheet or clamp and support where possible to keep the sheet firm when cutting.

If varnishing the hardboard and using it as a decorative surface (or if laying thin vinyl floor tiles on it) lay the shiny side uppermost; for any other decorative floor covering lay the rough side upwards.

The hardboard sheets should be laid, as far as possible, in staggered brickwork fashion so the joints do not align. Fix down the boards with hardboard nails 25mm (1in) long at 100mm (or 4 in) intervals along the edges and at 150mm (or 6in) intervals over the whole board surface (**see 9**).

Where floorboards may have to be lifted from time to time to give access to cables and pipes, the hardboard should be fixed in small panels with No 6 countersunk screws.

Relaying a floor

If the boards are badly worn and there are a lot of wide gaps between them, it is best to relay the floor. You can then refix worn boards upside down to give a new surface. It is possible to fill gaps between boards with papier mâché, wood filler or wood strips, but this is generally too time-consuming except where there are only a few gaps to fill.

If you are relaying the floor, it is a good oppor-tunity while the boards are lifted to check for damp, rot and woodworm – and carry out treatment if necessary. You may also decide it is worth while insulating under the floor, if working downstairs.

Normally gaps between boards can be eliminated by pushing the boards together as they are renailed. If they are warped, however, you will have to fill the gaps with wedges or plane the edges level.

Nail the first board into place with 63mm (2$\frac{1}{2}$in) cut floor brads or lost head nails, then position four or five boards together. Place folding wedges at intervals against the boards and nail pieces of scrap timber to the joists against the wedges to stop them moving. Hammer the wedges together to close the gaps in the boards, then nail the boards to the joists when the boards are in the correct position (**see 10**).

Replace damaged boards with new timber or with second-hand floorboards, which are usually available from demolition yards. All second-hand timber should be carefully examined for rot and woodworm damage. It is advisable to take a sample of the existing floorboards to compare for width and thickness.

You can make a very hard and smooth floor by replacing the timber floorboards with flooring grade chipboard panels. The tongued and grooved type makes an exceptionally smooth floor, but because it is difficult to lift make sure to leave small, screwed down access panels over cables and pipes which may have to be reached from time to time.

Use 19mm ($\frac{3}{4}$in) chipboard for joists up to 450mm (or 18in) apart and 22mm ($\frac{7}{8}$in) chipboard for joists from 450–600mm (or 18–24in) apart. Fit the panels together and nail in place through the tongues with round head nails.

9 Order of laying cut hardboard sheets to level uneven floor surface
10 Using folding wedges and nailed blocks to close gaps between boards when relaying timber floor

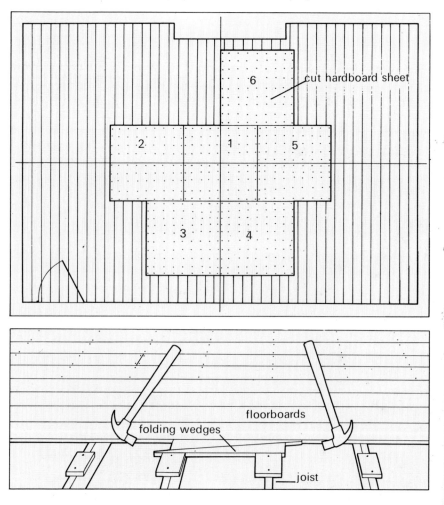

cut hardboard sheet

floorboards

folding wedges

joist

Fitting carpets

Carpets are always a major item in any home improvement budget. If you cannot buy them with free fitting, you can fit them yourself following carefully the correct methods; these depend on the type of carpet to be laid and the different ways of fitting available, whether you use carpet grippers attached to the floor or carpet tacks. Properly laid, a good carpet will enhance the room and last for years.

What you need

A good quality carpet is expensive but well worth the outlay since it will withstand wear and tear far better than a cheaper one; it must, however, be laid correctly. This means it must be properly stretched and fitted over a suitable underlay on a sound sub-floor. A well laid carpet will retain its tension, remain flat and not ruck up. An unstretched or poorly stretched carpet will ruck up easily even under normal use and will be disturbed even more if furniture is moved over it; and apart from looking unattractive, it will also wear prematurely and unevenly.

Genuine free-fitting offers do arise occasionally so it is worth taking advantage of them. If there is no free-fitting offer available, you can lay a carpet successfully yourself; but you should make sure the job is within your capabilities since mistakes can be costly.

Well over half the carpets now sold are non-fray tufted types with a foam or hessian backing. Foam-backs need not be stretched during fitting and are therefore quite straightforward to lay. They can be loose-laid, but you will still have to secure edges in doorways. Some hessian-backs may need stretching; check with your supplier before you buy.

Other carpets will have to be stretched, a job you can do yourself if the carpet is plain and the room does not exceed 4.6m (or 15ft) in width or length. Above this size stretching is done at differing angles to suit the installation and you should seek professional advice before tackling this job. In the case of a patterned carpet, incorrect stretching can distort the pattern, so great care is needed.

If you are using body carpet, you will not have to join seams yourself. If you give your supplier the room measurements, the carpet will be delivered to you in a single piece – with an allowance for trimming the edges.

Estimating quantity

Free measuring and estimating is a widespread feature of the carpet trade and it is worth taking advantage of this service, particularly if you have an awkward-shaped room – the supplier will work out the most economical way of carpeting it. If this service is not available, make an accurate scale plan of the room – including doors and windows – and give it to your supplier when ordering.

Types of underlay

All carpets except for felt require an underlay even those with a foam backing; without this, the performance of the carpet – whatever its quality – will suffer. It is therefore false economy to skimp on underlay – and you should never use just old newspaper or old carpet in its place.

Good quality underlay not only improves the feel of a carpet underfoot, but also provides a buffer between the carpet and the floor; this will ensure even wear. Although it is important to lay carpet on a level sub-floor, it is not always possible to achieve perfect smoothness and so a good underlay will help overcome any minor defects. It also protects the carpet from dirt and dust rising through the floorboards and will help reduce noise and heat loss.

Felt Sold in 1.4m (4½ft) widths, various types are available which include jute, animal hair, wool waste and a combination of these materials. In some cases rubber is incorporated in layers into the construction – or a solution of rubber impregnated into the felt.

Polyurethane foam or rubber More springy and resilient than felt, this type gives the carpet a softer feel. When used beneath carpet composed of seamed strips, however, it may not allow the

1 Knee kicker
2 Gripper for ordinary carpet
3 Gripper for foam-backed carpet
4 Felt underlay
5 Bonded felt underlay
6 Polyurethane foam underlay
7 Two kinds of rubber underlay
8 Felt paper
9 Using a knee kicker to stretch carpet taut

1

2

3

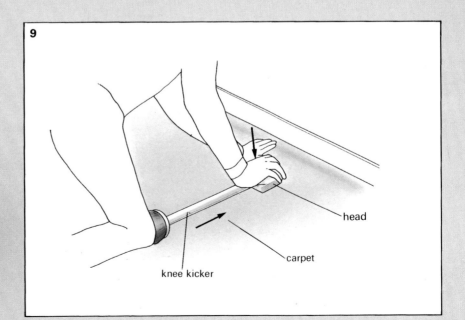

knee kicker

head

carpet

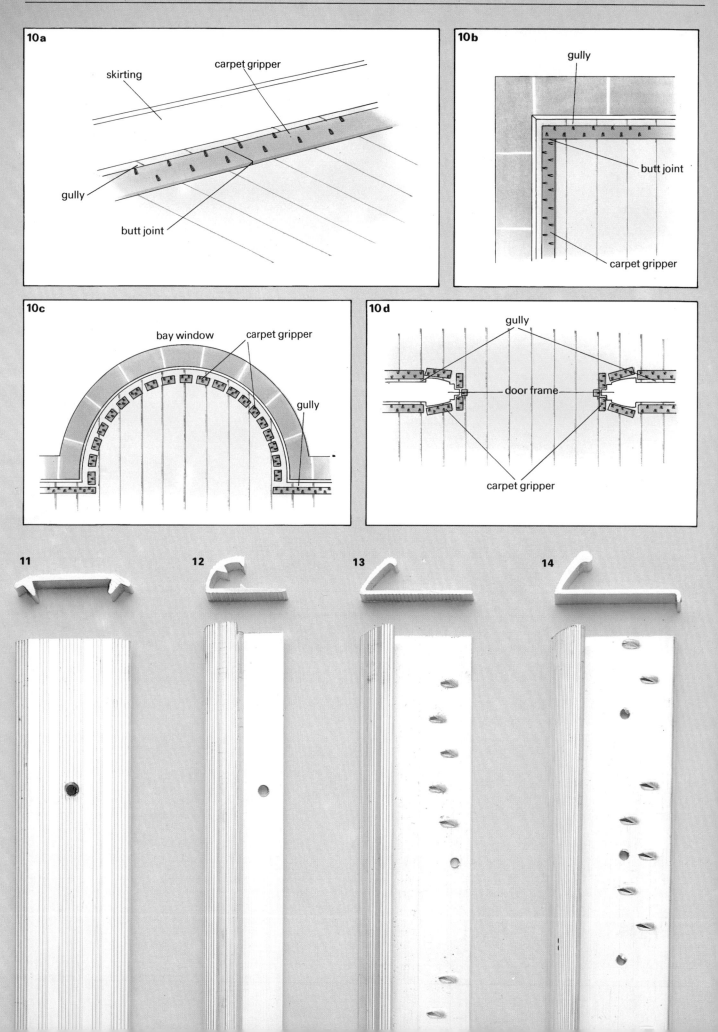

10a

skirting

carpet gripper

gully

butt joint

10b

gully

butt joint

carpet gripper

10c

bay window

carpet gripper

gully

10d

gully

door frame

carpet gripper

11

12

13

14

10a Position the carpet gripper about 6mm away from the wall, butt-joining the lengths
10b When you reach a corner, butt lengths together at right-angles
10c For awkward areas such as bay windows, cut the gripper into short lengths and position these on the floor so there is a small gap between each piece
10d At doorways, cut the gripper into short lengths to follow the line of the door frame
Types of binder:
11 Joint cover strip
12 Bar for foam-backed carpet
13 Ordinary binder bar
14 Bar for joining carpet to hard flooring such as vinyl
15 Double-sided bar with fixed central covering strip for joining carpet to carpet
16 Double-sided bar with separate covering strip

seams to bed down as well as they would on felt. Rubber underlay should never be used where there is underfloor heating since the rubber will smell and may eventually disintegrate.
Felt paper This under-carpet covering is used beneath traditional underlay where narrow gaps between the floorboards have not been filled, since it will provide an additional barrier against dirt and dust from underneath the floor. Felt paper is also used underneath foam-backed carpet to prevent the backing sticking to the floor; brown paper can be used instead if there are no gaps between the floorboards. Such protection is essential; if the foam backing sticks to the floor, it is difficult to remove the carpet intact. The backing may also disintegrate under normal use, causing uneven and premature wear to the carpet.

Fitting underlay
To prevent strips of underlay moving, join them at the edges with self-adhesive tape or by tacking or stapling them down; use adhesive on concrete floors. Underlay is never stretched to the same extent as carpet, but it must be pulled taut to eliminate any wrinkles.

Never allow an extra thickness of underlay in areas subjected to excessive wear and tear, such as doorways. Not only is it unnecessary, but the extra thickness will cause a bump in the carpet and result in uneven wear.

Tools and equipment
For successful carpet fitting you must have the right tools and equipment. If you are stretching carpet, for example, a knee kicker is essential; although an expensive item to buy unless you are

going to use it several times, you can hire one. Carpet grippers are the ideal fixings for carpets that have to be stretched, while for those carpets that do not stretch you will have to use the traditional turn-and-tack method. Two basic items needed when fitting carpets are a sharp trimming knife and self-adhesive tape.

Knee kicker
A knee kicker is used to stretch the carpet taut – but not too tight – onto carpet grippers. It is never used on foam-backed carpets, or hessian-backed ones which do not need to be stretched.

In the head of the knee kicker are two sets of pins. The thinner pins are adjustable, so the amount they can project from the head can be increased or reduced. These pins are necessary when stretching shag pile carpets and must be set accurately to grip the carpet backing. If they are set too short, they will snare the pile as the tool is projected forward; if they are too long, they will become embedded into the underlay and pull it out of place or catch the floor underneath. The thicker fixed pins (called nap grips) give the added purchase required for smooth pile carpets.
Using a kicker The knee kicker is literally kicked with the muscle above the knee cap – never with the knee cap itself since this might cause injury. At each point of stretching, only one kick should be used to stretch the carpet onto the carpet gripper; if a succession of kicks is made, the carpet will spring back to its original position between kicks.

The hands play an important part in the technique of using a kicker. The tool is rested on the carpet with the palm of one hand exerting downward pressure on the head of the kicker while the fingers are used to bring the carpet into contact with the gripper pins at the peak of the stretch. The other hand is used to press down on the stretched carpet in front of the head. As the carpet is stretched and pushed over the gripper pins, the natural elasticity will enable it to spring back securely onto the pins.

Generally the better the quality of carpet, the less stretch is needed. But remember the carpet should be taut – never tight.

Carpet gripper
There are two basic types of carpet gripper – one with nails for fixing to timber floors and one with hardened pins for fixing to concrete floors. The gripper consists of a strip of wood about 25mm (1in) wide and 6mm ($\frac{1}{4}$in) thick with two rows of pins protruding from the upper face at an angle. The pins which grip the carpet are positioned every 50mm (2in) along the gripper and strips are available in 750, 1200 and 1500mm (or 30, 48 and 60in) lengths. The carpet is stretched onto the pins, which hold it firmly in place. This is a superior method to tacking since the carpet is held continuously along its edge; carpet tacks normally hold the carpet at 150mm (or 6in) intervals, often producing a scalloped-edge appearance.

A special flat steel strip containing dome-shaped pins has been designed for foam-backed carpets; the pins are made to penetrate cleanly through the foam. This strip is supplied in 2 and 3m (or 6$\frac{1}{2}$ and 10ft) lengths in boxes containing 60 pieces. A normal carpet gripper can be used on foam-backed carpet if preferred.
Fixing a gripper The carpet gripper is fixed to the floor around the edge of the room, except in door-

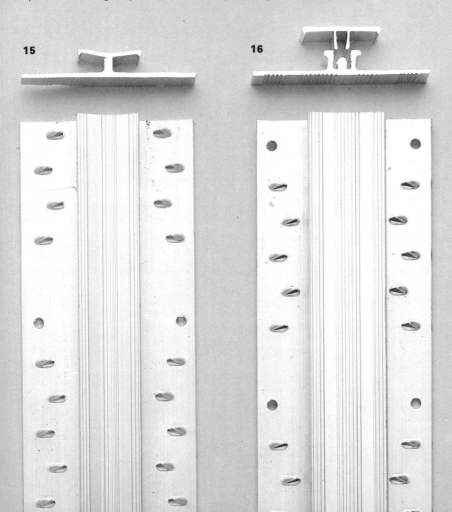

ways. Lengths should butt up against each other at the edges; where short lengths are needed – at corners, for example – cut the gripper with a saw or tinsnips. There is no need to mitre joins at corners; simply butt together the adjoining pieces at right-angles.

Always allow a space between the back edge of the gripper and the wall. The gully formed should be slightly less than the thickness of the carpet – 6mm (¼in) is usually about the right allowance. Keep a uniform space all round to achieve a smooth, level finish to the carpet edge and make sure the angled pins project towards the wall.

The gripper cannot be bent so in bay windows, for example, cut it into short lengths and fix these to the floor, leaving a small space between each piece. Arrange the gripper to follow the shape of the bay. At doorways, cut short lengths to follow the line of the door frame. If the carpet continues into an adjoining room, fix the gripper around the frame into the next room.

With timber floors the gripper should be nailed down; use a hammer and nail punch to avoid any possible damage to the pins. Where short lengths have been cut off the gripper, insert at least two nails – one at each end.

With concrete floors specially hardened pins are used to secure the gripper, although you can stick it down with PVA adhesive or an adhesive recommended by the manufacturer. Make sure the floor has been cleaned thoroughly or the adhesive will not hold the gripper firmly in place. Spread any surplus adhesive with your thumb onto the edge of the gripper that faces the carpet; by continuing the bond in this way you will ensure a firmer fixing. Allow two days for the adhesive to set.

Even after levelling a concrete floor (if this is necessary), you may still find small uneven patches; in this case, if the longer lengths of gripper will not lie flat, cut them into smaller sections.

Carpet tacks

If you choose to tack down a carpet to a timber floor, you will need two lengths of carpet tacks. To fix the carpet around the edges use 19mm (¾in) tacks; these will go through a double thickness of carpet (where it has been folded under at the edge) and into the floor. In corners, where three thicknesses of carpet result from folding under the edges, use 25mm (1in) tacks.

Use only rustproof tacks or rust marks could form around the fixing points if the tacks ever got wet. Space the tacks at 150mm (6in) intervals around the room; closer spacing will be needed at corners and other awkward areas.

Binder bar

To give a neat, protective finish to the carpet edge, use a binder bar at the doorway. You can tack down the carpet or sew adjoining carpets together, but the edges may eventually work loose. Binders are available in aluminium or brass and in various finishes such as fluted, satin and polished. They are normally supplied in 813mm (2ft 8in) lengths, which is the common distance across the threshold; trim the binder bar with a hacksaw to fit smaller openings. Since the bars contain evenly spaced pre-drilled holes for fixing points, when trimming a bar you may have to take a little off each end to ensure the fixing points remain evenly spaced.

The underside of the bar is usually ribbed to provide a key, if you want to fix it to a concrete

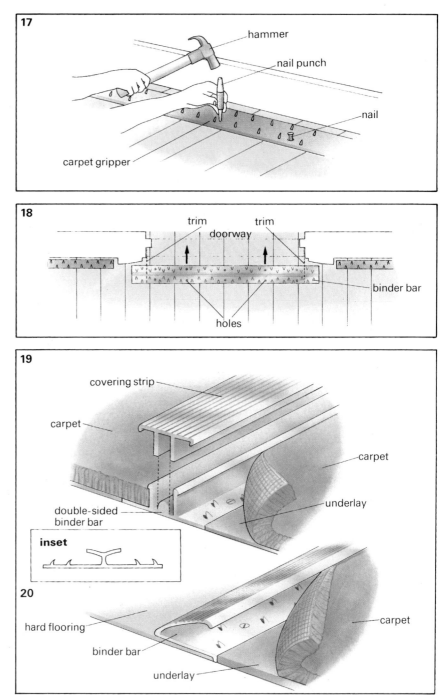

floor with adhesive; but normally it is fitted with screws or nails.

Joining carpet to carpet There is a double-sided bar available which enables you to make a neat join between two carpets at a threshold. Both carpets are stretched onto the angled pins so the respective edges lie close against the centre channel. A central covering strip is then tapped over to conceal the carpet edges and help keep them in place.

Joining carpet to hard flooring For this operation there is a bar with both plain and fitting lips; the plain lip is placed over the edge of the adjoining flooring while the carpet edge is pressed onto the pins projecting from the other side of the bar and tucked under the protective lip. The lip is then hammered down lightly to hold the carpet edge securely. Place a block of wood between the hammer and the binder bar to prevent damage when tapping down the lip.

17 Grippers should be nailed to a timber floor. **18** When trimming a binder bar, cut the same amount off each end; the bar fits under the door stop. **19** Joining carpet to carpet with a double binder bar; the central covering strip may be separate or fixed (**inset**). **20** Joining carpet to hard flooring

Laying carpets

Before laying carpet it is essential to prepare the sub-floor carefully to make sure it is dry, level, flat and clean. Any bumps in the surface will cause the carpet to wear prematurely and unevenly.

Preparing the sub-floor
Clear the room of furniture and inspect the floor thoroughly, walking all over it to check for squeaks, uneven or loose boards and protruding nail heads. If there are any signs of damp or rot, deal with the problem immediately.

Loose and squeaking floorboards Squeaks below a fitted carpet are irritating and not easily remedied once the carpet is laid. They can indicate the nails securing the boards are working loose, causing a floorboard to rise and fall when walked on. Some squeaks may be cured by sprinkling talcum powder or French chalk between the boards. Where squeaking persists, if the boards are loose, secure them with screws. First sink protruding nails below the surface with a nail punch. Drill countersunk clearance holes through the boards for the screws, about 13mm ($\frac{1}{2}$in) from each nail head, drill pilot holes into the joists and tighten the screws firmly,

making sure the heads are below the surface.

Always be careful when hammering nails or inserting screws into floorboards. If you are doubtful about what lies below, lift the board and make sure there are no pipes or wires nearby.

Levelling the surface Check for any sharp edges or uneven boards. Where possible, plane down protruding boards flush with the surround. If, as sometimes happens, a board cannot be levelled off completely, at least round off any sharp edges.

Fill any wide gaps between boards with wedge-shaped wood strips, cut to length and coated on both sides with woodworking adhesive. Tap the strips down firmly and plane down any protruding edges. Fill smaller gaps with mastic.

If the floor is very uneven and cannot be levelled successfully, cover it with hardboard or replace the boards. Level concrete with screeding compound.

Warning Do not lay carpet over thermoplastic tiles unless you have taken measures to eliminate condensation in the room. Otherwise the tiles will 'sweat' and moisture will work through to the carpet, causing mildew stains on the pile. Never use rubber or foam underlays over thermoplastic tiles

Above Fitted carpet not only gives an impression of warmth and cosiness to a room, but it also goes a long way towards improving both heat and sound insulation. Cleaning will be much easier too when there is only one type of surface to look after

– always choose felt. When the sub-floor has been prepared, clean it thoroughly.

Checking doors

Check to see if the new carpet will raise the floor level to a point where the door will not pass easily over it. The door must clear the carpet completely; if it brushes over it as it opens and closes, it wears the pile. The solution is to remove the door and plane off enough from its bottom edge to ensure it clears the carpet. Do this before laying the carpet since it will make the job easier; even if the door does not need modifying, it is easier to lay carpet with the door removed.

Laying the carpet

If you are using carpet grippers to secure the carpet, fix them in position around the edges of the room and fit a binder bar in the doorway (as described).

Take the carpet into the room, open it up fully and position it roughly with excess carpet lapping up the walls. It is usual to lay the carpet with the pile leaning away from the light since this prevents uneven shading in daylight, which may be particularly noticeable in the case of plain carpets. If the carpet has a definite pattern, this should be the right way up as you enter the room.

Fitting the underlay

When the carpet is arranged, roll half of it back to expose half of the floor area. This is to enable you to put down your underlay one half at a time. If you try to put down all the underlay and then the carpet, you will almost certainly disturb the underlay as the heavy carpet is dragged over it.

If you are using felt paper, lay it in strips across the room, butt-joining the edges with self-adhesive tape. Trim the edges of the paper to butt against the carpet grippers. Stick it to the floor with double-sided adhesive tape at the edges of the room and around any projections. An alternative method of fixing felt paper is to use latex adhesive applied from a washing-up liquid bottle.

Put down the underlay in strips across the room, joining the edges with self-adhesive tape. To do this, turn the two lengths of underlay reverse side up and butt the adjoining edges. Remove the protective paper from the tape and press the sticky side down along the joint (**see 1**). Fix the underlay to a timber floor with tacks or staples and with adhesive to a concrete floor. Trim it to butt up against the carpet grippers.

Unroll the carpet to cover the floor and roll up the other half, laying the felt paper and underlay as before. Finally, unroll the carpet again to cover the entire floor.

Fitting a stretched carpet

If possible, start fitting the carpet in a corner where you have a reasonably uninterrupted run of walls – that is, without recesses, radiators or other obstructions. During the initial positioning try to leave only about 10mm (⅜in) of carpet lapping up against the starting walls. This will save you having to trim these two edges.

Starting edge technique A special method is used to engage the starting edge of the carpet onto the carpet gripper to ensure the carpet is firmly held during stretching. Using the fingertips with steady downward pressure, press the edge of the carpet

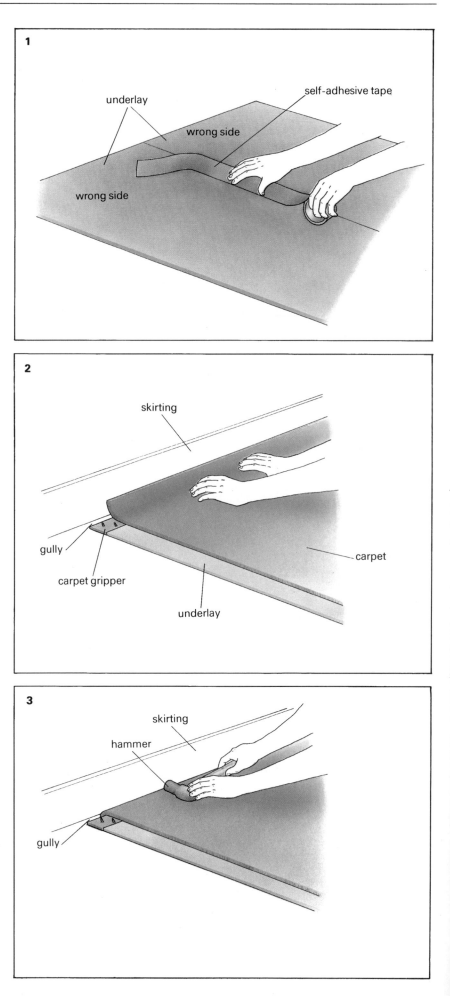

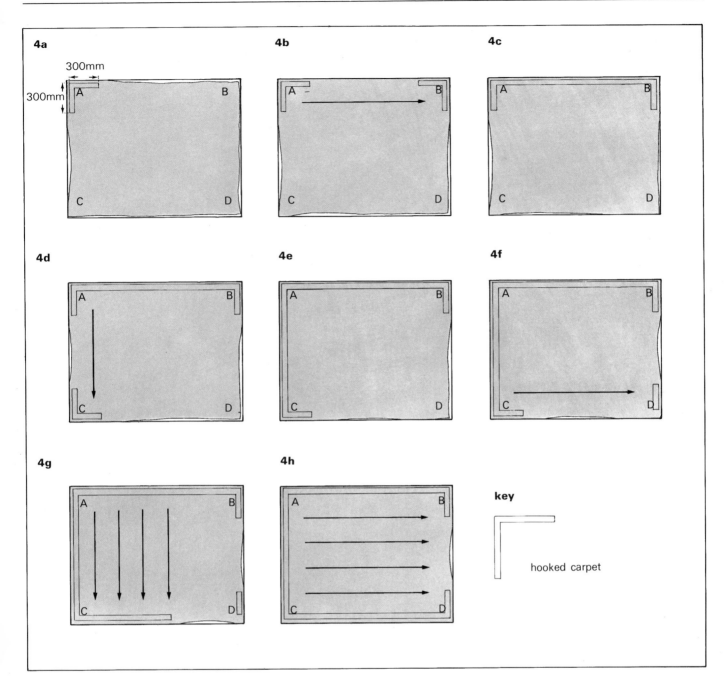

4a

300mm

300mm

A   B

C   D

4b

A   B

C   D

4c

A   B

C   D

4d

A   B

C   D

4e

A   B

C   D

4f

A   B

C   D

4g

A   B

C   D

4h

A   B

C   D

key

hooked carpet

along the wall onto the back row of pins (**see 2**). With a hammer, press the surplus carpet down to form a 'U' shape of carpet between the gripper and the wall (**see 3**). The starting edge technique is used along the first two walls to be fitted; the carpet is hooked along the other two walls by stretching.

Stretching As work progresses, use a knee kicker (as described earlier) if the carpet needs to be stretched. Stretch one part of the carpet and hook it into the pins. Move along a few feet and stretch the next portion, continuing in this way until all the carpet is gripped.

Order of work Using the starting edge technique, begin at corner A and hook about 300mm (12in) of carpet along each wall forming the corner (**see 4a**). Stretch the carpet towards B and hook corner B, using the kicker. Again hook the carpet about 300mm (12in) along each wall (**see 4b**). With the two corners secured, hook the carpet along the length of the wall AB, using the starting edge technique (**see 4c**). Then stretch the carpet from A to C and hook as for corner B (**see 4d**). Hook the

carpet along the wall AC, again using the starting edge technique (**see 4e**).

Stretch the carpet from C to D and hook a section of carpet near D on wall BD (**see 4f**). Then stretch the carpet from wall AB to CD, using the kicker and hooking from C to D (**see 4g**). This will have the effect of securing the carpet along wall AB firmly on the hooks. Three edges of the carpet are now hooked and surplus will be lapping up wall CD.

Finally stretch the carpet from wall AC to wall BD (**see 4h**), working from B to D with surplus carpet lapping up against wall BD. The carpet is now fully stretched and ready to be trimmed and fitted at corners and round any pipes.

Warning Check the carpet carefully to make sure it is evenly stretched. Distorted pattern lines and crooked seams indicate faulty stretching. If the carpet is plain, unseamed faults are not so obvious; look closely to see if the pile is running straight. If there are any distortions, unhook the affected part and restretch it. Do not hook the carpet onto any binder bars at this stage.

Trimming the carpet

Trim the carpet with a sharp trimming knife. At straight edges take off just enough surplus to leave a 10mm (⅜in) overlap to be pressed behind the carpet grippers. Use an awl or spoon handle to turn the trimmed edge into the gulley.

Right-angle projection Press the carpet into the front edge of the projection, using a length of hardboard to hold it firmly in the angle between wall and floor. Trim along the front edge with a knife (**see 5a**), leaving about a 25mm (1in) overlap to avoid overtrimming – you can trim it accurately later. Fold back the carpet towards you. Place a piece of hardboard underneath to protect the carpet below and cut it to fit from the corners of the fireplace, or projection, to the wall (**see 5b**); still leave about a 25mm (1in) overlap.

Corners Cut slits in the carpet at the corners of the room and any right-angle projection so the carpet lies flat around the corner (**see 5c**). Stretch the carpet onto the carpet gripper and trim.

Pipes Lap up the carpet against the front of the pipe, apply latex adhesive to the back of the carpet at roughly the centre of the pipe and cut a slit in the carpet (**see 6a**). Ease the carpet round the pipe and tuck under the edges. For large diameter pipes, it is better to use a card template or a shape-tracer to draw the outline of each half of the pipe on the corresponding sides of the split in the carpet (**see 6b**). Cut out the shapes and ease the carpet round the pipe.

Fitting carpet to binder bar

Tuck the edge of the carpet under the lip and stretch the carpet onto the hooks (**see 7**). Place a piece of hardboard onto the lip to protect it and hammer the lip down.

Fitting foam and hessian-backed carpet

To fit foam and hessian-backed carpets which do not need to be stretched, follow the above instructions but omit stretching. All sides of the carpet should be fitted using the starting edge technique (as described above). Some tufted carpets, however, do stretch through use and this type should be loose laid for a few weeks before fixing. Once it has stretched, you can secure the carpet.

The thickness of foam on a foam-backed carpet may create a slight bump if fitted under an ordinary binder bar; to avoid this, remove some of the backing. Lay the carpet on the top of the metal lip (**see 8a**), then fold it back and with a felt tip pen mark the foam where it meets the edge of the binder bar (**see 8b**). Place a length of hardboard under the folded part and score the foam along the marked line with a trimming knife (**see 8c**); take care not to go right through to the pile. Peel off the section of foam from the edge of the carpet to the scored line (**see 8d**). Tuck the edge under the lip, place a piece of hardboard on top and hammer the lip down.

Warning If the carpet is bonded in foam, it is impossible to trim off the foam.

Joining seams with tape

Although carpet suppliers will seam body widths for you, you may find you have to make a seam to fit carpet into a recess. You may need to make seams if you move house and fit your old carpet into a different shape room. Professionals use stitching or heat-bonding to join seams, but the simplest method for the amateur is to use 50mm (2in) carpet tape and latex adhesive.

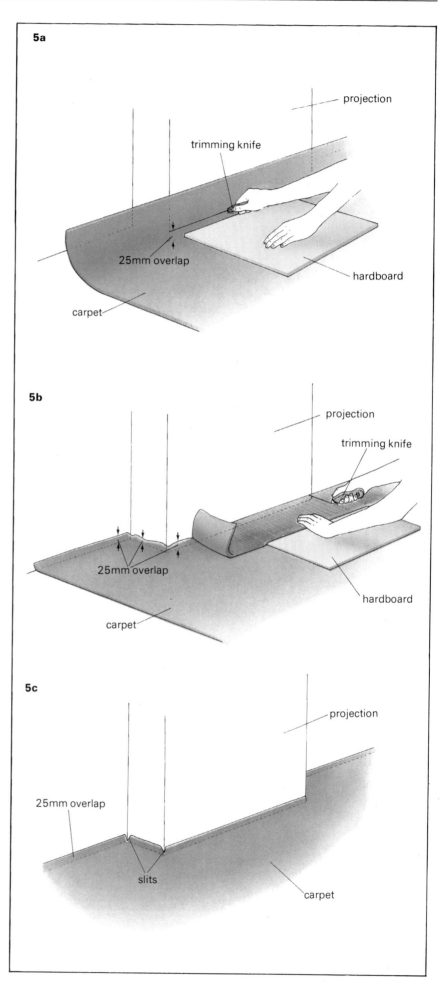

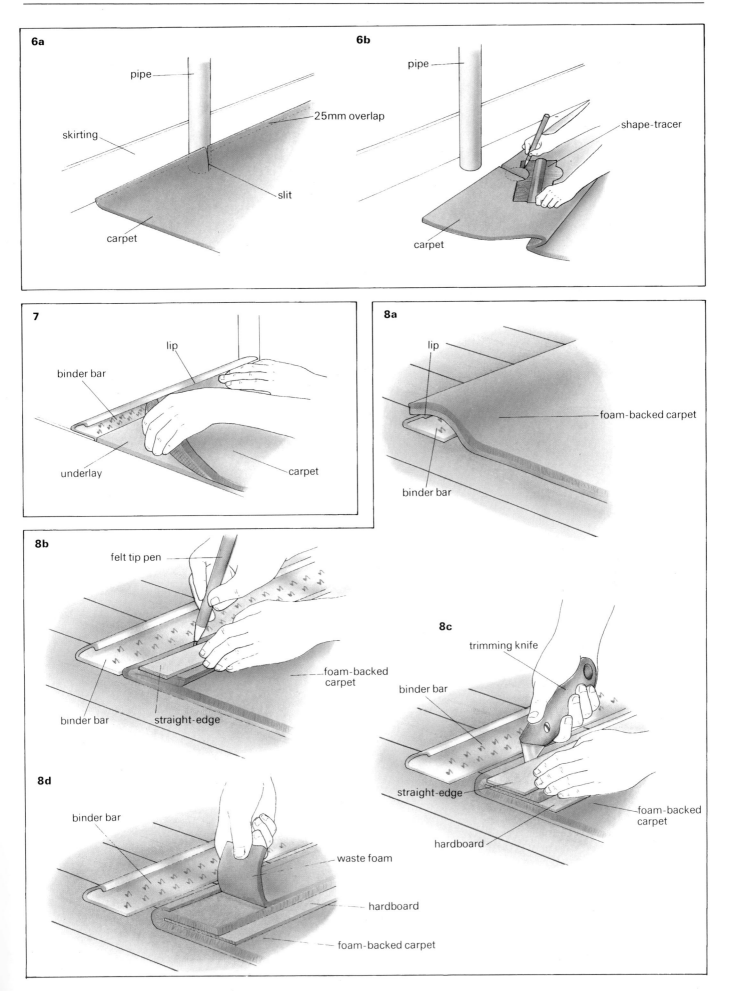

6a

pipe

skirting

25mm overlap

slit

carpet

6b

pipe

shape-tracer

carpet

7

lip

binder bar

underlay

carpet

8a

lip

foam-backed carpet

binder bar

8b

felt tip pen

binder bar

straight-edge

foam-backed carpet

8c

trimming knife

binder bar

straight-edge

foam-backed carpet

hardboard

8d

binder bar

waste foam

hardboard

foam-backed carpet

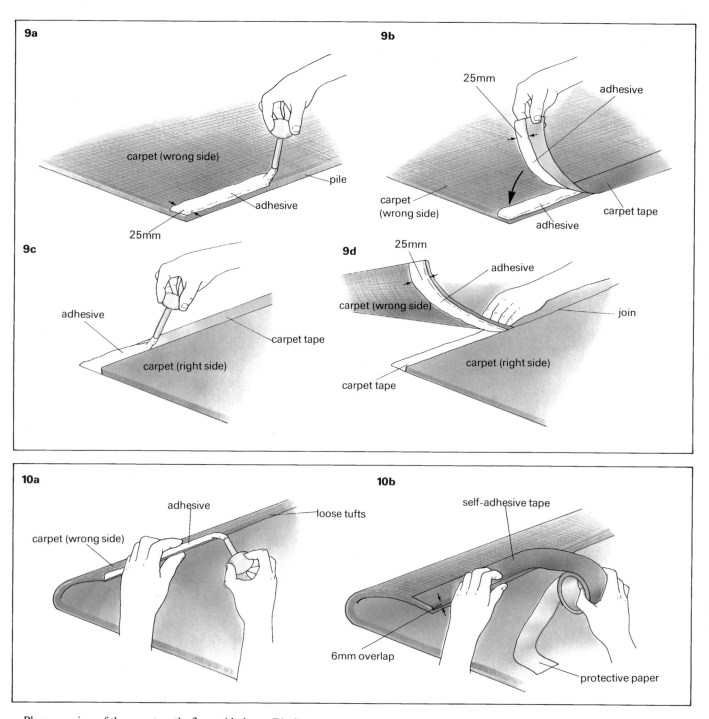

Place one piece of the carpet on the floor with the backing uppermost. Brush a 25mm (1in) band of adhesive along the edge, then halfway down the pile (**see 9a**). Apply a 25mm (1in) band of adhesive to one side of the carpet tape, wait for a few minutes until the adhesive is tacky and then bring into contact the bands of adhesive on the tape and the carpet edge (**see 9b**). Press down firmly along the join. The untreated half of the tape will now be protruding beyond the edge of the carpet.

Turn the carpet over so the pile is facing upwards. Carefully brush adhesive along the protruding half of the tape (**see 9c**). Apply adhesive to the edge of the other piece of carpet as before. When the adhesive is tacky, turn over the second piece of carpet so the pile is uppermost and press the edges of the two pieces of carpet carefully together (**see 9d**), making sure any pattern is aligned. Press down along the seam to ensure a firm join.

Binding edges

If you want to cut a fitted carpet to make a carpet square, you will need to bind the edges – when the carpet does not have an anti-fray backing.

The easiest way to do this is with self-adhesive tape. Turn the carpet edge back to expose the backing and seal any loose tufts with latex adhesive (**see 10a**); apply this with a small brush to make sure it does not come into contact with the surface of the pile. You can take the precaution of brushing adhesive along the whole length, whether loose tufts are evident or not.

Peel the protective paper backing off the tape and press the sticky surface onto the back edge of the carpet, allowing 6mm (¼in) to overlap the edge. Fold the overlap over to adhere tightly against the base of the tufts (**see 10b**). Finish off by pressing the tape firmly down or by tapping it lightly with a hammer.

Laying carpet tiles

The advantage of carpet tiles is they can be loose laid; this means you can move them around from time to time to distribute the wear evenly and replace individual tiles should they become damaged. If you spill something you can simply remove the affected square, wash it clean and leave it to dry flat, away from direct heat, before replacing it.

Carpet tiles are easy to lay and awkward shapes can be dealt with one by one so mistakes in cutting will be confined to individual tiles. They are available in a variety of fibres, surfaces and colours and are usually either mottled or plain; you can achieve a patterned or chequerboard effect by using different colours together or by laying tiles of the same colour so the piles run at right-angles to each other – or you can make a contrasting border. The backing is usually PVC or rubber and some tiles have a self-adhesive backing which is reusable should you want, or need, to move them about.

Warning When buying carpet tiles, check there is a guarantee on the stability of their dimensions so there is no expansion or contraction after they have been laid.

Sizes Carpet tiles are widely available in 500mm (19½in) squares, so four of these will cover one square metre. Some manufacturers have not changed to metric sizes and produce 18in square tiles, four of which will cover one square yard. Another popular size is the 12in square; these tiles are sold in packs of nine to cover a square yard.

Estimating quantity Since there may be a variation in shade between different batches, buy all you need at the same time. Even so, it is a good idea to open several packets of tiles and mix them up before you lay them so any slight variation in shade is barely noticeable.

The sizes available make it easy to calculate the quantity you need. Make a plan of the room on squared paper and work out the area to be covered. You may have to cut tiles to fit round the edges of the room but, if the border is less than half of one tile, allow only one for every two border tiles.

Preparing the sub-floor

The sub-floor must be clean, dry, level and sound. If it is bumpy, it will cause the carpet to wear in patches; so always remove old or damaged floor coverings. If there is a gap between the skirting and the floor, the tiles may work their way underneath the skirting. Prevent this by closing the gap with hardwood beading (this will also keep out draughts) or by sticking down the border tiles.

Timber floors Make sure there is adequate ventilation below the floor. Fill any gaps between the floorboards with a tough wood filler. Make sure all floorboards are nailed securely down so there is no movement and punch all nail heads well below the surface of the timber with a nail punch.

If the floor is very uneven, cover it with hardboard before laying the tiles. Timber floors treated with wood preservative are unsuitable for most types of carpet tiles, so check first with the tile manufacturer's instructions.

Solid floors Don't lay carpet tiles on a concrete floor which has underfloor heating. If the concrete floor is laid directly onto the ground, bear in mind

Above Carpet tiles will stand up to a great deal of heavy wear and are particularly suitable in a child's room. They are easy to look after since you can clean or replace individual tiles. The best way of equalizing wear on tiles is to move them around at regular intervals

it must have a damp proof membrane. Fill any cracks or holes and smooth off an uneven floor with a levelling compound – you may be able to rub down any bumps or rough spots.

Laying the tiles

If you cannot clear all the furniture out of the room, tile one half at a time. Generally speaking it is better to loose-lay the tiles so they are movable, but you should stick them down in areas where there is likely to be a lot of movement.

You can fix them down permanently with a flooring adhesive (use the one recommended by the manufacturer) or with double-sided adhesive tape so you can move them if necessary. If you place the tape round three sides only, you will find it easier to remove the tile. Always fix the first tile with tape so you have a stable base to work from.

Marking out the room Lay the tiles from the centre of the room so you get an even border round the edges. To find the centre, fix a chalked string line between the centre points of each pair of opposite walls. Snap each string line so it leaves a chalk mark on the floor; the centre point will be where the two lines cross.

Before you stick down the first tile, lay out two lines to the edges of the room to find out how wide the border tiles will be. If only a very narrow space is left on either edge, adjust the string lines to give a wider border; this not only looks better but means you will not have to cut fiddly narrow pieces to fit.

Place the double-sided adhesive tape on three bottom edges of the first tile and press it firmly down in the angle between the two string lines. Loose lay the second tile, butting it up against the first, along the string line; press it down firmly so it lies flat. Lay the tiles along the two string lines in one quarter of the room then fill in so that quarter

is complete except for the border tiles.

Some manufacturers suggest laying the tiles in alternate directions and the tiles are arrowed on the back to make this easy.

Stick down tiles where necessary and make sure all are butted firmly against each other so there are no gaps. Lay tiles over the remainder of the room, a quarter at a time, leaving the border uncovered.

Border tiles To get a tight fit at the edge of the wall, mark out and cut each tile individually. To do this, place a border tile on the last complete tile to be laid and butt another tile firmly against the wall on top of this one. Draw a line where the top tile touches the tile below, marking with a ball-point pen on the bottom face of the tile. Cut along this line with a sharp trimming knife held against a metal straight-edge and fix the cut edge of the tile against the wall.

To fit a tile round a corner mark one line as before and slide the tile round the corner, without turning it; draw another line so you have two lines crossing at right-angles. Cut out the rectangular piece, leaving an L-shaped portion which will fit neatly round the corner.

Awkward areas For more awkward shapes, make a card template or use a shape-tracer (or contour gauge) and mark the outline on the tile. When cutting a tile to fit round a pipe, first make a card template of the required shape then trace that shape onto the back of the tile. Cut a slit from the hole made for the pipe directly to the skirting board. When the tile is fixed, this line will be invisible.

Doorways Fit a metal binder bar or threshold strip in every doorway to hold the tiles in position in an area where there is always a lot of wear and tear. Available in a variety of finishes, the bar or strip will also provide a neat join between the carpet tiles and the adjoining floor covering.

1 Start tiling from the centre of the room so you get an even border round the edge
2 To cut an edge tile to fit, place it on the last whole tile, put another tile on top of this so it butts up against the wall and mark where the top tile touches the tile below; you can place a piece of wood between the tiles to prevent scoring right through
3 Cut along the marked line with a trimming knife held against a metal straight-edge
4 Fix the cut edge of the tile against the wall and secure with double-sided adhesive tape
5 To fit a tile round a pipe, make a template of the required shape and trace the shape onto the back of the tile; cut a slit from the hole made for the pipe to the skirting
6 Fit the tile round the pipe and secure with tape for an invisible join

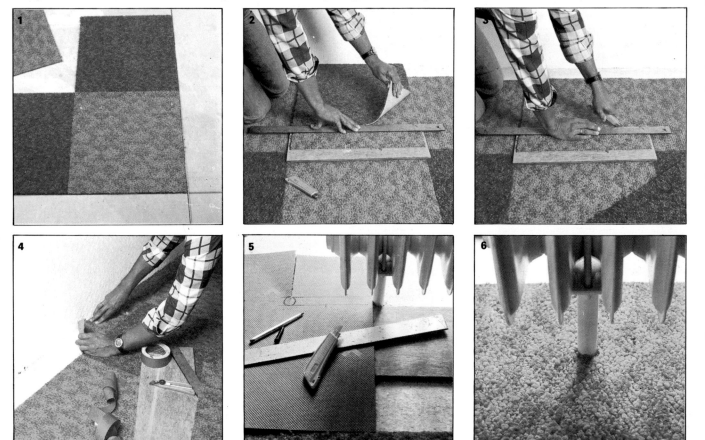

Fitting a stair carpet

Your stair carpet receives more wear than you might expect, so make sure you buy the right type and fit it correctly – for safety and maximum economy.

When selecting a carpet for stairs, bear in mind the heavy wear to which it is going to be subjected. Most people do not realize how many times even a small family use the stairs every day. Wear is not only caused by treading but also by the scraping of heels against the risers and by strong rubbing against the nosing. Long pile carpets (for example shag and semi-shag) are not suitable for staircases and foam-backed carpets are best avoided, if possible, since they are complicated to install.

As in all carpet installations underlay is essential since it provides longer life, increases sound insulation and gives greater comfort. Don't use stair pads, which only cover the tread area. When fitting underlay, make sure there is enough to pass round the nosing of the stair.

To give longer life, a stair carpet should be moved about six months after laying; this enables those parts of the carpet covering the risers to be placed over the treads and vice versa. Subsequently, at longer intervals, the carpet should be slightly moved to equalize the wear. When the carpet is laid, the extra amount is folded against the riser at the bottom of the staircase. Before fitting the carpet, make sure the natural inclination of the pile faces downwards.

Measuring up When buying a carpet, first measure the length you require. Assume the method of installation you are going to use will cause the carpet on the upper landing to overlap the top riser. Begin measuring from the base of the top riser and take the tape lightly over each tread and riser. Add to the total measured length an additional 38mm ($1\frac{1}{2}$in) for each step to allow for the space taken by the underlay. Add a further 457mm (18in) to enable the carpet to be moved to increase its life. If the staircase includes a winder, measure along the path taken by the outer edge of the carpet.

Laying the carpet

The two main methods of laying stair carpets are by tacking down and by using tackless strip. Whichever method you use, it is necessary to mark on the stairs the positions of the edges of the carpet and the underlay; the marking for the underlay will also apply to the tackless strips when they are used. The purpose of this marking is to ensure the carpet is laid centrally when it is not wide enough to cover the stair fully. If the steps are 813mm (32in) wide and the carpet is 686mm (27in) wide, a mark should be made on the riser 63mm ($2\frac{1}{2}$in) in from each edge. Then make a mark 19mm ($\frac{3}{4}$in) inside the first ones to indicate the width and position of the underlay and of the tackless strip.

Tack-down method

For tacking down a special type of tack is used which is less visible than the normal type. First attach all the underlay, using a separate piece for each step; the width should be 38mm ($1\frac{1}{2}$in) less

than the width of the carpet and it must be long enough to cover the tread and lap round the nosing so the lower edge can be secured to the riser below. Align the sides of each pad with the inner pair of marks and position the back edge 25mm (1in) in from the riser. Tack it down at intervals of 150mm (6in) across the back of the tread, stretch it over the nosing and tack it across the riser below.

Starting at the top tread, position the end of the carpet as indicated by the marks so it is properly centred; allow an extra 13mm ($\frac{1}{2}$in) for turning under where the material reaches the top riser. Unwrap enough material from the roll to cover the first two or three steps. Before starting to tack, make sure the tuft rows across the carpet are parallel with the nosing. Turn the end of the carpet under so the cut end is not exposed and tack down one corner; stretch the carpet to make it even and

Above By fitting carpet to your stairs you can not only make them safer to use, but you can also draw them into the home's overall design; here the stairs have been covered with the same carpet as that used in the rest of the house, which brings the many different levels together and makes the house seem larger

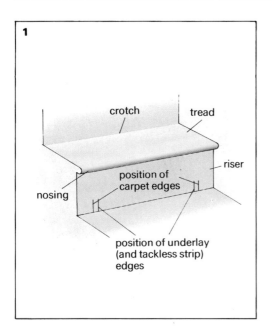

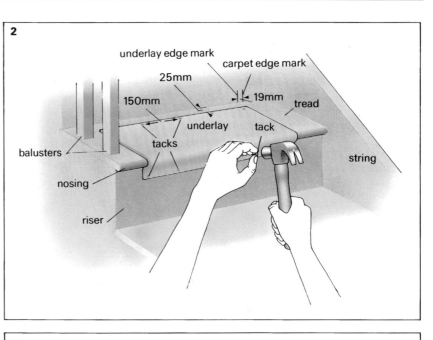

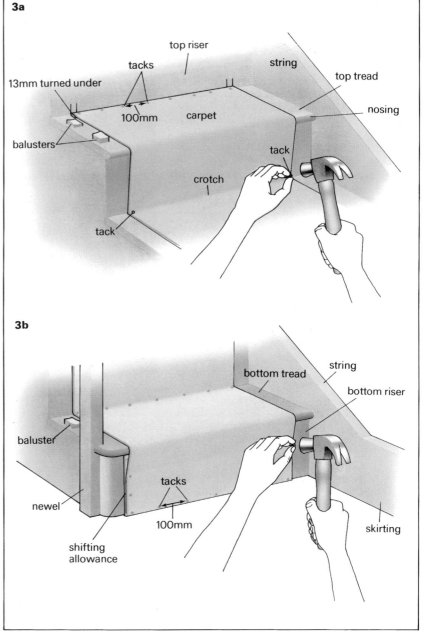

1 To ensure the carpet lies centrally on the stair, mark on the riser the position of the edges of the underlay and the carpet; the marks for the underlay will also apply to tackless strip, if this is used
2 Fitting underlay for tacked carpet
3a Tacking down the carpet, starting at the first tread; the landing carpet should cover the first riser
3b Fitting the carpet at the bottom

tack across the riser at intervals of about 100mm (4in). Continue down the stairs, stretching the carpet over the nosing and tacking the edges in at the crotch. Then insert tacks across the crotch at 100mm (4in) intervals.

Where additional material has been included to allow for shifting, the material is folded in and held against the bottom riser by tacking up the sides. A slight overlap is needed at the bottom end of the carpet so it can be folded back when the carpet is finally tacked at the base of the lowest riser; take this into account also when measuring the shifting allowance. The same is done to the overlap of the landing carpet which covers the top riser.

Tackless strip method
Tackless strip is a flat narrow strip of wood, which is nailed to the floor; it is fitted with pins set at an angle, onto which the carpet is hooked. For laying stair carpets the strip is sold in 762mm (30in) lengths, so to fit a carpet 686mm (27in) wide, cut the lengths down to 648mm (25½in). When installing tackless strips, first mark the stairs as explained above, then fix the strips on the stairs. One strip is nailed across the riser, parallel with and 16mm (⅝in) above the crotch. Another strip is nailed across the tread the same distance from the crotch; this provides a gap into which the carpet is tucked. These distances will have to be increased or decreased according to the thickness of the carpet, since it is important to ensure a tight fit. The pins of both strips should lean towards the crotch.

Next attach the pieces of underlay, which should be longer than those used in the tack-down method. The rear edge of the underlay butts up against the tackless strip on the tread and is tacked down. The front edge is taken over the nosing, stretched down

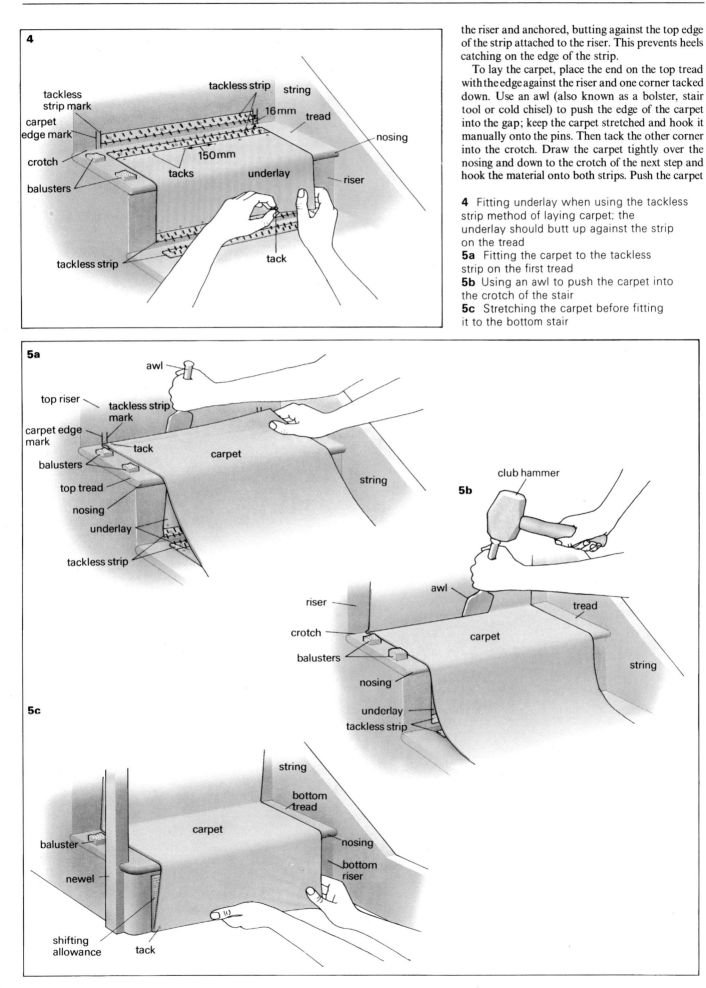

4

tackless
strip mark

carpet
edge mark

crotch

balusters

tackless strip

tackless strip

string

16mm

tread

nosing

150mm

tacks

underlay

riser

tack

the riser and anchored, butting against the top edge of the riser and anchored, butting against the top edge of the strip attached to the riser. This prevents heels catching on the edge of the strip.

To lay the carpet, place the end on the top tread with the edge against the riser and one corner tacked down. Use an awl (also known as a bolster, stair tool or cold chisel) to push the edge of the carpet into the gap; keep the carpet stretched and hook it manually onto the pins. Then tack the other corner into the crotch. Draw the carpet tightly over the nosing and down to the crotch of the next step and hook the material onto both strips. Push the carpet

4 Fitting underlay when using the tackless strip method of laying carpet; the underlay should butt up against the strip on the tread
5a Fitting the carpet to the tackless strip on the first tread
5b Using an awl to push the carpet into the crotch of the stair
5c Stretching the carpet before fitting it to the bottom stair

5a

awl

top riser

tackless strip
mark

carpet edge
mark

balusters

top tread

nosing

underlay

tackless strip

tack

carpet

string

5b

club hammer

riser

crotch

balusters

nosing

underlay

tackless strip

awl

tread

carpet

string

5c

string

bottom
tread

carpet

nosing

bottom
riser

baluster

newel

shifting
allowance

tack

into the gap between the strips, using the awl to help tighten the carpet and prevent rucking. Repeat this procedure down the staircase. At the bottom, fold in the end of the carpet and tack across the bottom riser to give a neat finish.

Edge-to-edge fitting
In edge-to-edge fitting, where the steps are covered completely, the tackless strip and underlay have to be wider, although still slightly narrower than the carpet. If the carpet has been cut to width from wider material, latex adhesive should be applied along the edges to prevent the backing fraying and tufts working loose at the edges. Trim those parts that are too wide.

An even simpler method of tackless strip fitting is to use an angled metal strip with bevelled gripper pins along each of the inside faces. The strip fits into the crotch and the carpet is held by the pins. This is similar to the tackless strip although there is no gap into which you can tuck the carpet to tighten it. Another version has two faces to provide extra stretch and is particularly suitable for hessian,

secondary-backed fabric. If you have to use a foam-backed carpet, you can buy pairs of tongued plastic strips. These are fitted close to the crotch of the step, similar to the tackless strip; this enables the foam-backed carpet to be wedged between them. It is essential these components are positioned accurately and conform with the thickness of the material.

Fitting onto winders
Fitting carpets for winding stairs can be difficult. The easiest way is to cut separate pieces for each tread and the riser below, using a paper template to get the right shape. Cut the carpet so the tuft rows are parallel with the nosings and tack the pieces into position. When using tackless strip for edge-to-edge fitting, fit a length of strip along the skirting to hold the carpet along the three sides of the triangle.

By following carefully the methods described either using tacks or tackless strips, you should make a neat job of covering your stairs.

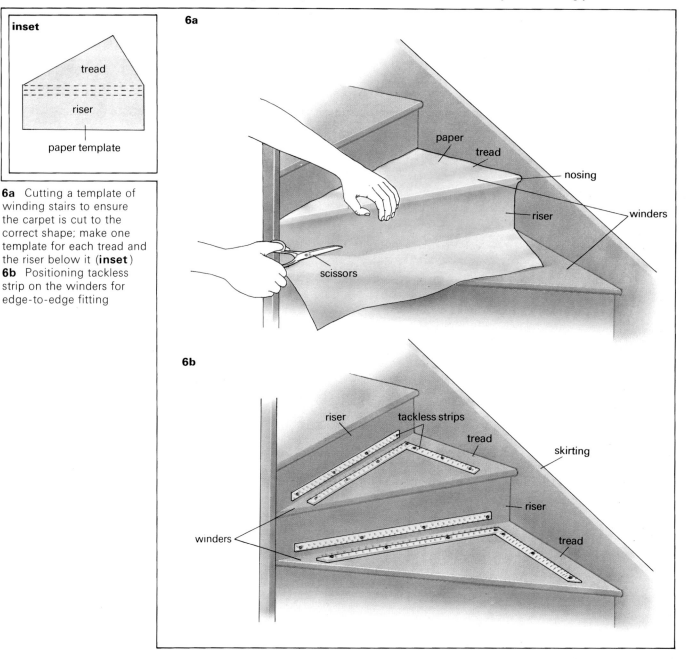

inset

tread

riser

paper template

6a Cutting a template of winding stairs to ensure the carpet is cut to the correct shape; make one template for each tread and the riser below it (**inset**)
6b Positioning tackless strip on the winders for edge-to-edge fitting

6a

paper
tread
nosing
riser
winders
scissors

6b

riser
tackless strips
tread
skirting
riser
tread
winders

Cleaning & repairing carpets

Carpets will become worn or damaged in the course of everyday use. There is no need to go to the expense of replacing them when you can patch and repair minor damage easily and at a fraction of the cost. You should remember to save remnants and offcuts when carpets are being fitted so you will be able to carry out repairs in the future.

Regular vacuum cleaning, ideally every day, will remove grit which cuts into carpet fibres and backing as it is trodden in. Fluff will form on the surface of new carpets; this consists of short fibres which do not reach the base of the carpet and should be removed for the first few weeks with a hand brush, carpet sweeper or vacuum cleaner. Sometimes, while a carpet is bedding down, short loose fibres may become tangled with stronger fibres, causing small balls or pills of fibre on the surface. These should be trimmed off with scissors; never attempt to pull protruding fibres out of the carpet.

Often the surface of a looped pile carpet may be caught up with a nail, in the base of a piece of furniture for example; this will cause a pulled loop. Look carefully to see if an adjacent loop has been pulled into the base of the carpet; if one has, you may be able to tease it up with a piece of hooked wire and draw the pulled loop back into the surface. If not, you will need to trim the loop level with the surface.

Cleaning carpets

Lightly soiled carpets can be cleaned with carpet shampoo, applied by a manual or electric carpet shampooer following manufacturer's instructions. Treat heavily stained areas separately and test a small area before treating the whole carpet to check for discolouration. The best shampoos produce a dry foam which does not wet the carpet excessively; if the carpet is too wet, this could cause shrinkage and discolouration. After shampooing, leave the pile sloping in one direction and allow the carpet to dry before walking or replacing furniture on it: vacuum it clean when it is dry.

Heavily soiled carpet will have to be treated by professionals – or you can hire a 'steam' carpet cleaner; this is a large vacuum cleaner with a wet shampoo applicator. A hand-held nozzle sprays shampoo and hot water and the carpet is vacuumed so the shampoo, dirt and most of the water is drawn into the waste tank of the cleaner. The carpet is left drier than after ordinary shampooing, so the furniture may be replaced within about an hour.

Removing stains

When treating stains on carpets you should always test an area to discover whether the treatment has any effect on the colour dyes in the carpet. Remember it is much harder to remove all liquids and semi-solids if they are allowed to dry. Stains fall into two basic categories and there are specific treatments for each type of carpet stain.

Water soluble stains These should yield to a carpet

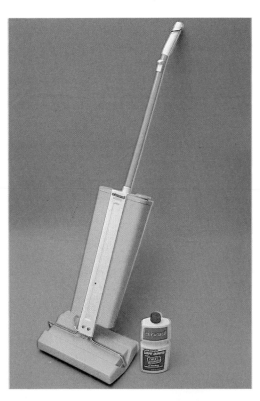

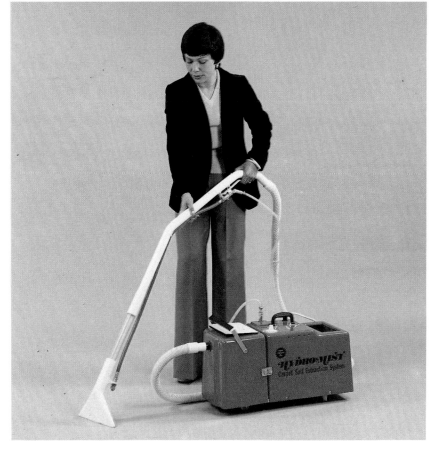

Left Carpet shampooer, suitable for cleaning lightly soiled carpets
Below 'Steam' cleaner, suitable for heavily soiled carpets

Following page
1a When patching woven back carpet, first mark out the damaged area on the back of the carpet and apply adhesive along the marked lines
1b Cut out the damaged area with a sharp knife, placing a piece of hardboard under the carpet for protection
1c Place the damaged piece on a carpet offcut and mark its exact shape with a felt pen
1d Fix strips of carpet tape to overlap the edges of the hole
1e Place the patch over the carpet tape and hammer it down along the edges to ensure a firm bond

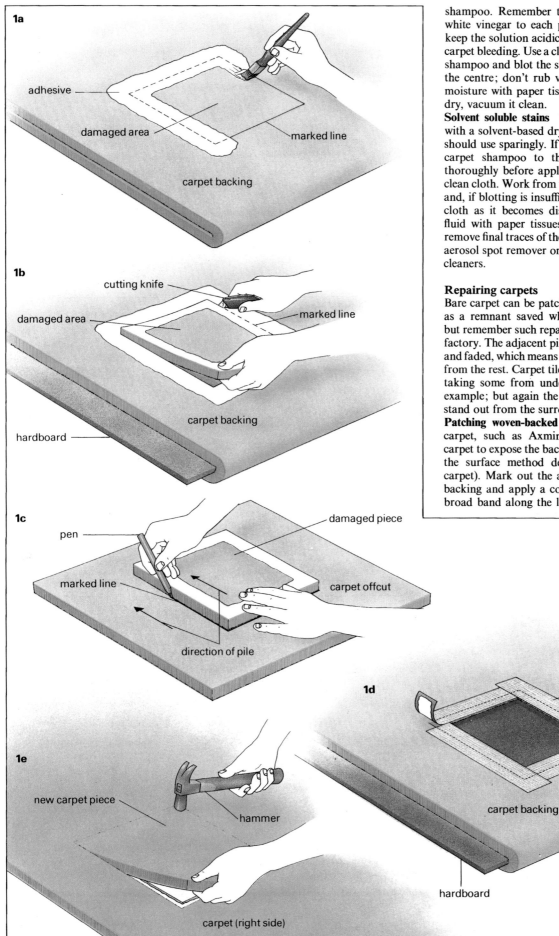

1a
adhesive
damaged area
marked line
carpet backing

1b
cutting knife
damaged area
marked line
hardboard
carpet backing

1c
pen
damaged piece
marked line
carpet offcut
direction of pile

1d
carpet tape
carpet backing

1e
new carpet piece
hammer
hardboard
carpet (right side)

shampoo. Remember to add one teaspoonful of white vinegar to each pint of shampoo; this will keep the solution acidic and prevent the dye in the carpet bleeding. Use a clean white cloth to apply the shampoo and blot the stain from the edge towards the centre; don't rub vigorously. Mop up excess moisture with paper tissues and, when the area is dry, vacuum it clean.

Solvent soluble stains These should be removed with a solvent-based dry cleaning fluid, which you should use sparingly. If you have applied water or carpet shampoo to the stain, allow it to dry thoroughly before applying the fluid on a pad of clean cloth. Work from the edge towards the centre and, if blotting is insufficient, rub gently. Turn the cloth as it becomes discoloured and blot excess fluid with paper tissues. Use carpet shampoo to remove final traces of the stain; if it does not, use an aerosol spot remover or call in professional carpet cleaners.

Repairing carpets
Bare carpet can be patched with a new piece, such as a remnant saved when the carpet was fitted; but remember such repairs are rarely entirely satisfactory. The adjacent pile is likely to have flattened and faded, which means the new piece will stand out from the rest. Carpet tiles can be moved around by taking some from under pieces of furniture, for example; but again the replacements are likely to stand out from the surrounding tiles.

Patching woven-backed carpet To patch woven carpet, such as Axminster or Wilton, turn the carpet to expose the backing (although you can use the surface method described for foam-backed carpet). Mark out the area of the damage on the backing and apply a coat of carpet adhesive in a broad band along the lines you have drawn; this will prevent the carpet fraying when you cut out the damaged area. Place a sheet of hardboard under the carpet and cut along the marked lines with a sharp knife. Put the piece you have cut out upside down on the back of an offcut of the carpet and carefully match the direction of pile and pattern (the pattern will usually show through the back of a woven carpet). Mark out the exact shape of the worn piece onto the new one, coat with adhesive and cut out as before. Lay strips of 50mm (2in) carpet tape around the edge of the hole in the carpet to accept the patch; you can use either self-adhesive tape or woven fabric tape (which requires carpet adhesive). Re-lay the carpet and press the patch into place over the carpet tape; take great care not to push down the surrounding pile as you press the patch into place. Hammer it down along the edges to ensure firm contact with the carpet tape beneath.

Patching foam-backed carpet This is easier because you can patch from above the surface of the carpet. Lay a large offcut over the worn area and match the pile direction and pattern; very carefully cut both layers at the same time with a sharp knife. If it is a large patch, you can tack the pieces down to prevent movement as you cut through. The foam backing will prevent fraying. If you intend to use this method with woven carpet, you will need to apply carpet adhesive along edges of both the hole and the patch roughly halfway up the pile. Cut strips of carpet tape so they will overlap around the hole, raise the edges of the carpet and apply the tape so half its width is exposed (sticky side up). Place the patch in position and hammer down the edges to ensure sound contact with the tape.

Repairing tears Tears in carpet are usually caused by movement of the underfloor; this should be rectified before you make the repair. Tears often occur at the back and front edges of stair treads because of movement between treads and risers. To repair a tear, turn the carpet over and hold the tear closed before sticking 75mm (3in) wide self-adhesive or woven carpet tape along it. If you use woven tape with carpet adhesive, you can make the repair stronger by stitching along the sides of the tear with a curved needle and strong thread.

Repairing frayed edges Frayed edges occur most frequently at doorways and they can be repaired by fitting aluminium binder bars, which are available

in various designs. Use bars with small teeth for woven-backed carpets and bars with small lips to hold foam-backed carpets. Cut the binder bar to length (to fit the doorway) and nail it down; on a concrete floor you can fix the bar with masonry pins or use adhesive. If the carpet has a woven backing, you should seal the edge by working in a 25mm (1in) strip of carpet adhesive and trimming off the loose ends. Make sure the carpet lies flat without rucks or wrinkles before hammering down the lip of the binder bar, using a wood block as protection.

You can also seal frayed edges with carpet tape; this is especially useful for frayed carpet squares. If the carpet has a woven back, cut off a small amount of carpet to give a neat, straight edge. Seal this edge with adhesive, taking care not to get the adhesive higher than the base of the tufts. Stick carpet tape along the edge, allowing $3-6mm$ ($\frac{1}{8}-\frac{1}{4}$in) to overlap; turn the overlap over so it sticks to the base of the tufts all along the edge.

It is more difficult to bind the edges of foam-backed carpet because it crumbles at the edges. The foam may make binding difficult because you need a good key for the adhesive or self-adhesive tape. It may be necessary to experiment with different adhesives to find one which gives the best bond.

Repairing burns You may be able to trim off the tips of burnt fibres to remove a mild cigarette burn; more serious burns on woollen rugs and carpets can be patched with thick knitting wool. Trim off the burnt tufts with a small pair of nail scissors and cut the patching wool into 13mm ($\frac{1}{2}$in) pieces. Hold back the carpet pile around the damaged area and work carpet adhesive into the trimmed tufts with a matchstick. Ease a bunch of wool pieces into the damaged area with a matchstick, filling the hole as tightly as possible. When the adhesive is dry, cut the ends level with the pile and pull out any loose ends. Use a needle to tease the new wool fibres into the fibres of the carpet.

Serious burns in woven, nylon and man-made carpets must be patched using the technique described for worn carpets.

Repairing rush matting This type of floor covering is not easily repaired, but you may be able to stitch loose pieces back into position. Replacement pieces are available for square rush matting, which you can stitch into place to repair worn areas.

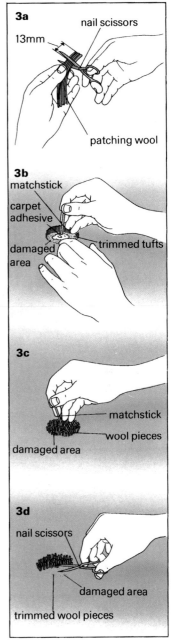

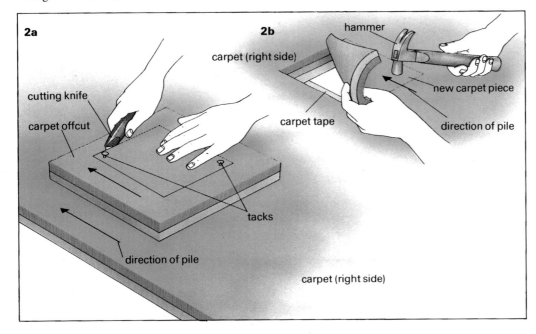

2a When patching foam-backed carpet, place a large offcut on top of the damaged area and cut through both layers at the same time; you can tack down the offcut to stop it moving as you cut through
2b Fix carpet tape to overlap the edges of the hole, place the patch in position and hammer it down firmly
3a To repair a burn, cut strands of patching wool into 13mm lengths
3b Trim off the burnt carpet fibres and work adhesive into the tufts with a matchstick
3c Ease a bunch of wool pieces into the hole, packing them in as tightly as possible
3d When the adhesive is dry, trim the ends of the wool level with the pile

Carpet stains and how to remove them

Stain	Treatment	Method
Animal or baby soiling	Carpet shampoo or biological detergent	Blot or scrape then apply treatment
Beer, wine, spirits	Clean warm water or, if persistent, carpet shampoo	Blot with clean cloth and sponge
Blood	Cold water or, if persistent, carpet shampoo or biological detergent	Sponge with water before stain dries
Burns	Stiff brush or nail scissors then carpet shampoo	Brush or cut away lightly scorched areas then shampoo (serious burns will require retufting or patching)
Chewing gum	Dry cleaning fluid	Scrape off as much as possible then apply treatment
Chocolate, egg, ice cream, soft drinks, vomit	Carpet shampoo or, if persistent, solution of 7ml ($\frac{1}{4}$fl oz) borax with 248ml (10fl oz) water then shampoo	Scrape off then apply treatment
Fruit juice	Carpet shampoo or biological detergent	Blot then apply treatment
Cocoa, coffee, tea, milk	Clean warm water or, if persistent, carpet shampoo or detergent followed by borax solution as for **Chocolate**	Blot with cloth and sponge with water
Adhesive	As for **Chocolate**	Blot or scrape while adhesive is still liquid then apply treatment (old adhesive stains may yield to dry cleaning fluid; if not, seek professional help)
Grass	Methylated spirit then carpet shampoo or biological detergent	Wipe with methylated spirit before applying treatment
Grease, oil, fat, butter, margarine, ointment, perfume, tar, candle wax, shoe polish	Carpet shampoo or solvent-based dry cleaning fluid	Blot or scrape then shampoo; blot excess with tissues, allow to dry and apply treatment with cloth; shampoo again to remove traces
Ink	Carpet shampoo, biological detergent, methylated spirit or dry cleaning fluid	Soak up with tissues then apply treatment; ball pen stains can be removed with methylated spirit (old and indelible ink stains will require professional help)
Paint, varnish	Water for water-based paint such as emulsion, white spirit for oil-based paint such as gloss and varnishes and amyl-acetate (cellulose thinner) for cellulose paints and lacquers; then carpet shampoo	Scrape or wipe off excess, treat with thinner then use carpet shampoo (dried stains may yield to paint stripper applied with care — test a corner first; alternatively seek professional help)
Rust	Carpet shampoo then vacuum cleaner	Blot fresh stains with carpet shampoo on cloth, allow to dry then vacuum (old stains require professional help)
Soot	Carpet shampoo	Blot with treatment on cloth

Upholstery & curtains

However hard-wearing your chairs may be, sooner or
later they will need repairing or re-covering.
Replacing furniture is costly; repairs and new covers
will make chairs like new. This section gives detailed
guidance on how to restore a range of chairs and
keep them clean. It also shows you how to choose
and make your own curtains and how to hang them.
Although sewing is obviously involved in these
operations, expert skills are not necessarily required
and the simple, explanatory illustrations will help
even the beginner to achieve satisfactory results on
the furniture or windows.

Upholstery: cleaning & general repairs

It is worth getting into the habit of vacuuming your upholstery on a regular basis, since if you spring-clean it once a year, dirt will be ground into the fabric. Most suction cleaners have a special attachment for cleaning upholstery and for removing dust and dirt from awkward places in the backs and sides of chairs.

If possible, you should remove any spillage immediately after it happens. Treatment will depend on the type of fabric, so before you begin always check the manufacturer's instructions to make sure the cleaner you have in mind is suitable. You should check for such things as shrinkage and colour-fastness by making a small test with the cleaner in an inconspicuous place on the upholstery. To avoid overdampening the fabric and the padding beneath, it is best to use a dry cleaner on fabrics to get rid of spots and stains. This type of cleaner only wets the surface and dries very quickly to a powder; when you brush off the powder, it should take the stain with it. At least one make of this type is suitable for cleaning both upholstery and carpet.

Loose covers These can be either dry-cleaned or washed, depending on the composition of the fabric. If you are in doubt, check with the manufacturer's washing instructions or go to a reputable cleaner for advice. Some materials may be liable to shrink or run their colours in the wash and you should check for this before you begin washing.

Fixed covers Very badly soiled areas in fixed fabric covers can be cleaned by using a special upholstery shampoo. Again, to avoid overdampening the fabric, you can use a dry shampoo with an applicator. The shampoo foam is forced through a sponge head in a controlled flow which eventually dries to a powder and is removed with an upholstery attachment on a vacuum cleaner. To make sure the shampoo will not harm the fabric, check on a small, hidden area first.

Alternatively, if you are going to spring-clean your carpets by hiring a hot water soil extraction machine, you can clean your upholstery at the same time. Ask for a special upholstery tool attachment when you are hiring one of these machines, which are available by the day or half-day from specialist hire shops and some carpet retailers. The machines are fairly heavy to manoeuvre; but this should not be a problem when you are cleaning upholstery, since you will probably be able to reach several chairs from one position. A shampoo is mixed with the hot water, 'vacuumed' over the upholstery with one sweep and sucked back with the grime and dirt in the next sweep, which takes out most of the moisture. It is best to treat very dirty areas with a spot remover to loosen the stain before starting to clean with the machine. The upholstery will dry out in a warm room.

Methods of repairing

Burst or frayed machine seams or tears near piping can be repaired by slip-stitching, which if done with care will conceal the damage. Neaten any frayed

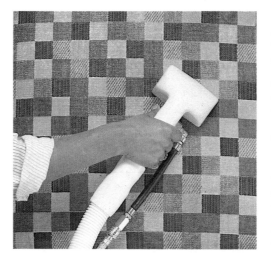

edges by trimming, but don't cut into the fabric itself. If necessary, turn in a tiny piece along either side of the torn edges to make them neat. Use large darning needles fixed down firmly into the padding along the torn edges to hold them together while slip-stitching the tear.

You will need matching strong thread and an upholsterer's half circle 'slipping' needle, which you can buy from the haberdashery department of a large store or possibly an upholsterer's shop. Tie a knot in one end of the thread and insert the needle into one side of the tear a little way in from the end, hiding the knot on the underside of the upholstery. Bring the two edges together by using very tiny stitches on either side, pulling the thread through very firmly each time and keeping the stitches parallel. Remove the darning needles as you go along and finish by fastening off the thread, working the thread end into the seam.

Patches A hole can be successfully repaired by taking replacement fabric from elsewhere (from the underside of the chair or sofa, for example) and patching it in. If this is not possible and you feel it is worth the effort, try locating an extra piece of matching fabric from the manufacturer. Carefully cut away all the damaged fabric, tidying up the edges as you cut. The replacement patch should be slightly larger than the actual hole size and, where necessary, you should carefully match the pattern; if there is a pile make sure it is the right way up. Push the patch down into position onto the padding and underneath the hole edges. Coat round the edges of the patch and the undersides of the fabric edges round the hole with a fabric adhesive, taking care not to let the adhesive touch anywhere else. Wait until the adhesive becomes fairly tacky, press the two surfaces together and leave them to dry. This type of patch will satisfactorily disguise small damaged areas. For anything larger you will need to fit a replacement cover for that particular section: this is covered later in the book.

Leather and vinyl Covers in leather and vinyl cannot be slip-stitched, but provided they are soft

Left A carpet soil extraction machine fitted with a special attachment can be used to clean upholstery

1 When slip-stitching torn fabric, hold the edges together with large darning needles fixed firmly into the padding

2 To patch damaged fabric, position the patch beneath the hole edges, matching any pattern; coat the hole edges and the edges of the patch with adhesive and, when this is tacky, press the two surfaces together

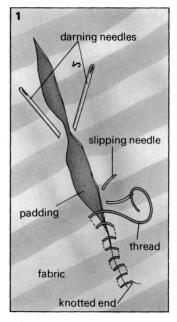

1
darning needles
slipping needle
padding
thread
fabric
knotted end

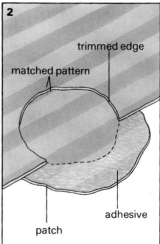

2
trimmed edge
matched pattern
adhesive
patch

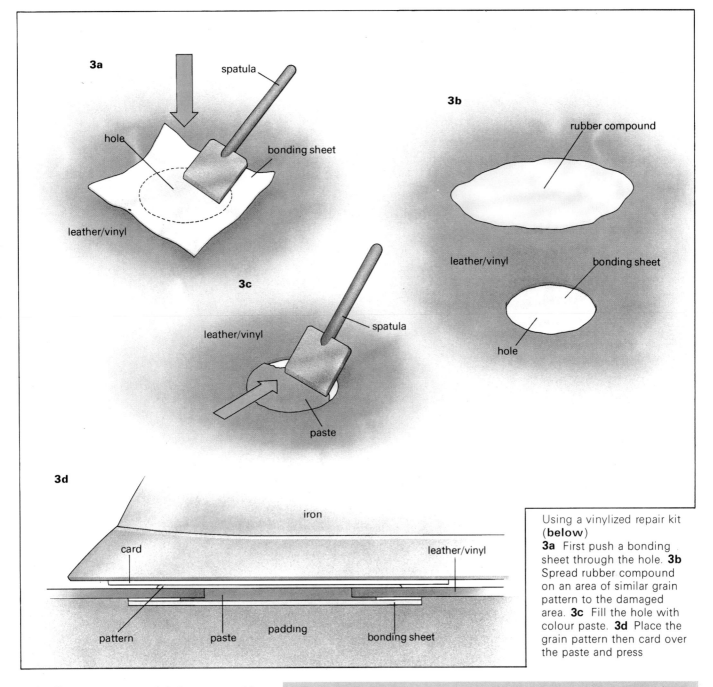

3a spatula

hole

bonding sheet

leather/vinyl

3b rubber compound

leather/vinyl   bonding sheet

hole

3c

leather/vinyl   spatula

paste

3d

iron

card   leather/vinyl

pattern   paste   padding   bonding sheet

Using a vinylized repair kit
(**below**)
3a First push a bonding
sheet through the hole. **3b**
Spread rubber compound
on an area of similar grain
pattern to the damaged
area. **3c** Fill the hole with
colour paste. **3d** Place the
grain pattern then card over
the paste and press

and well worn you can repair holes or tears with a special repair kit available from a hardware store or haberdashers. The kit enables you not only to match up the upholstery colour but also the grain, which is particularly important if you want to achieve a good repair.

Clean the surface with white spirit to remove grease and dirt and insert a small piece of bonding sheet (provided with the kit) through the tear to form the base for the repair paste. Mix the paste to the exact colour and use a knife or spatula to spread it into the area. To match the upholstery grain use one of the patterns which come with the kit; alternatively for an unusual grain pattern you can use the rubber compound (which is also supplied) to make a mould of an area identical to that which is damaged to provide a pattern. Place the grain pattern or rubber mould face down over the paste, place a piece of card on top and press down on it for two minutes with a warm iron to imprint the pattern on the paste.

Button & foam cushion repairs

Some chairs and sofas have decorative buttons on the seat and back; these often work loose and fall off and can mar the appearance of upholstery which is otherwise in a good state of repair. Fortunately, replacing them is a relatively simple task. If only one or two buttons are missing, you could cover the new ones with pieces of fabric taken from an inconspicious part of the chair or sofa; if several are missing, you may find it easier to replace all the buttons and cover them in a contrasting fabric.

Metal button trims These, which you cover with fabric yourself, are available in a range of sizes from haberdashery departments of large stores. They are in two sections: the round main part has small claws on the bottom onto which fabric is pressed and the other part is a cap which clamps the fabric down and secures it in position.

If you are using the same fabric, take a piece out of the underside of the chair or sofa or from the tuck-ins of the lower inside arms. You will find it worth experimenting with the fabric and the button trims until you achieve the correct tension across the button face. If the fabric is very thick, which upholstery fabric often is, you may find it very difficult to fit it onto the button trims. You can take the spare fabric to the fabrics department of a large store where you should be able to have the buttons covered at a reasonable cost.

Fixing buttons

When you are fixing a button to the inside back of a chair or settee, it is worth taking the back cover off so you have access to the inside padding. Thread a length of thin stitching twine through the button and then thread the two ends of the length of twine through the eye of a long upholstery stitching needle.

Mark the position of the button with a piece of tailor's chalk on the inside back cover, push the needle through this mark and through the inside padding, making sure the twine comes right through with the needle. Use a slip knot to join the two pieces of twine securely together; but before pulling the knot tight insert a small piece or tuft of felt or cloth between the stuffing and the slip knot to prevent the knot pulling through later and making an unsightly hole.

Tighten the slip knot by pulling one end of the twine. At the same time check the other buttons already in place; if they are deep-buttoned (pulled in very tightly into the upholstery), make sure you match up the depth of the button you are fixing with their depth and pull in accordingly. When the buttons are all the same depth, tie a reef knot to stop the slip knot coming undone later; cut off the twine ends for a neat finish.

Where it is not possible to take off the back cover without a great deal of trouble, you can make a quick repair with the cover on. Thread a long upholstery needle with twine and insert it into the upholstery on the side where you are going to replace the button. Push it through until the eye has

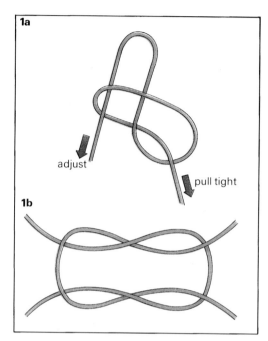

1a Tying a slip knot
1b Tying a reef knot
2a To replace a button, thread a length of twine through the button and then thread both ends through the eye of an upholstery needle
2b Mark the position of the button on the inside back cover; push the needle through the mark and the padding, making sure the twine comes right through with the needle
2c Tie the two pieces of twine with a slip knot; before tightening this insert a small tuft of felt or cloth between the knot and the padding
2d Tighten the slip knot until the button is at the same depth as other buttons on the chair; secure with a reef knot

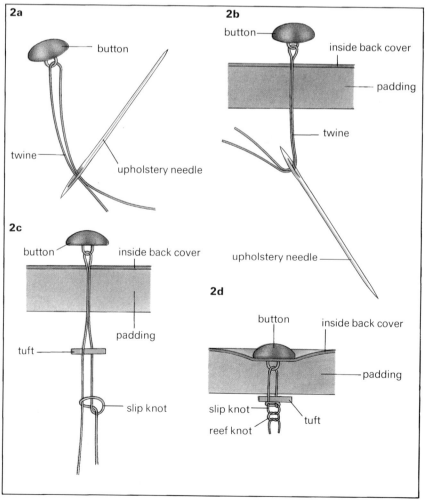

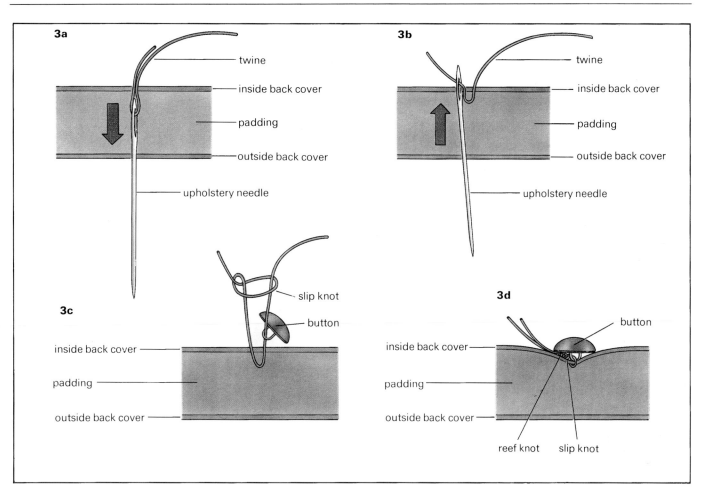

3a

twine
inside back cover
padding
outside back cover
upholstery needle

3b

twine
inside back cover
padding
outside back cover
upholstery needle

slip knot
button

3c

inside back cover
padding
outside back cover

3d

button
inside back cover
padding
outside back cover

reef knot   slip knot

passed through the front fabric and the inside padding, leaving one end of the twine about 100mm (or 4in) long on the side where the button will be replaced. Push the eye back so it emerges close to the insertion point; pull the needle and take off the thread. Pull in both ends of the twine and trim to even them up, leaving enough to allow you to make a slip knot.

Take one end and thread the button on, fixing it with a slip knot and pulling in both ends of the twine to secure it tightly. Check the button is in the correct position and finish off with a reef knot. Cut the ends back as far as possible and tuck them under the button.

Reversible cushions These can be rebuttoned fairly easily but the technique is slightly different. Since you will be working with buttons which have to be sewn in the same position on opposite sides of the cushion, it is best to remove the odd one on the opposite side to the one you are replacing so you can start from scratch. If the stitch holes have enlarged through wear, carefully stitch up this area using a fabric thread pulled out from a place on the cushion which is normally invisible. Fix the buttons slightly away from this point, making sure they are not drastically out of alignment with the rest of the buttons on the cushion.

Where necessary, carefully mark new positions for the buttons on each side of the cushion. Thread a length of twine through a button and thread both ends of the twine through the eye of a long upholstery needle. Push the needle through the marked point on one side, guiding it through the stuffing until it locates the marked point on the other side; pull it out and remove the thread from it.

Thread the other button on one end of the twine

and make a slip knot joining the two twine ends. Pull the slip knot tighter until both buttons are pulled in to the required depth. Secure the twine with a reef knot under the button and cut off the ends as short as possible so they are hidden under the button. Make sure you do not snip the upholstery fabric at the same time.

Repairing foam cushions
When a foam-padded cushion begins to sag at the edges (usually at the front) you will find it a simple matter to strengthen it. If the cushion cover has no zip, find the edge of the cover which has been handsewn and carefully cut along this edge to remove the stitches. Pull out the foam pad; you will need to squash it a little to free it from the cover. Where the cover has a zip, be careful not to catch the foam against the zip edges when you are pulling it out.

Locate the damaged part and, using a sharp knife or pair of scissors, remove it by making a cut across the foam at least 75mm (3in) away from the damaged section. Use the damaged piece as a pattern for cutting a replacement piece from the same kind of foam material, allowing an extra 25mm (1in).

Coat the edges of the replacement part and the places where they will meet the pad with impact adhesive, making sure you do so in a well ventilated room since this material is flammable. Allow the adhesive to become tacky and bring the two surfaces together, pushing them firmly in place. Allow the adhesive to dry completely, fold the foam and push it into the cover. Where necessary, sew the cover edges together using a half circle needle to make slipstitches.

You can make a quick repair with the back cover on:
3a Thread a long upholstery needle with twine and, working from the side on which you are going to replace the button, push the needle into the upholstery until the eye has passed through the inside back cover and into the padding
3b Push the eye back so it emerges close to the insertion point; pull out the needle and take off the thread
3c Pull the twine so both lengths are equal, thread the button onto the twine and tie a slip knot
3d Pull up the slip knot until the button is in the correct position and secure with a reef knot; trim back the ends of the twine and tuck them under the button

Rewebbing a chair

Left The completed webbing – it should be stretched taut over the frame (padding and springs are removed for clarity)

1 Using a web stretcher; wrap the webbing around the stretcher and pull it across the frame. Hold the stretcher against the frame edge at a 45 degree angle, press it down firmly and fix the webbing in place with tacks; you can make a web stretcher by cutting a deep 'V' across the end of a piece of timber (**inset**)

2 To fix the springs, tuck each one under the webbing where two pieces overlap and secure with twine; each spring should be held with four stitches (**inset**)

3 To replace the hessian backing, turn in the edges and tack it to the frame; fold the hessian round the legs and fix with tacks

A sagging or lumpy chair seat indicates the springs or the webbing have come away or the webbing has simply worn out; it also indicates the seat padding is in poor condition and needs replacing. Rewebbing a chair is a fairly straightforward job, but renewing the padding is slightly more difficult and is covered separately in the book.

Carrying out repairs

To examine the condition of the springing, turn the chair upside down and hold it steady by resting it on another chair or a workbench. Take off the hessian backing, using a chisel and mallet to remove the tacks which hold it to the frame; make sure you work very carefully in the direction of the grain to avoid damaging the wood. If the hessian is still in good condition, you will be able to use it again when you have completed the repair work. If, however, the backing looks worn or tatty, cut out a new one using the original as a pattern and allowing at least 25mm (1in) extra all around so you can make a neat, tucked-in finish.

Removing webbing When you have removed the hessian, check the condition of the webbing – and the springs if there are any; some chairs have only a padded base supported with webbing. Look to see whether any of the webbing has come away from the frame or become saggy and slack through wear; if this is the case, remove it using the chisel and mallet to knock out the tacks. Try not to enlarge the holes when you do this; if you do open them up a little, fill them with a fine wood filler and leave them to harden. Once the webbing is free from the frame, use a sharp knife to cut the spring twine which holds the webbing to the springs, disturbing the springs as little as possible.

Replacing webbing Turn over the end of the new

webbing 19mm (¾in) and, using the original tack holes as a guide, fix the webbing to the front edge of the frame with five tacks, placed in the shape of a 'W', so the wood will not split.

You will need to buy a web stretcher, or make one by cutting a deep 'V' across one end of a piece of 50 × 25mm (2 × 1in) wood. Stretch the webbing across the seat and wrap it around the stretcher from end to end. Pull the webbing across the frame and lay the V-shaped end of the stretcher onto the edge of the frame at about a 45 degree angle. Press

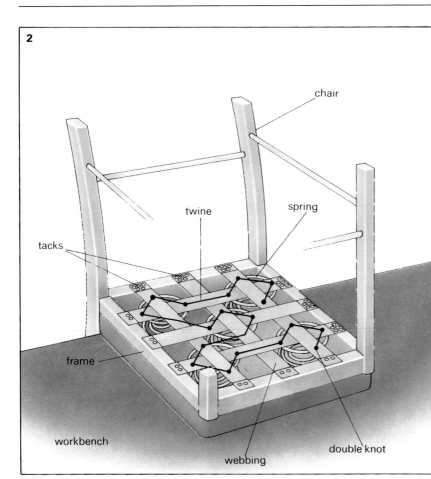

2

chair

twine

spring

tacks

frame

workbench

webbing

double knot

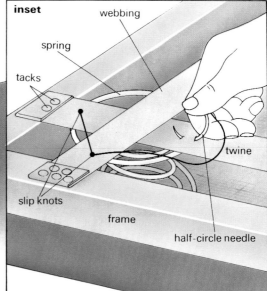

inset

webbing

spring

tacks

slip knots

frame

twine

half-circle needle

it down firmly until you feel the webbing will not stretch any more. Hold the stretcher in place and fix the webbing with a single row of three tacks. Remove the stretcher and cut off the webbing about 25mm (1in) from the tacks. Turn the end over and secure it with two more tacks.

Again using the old tack holes as a guide, complete the webbing along the length of the frame. Fix strips of webbing across the width of the frame, weaving them through the lengthwise pieces then stretching and tacking as before.

Fixing springs To make sure the springs are secure and will not tear through the hessian, tuck each one under a place where two pieces of webbing overlap. If the springs tend to squeak, put a small piece of felt or some other kind of padding between the two parts of the spring which are rubbing together.

When all the springs are in place, secure them to the webbing using spring twine and a half-circle or springing needle. Each spring should be fixed with four stitches equally spaced around it and caught at the same depth; finish off each stitch with a slip knot. Without breaking the twine, carry one stitch to an adjacent spring and stitch as before. When all the springs have been attached to the webbing in this way, finish off with a double knot and trim the twine.

Replace backing Once you have renewed the seat padding, you can replace the backing. Fold in the edges of the hessian and tack it to the frame with three tacks in the middle of each side. Adjust any creases by taking out the tacks, straightening and retacking. When the hessian is flat, continue fixing it down with tacks every 50mm (2in) along the frame, avoiding previous holes if possible. Fold the hessian into shape around the legs and fix with tacks close together for a neat finish.

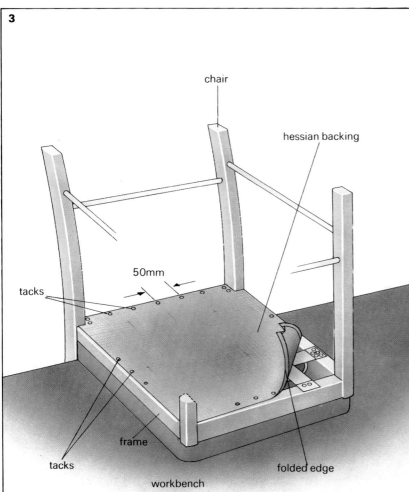

3

chair

hessian backing

50mm

tacks

frame

tacks

folded edge

workbench

Repadding a drop-seat dining chair

A dining chair is subjected to a fair amount of wear and will eventually become flattened and need a new cover. Repadding and recovering this type of chair is a relatively straightforward job.

It is likely the wood frame will have lost all its natural oils through years spent in a heated home and will be liable to split unless handled with care. When you are stripping off the old cover, carefully push an old wide-bladed screwdriver or an upholsterer's ripping chisel under each tack and ease it out with the aid of a mallet; make sure you work with the grain of the wood to avoid knocking out tiny pieces or splitting the frame.

When you have removed all the tacks, clean up the frame with medium fine glasspaper and check for cracks and woodworm. Treat woodworm with a proprietary brand of woodworm killer and fill any cracks with plastic wood. If the chair has been re-upholstered a number of times, there may be a lot of tack holes; it is best to fill the larger ones with plastic wood to give the frame extra strength.

Repadding the seat

A sagging seat usually results from damaged webbing or a broken plywood base; or the padding may have flattened through wear. Loose webbing should be replaced and covered with hessian as described earlier in the book.

Traditional hair and felt padding can be put back into shape if the hair has not become too knotted. Remove the felt layer first, then break up any large lumps of hair with your hands, distributing them evenly, and wash them in warm water. You may need more hair to build up the padding if it is old; this is fairly difficult to obtain and it may be easier to replace this type of padding with polyether foam.

Foam padding Use a medium-to-high density foam for replacing old stuffing; a type which is 25mm

(1in) thick would be most suitable. Carefully measure the frame seat and, using a sharp knife, cut a piece of foam which is slightly larger all round to ensure a good fit. Most dining chairs look better for a slightly raised effect and you can achieve this by sticking a piece of 13mm ($\frac{1}{2}$in) thick foam, about 75mm (3in) smaller all round, on the underside of the main piece in the centre.

Attach the foam directly to the frame by gluing

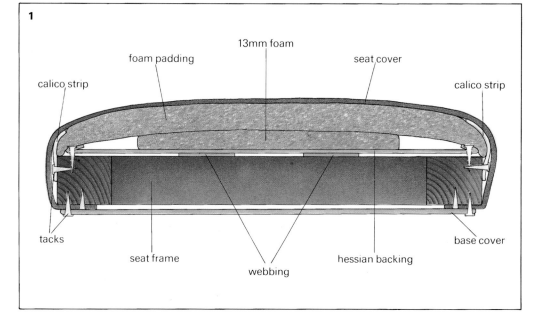

1 Section through a drop-in seat
2 When fitting hessian over the webbing, work from the centre of each side outwards
3 To give a foam padded seat a slightly raised effect, stick another smaller piece of foam onto the underside of the main piece
4 Attach the foam padding directly to the frame with strips of calico
5 Where the new cover is of thinner material than the old one, fix strips of card to the inside of the seat frame; this will pack out the frame and enable the seat to fit snugly
6 Fit the cover over the seat and tack it to the underside of the frame

Diagram labels: calico strip, foam padding, 13mm foam, seat cover, calico strip, tacks, seat frame, webbing, hessian backing, base cover

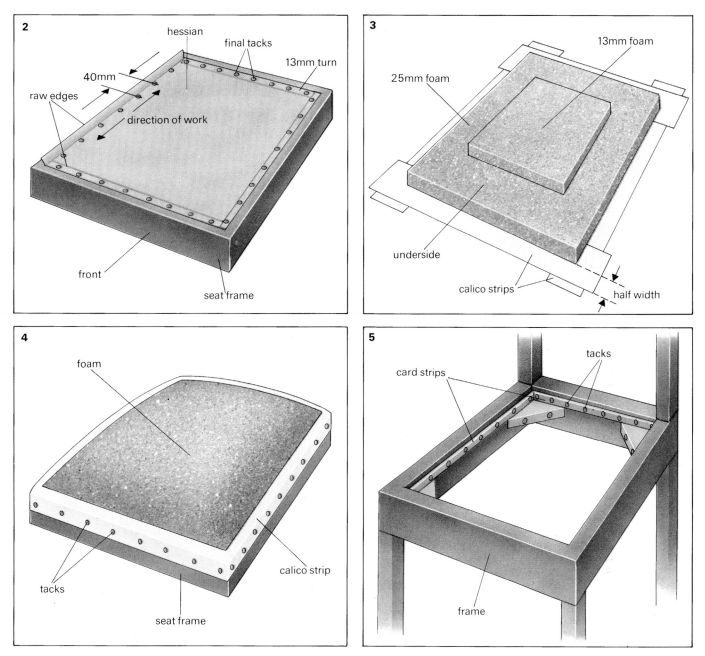

2
hessian
final tacks
13mm turn
40mm
raw edges
direction of work
front
seat frame

3
13mm foam
25mm foam
underside
calico strips
half width

4
foam
calico strip
tacks
seat frame

5
tacks
card strips
frame

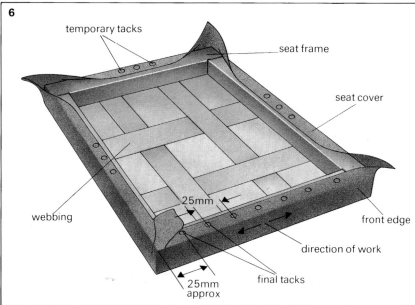

6
temporary tacks
seat frame
seat cover
webbing
25mm
front edge
direction of work
final tacks
25mm
approx

it into place around the sides; make sure the adhesive is completely dry before you fit the new cover. Alternatively you can use strips of calico which you stick down onto the foam top and then tack down onto the frame; use strips of calico slightly longer than each side of the foam and stick half the width onto the foam with the other half stretched over onto the frame edge and tacked down. Trim away any excess calico.

Re-covering the seat
You can use the old cover as a pattern for the new one, but allow slightly more material all round; you can trim away any surplus, if necessary. If you are going to use a slightly thicker material, it will be difficult for the seat to fit into the frame and you will need to shave back the inside frame a fraction with a cabinet scraper to allow for this.

If the cover is of a slightly thinner material than before, the seat will not fit snugly. You can remedy this by tacking or gluing strips of card round the insides of the chair frame, but remember to keep them below the top edge to avoid them showing

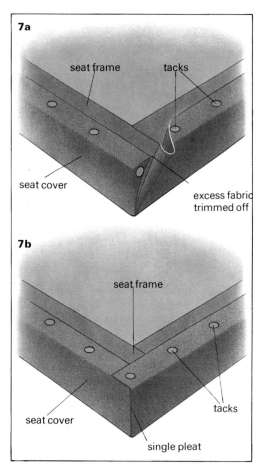

7a

seat frame   tacks

seat cover

excess fabric
trimmed off

7b

seat frame

seat cover   tacks

single pleat

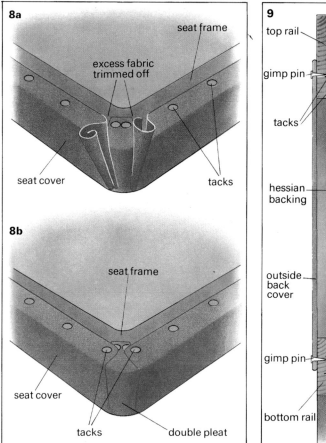

8a

seat frame

excess fabric
trimmed off

seat cover   tacks

8b

seat frame

seat cover

tacks   double pleat

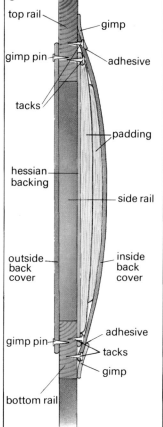

9

top rail   gimp

gimp pin   adhesive

tacks

padding

hessian
backing

side rail

outside
back
cover

inside
back
cover

gimp pin   adhesive

tacks

gimp

bottom rail

when the seat is in place. If there is a large pattern, make sure when you are cutting that it will be in the centre of the seat to get the best effect. If there is a pile to the fabric, this should brush forward.

Temporary tacking Remember to tack the cover down temporarily before you finish it so you can adjust any puckering or dragging of the fabric which occurs when you are stretching material in several directions. Do all the tacking on the underside of the frame. Fix down the front edge in the middle using three tacks, then fix the back edge and both sides, again using three tacks for each side. Remember to keep the fabric taut across the seat, taking any fullness into the corners. If necessary, adjust the cover by removing the tacks at the front, pulling the fabric tight and retacking.

Securing cover Once you are satisfied with the fit of the fabric, use small upholstery tacks to secure it at 25mm (1in) intervals along the seat frame. Start at the centre front and work to within 25mm (1in) of one corner, driving in the temporary tacks as you go. Then work from the centre front to within 25mm (1in) of the other corner. Repeat this procedure for the back edge, then the sides.

Corners These can be quite awkward to cover neatly, especially if bulky material is used. Where there are rounded edges, finish off the corners with a double pleat; to do this, stretch the material over the frame towards the underside and tack it there securely. Make sure there is an equal amount of fabric left on each side of the tacking point and make pleats with the excess fabric, facing them in towards the corner. Cut away any excess material underneath where it will not show, then pull both pleats taut and secure each with a tack.

Where there is a square corner, it is only necessary to use one pleat. Pull all the fabric round one

corner and fix it there with a tack. Dispose of the extra fabric on the underside by cutting it away; don't cut right to the top of the corner, where it might show. Pull the fabric down from the other side of the corner, taking it over the tacked piece and pleating and tacking it down as you go. Catch-stitch the pleat down, but hide the stitches on the inside.

Finishing off You can now fit the base cover to keep out dust; if the old one is in good condition, you can use this. Alternatively you can replace the base cover with one made from calico or hessian; use the old cover as a pattern for the new one. Turn in all the edges of the new base cover and fix it with tacks, spacing the tacks at equal intervals.

7a At a square corner, pull the fabric round one side of the frame and tack in place
7b Finish off by forming the fabric into a single pleat
8a At a rounded corner, pull the fabric over the frame and secure with tacks
8b Form the fabric into two pleats and tack in place
9 Section of a back pad
10 To retension the hessian backing, undo tacks on two adjacent edges, pull the hessian taut and retack

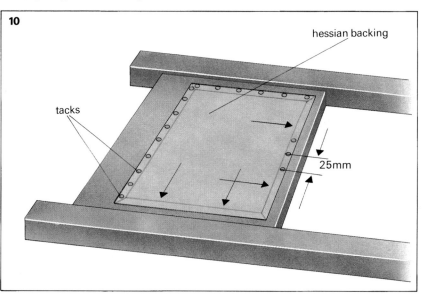

10

hessian backing

tacks

25mm

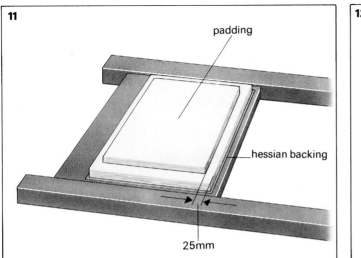

11
padding

hessian backing

25mm

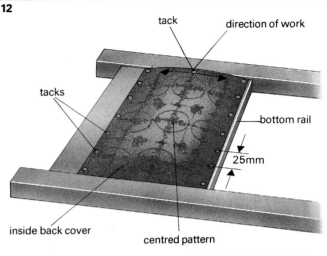

12
tack   direction of work

tacks

bottom rail

25mm

inside back cover   centred pattern

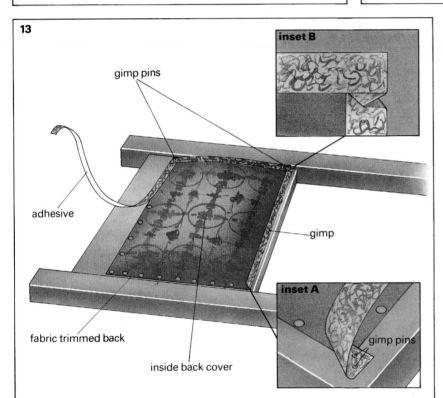

13
gimp pins

adhesive

gimp

fabric trimmed back

inside back cover

inset B

inset A

gimp pins

Repairing the backpad

Pull off any trimming on the front of the chair. Use an old chisel and mallet to remove the exposed tacks which hold the upholstery fabric in place, working carefully and in the direction of the grain to avoid damaging the wood.

Renewing padding Remove the covering and take out the old layers of flock or hair which were used as padding. Examine the calico or hessian backing; if it needs tensioning, undo two adjacent edges, pull the backing taut and retack every 25mm (1in). Lay on it a strip of flock or dacron wadding the size of the backing and then another strip 25mm (1in) smaller all around to give a domed appearance to the finished pad.

Replacing cover Cut a piece of covering material 50mm (2in) wider and deeper than the finished pad, making sure any pattern on the fabric is centred. Tack the fabric to the bottom rail at 25mm (1in) intervals, starting at the centre and working outwards. Continue in the same way until the fabric has been tacked down all around and with sharp scissors trim back the material in line with the wood.

Finishing off Fix one end of the gimp (trimming) by pinning it down with two gimp pins at one corner of the pad. Coat the underside of the trimming with latex-based adhesive and press it into position all around, folding it at the corners and pinning it down. When you reach the end, tuck the gimp under 13mm ($\frac{1}{2}$in) and pin.

Repairing outside back cover Remove the old cover and cut a new one 25mm (1in) larger all around. Attach it to the rails at 25mm (1in) intervals as before, turning under 13mm ($\frac{1}{2}$in) and using gimp pins instead of tacks since the back of this type of chair is not usually trimmed.

11 When fitting the padding, place a smaller piece of wadding on top of the main piece. **12** To fit the cover, centre the pattern and tack the fabric to the frame. **13** Trim the edges with gimp; fix one end with gimp pins (**inset A**) and fold the gimp to shape at corners before pinning (**inset B**). **14** Fix the outside back cover with gimp pins.

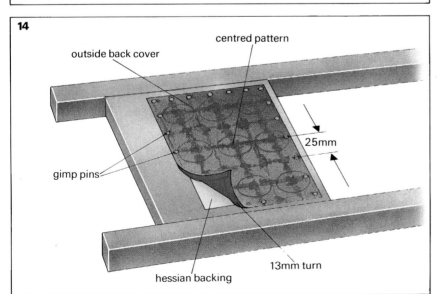

14
centred pattern

outside back cover

25mm

gimp pins

13mm turn

hessian backing

Reupholstering an armchair

Reupholstering a padded armchair may seem a daunting task; but as long as you are familiar with the basic reupholstery techniques described earlier in the book and are prepared to take time and effort over the job, you should be able to tackle it successfully. Here we explain how to strip an armchair to its frame and replace each part of the upholstery. It may not be necessary, however, for you to strip the chair completely; if, for example, only the stuffing needs replacing, you can leave the layers underneath intact.

Before you begin any work on the chair, it is important to make copious notes and clear diagrams of how and where each part of the final cover is fixed. Very few chairs are upholstered in exactly the same way and you may find some of our instructions will not apply to your particular chair; your notes and diagrams will ensure you replace everything correctly and retain the shape of the chair.

Stripping the chair

If the frame needs attention, you will have to strip the chair right down. Turn it upside down and place it on trestles or a firm table. Using a mallet and an upholsterer's ripping chisel, remove the tacks which secure the bottom canvas.

Turn the chair right side up and remove the outside back and outside arm covers; on some chairs these will be secured with tacks, but on others they will be slipstitched invisibly. Again, make notes and diagrams to ensure you can replace the covers correctly. Continue by stripping the seat; remove all tacks, including those holding the webbing, from the bottom frame of the chair and lift out the seat intact. Cut the twine holding the springs to the webbing and hessian, count the springs and note their size so you can replace them if necessary. Remove the seat cover and hessian from the stuffing by cutting the stitches; but leave the scrim in place so you do not disturb the shape.

Remove the inside back and inside arm covers which are tacked to the outside of the back and arm frames. Also detach the scrolls, if any; these will be stitched on. If the chair has a calico inner cover, this will be tacked on and should be removed. Take out the tacks securing the scrim which holds the stuffing in place and lift off both the scrim and the stuffing without disturbing the shape. Finally remove the hessian.

Repairing the frame

Check the condition of the frame; you may have to get a carpenter to repair any loose joints and replaced damaged sections of timber. Check the frame has not been attacked by woodworm; treat with woodworm fluid if necessary and allow it to dry before continuing, otherwise the furnishing fabric may be spoiled. Fill any holes left by the original tacks with filler or plastic wood and rub smooth with abrasive paper.

Replacing the webbing

Turn the chair upside down and, using a web stretcher, hammer and 16mm (or ⅝in) improved (heavy) tacks, fit new webbing over the base of the chair seat in the same way as the original webbing.

Turn the chair right side up and stretch two pieces of webbing vertically on the inside of each arm frame. On the inside back fix three vertical strips of webbing and weave two horizontal ones through them to support the back stuffing.

Replacing springs

Place the seat springs on the webbing in the same position as they were originally fixed. Keep the front ones well forward to take the strain of the front edge; the other springs should be placed slightly towards the centre of the seat to allow clearance at the arms and back for the stuffing.

Working from the inside of the seat and using twine and a springing needle, secure the base of each spring to the webbing; make three oversewing stitches in three places, with a long stitch underneath connecting each set of three. Lash the springs with lay cord or sisal.

Inside back If the chair has back springs, these should be placed at the junctions of the webbing and secured with oversewing stitches in the same way as the seat springs. There is no need to lash these back springs.

Above Although the final cover and stuffing on this chair need replacing, the rest of the upholstery is sound and can be left in place

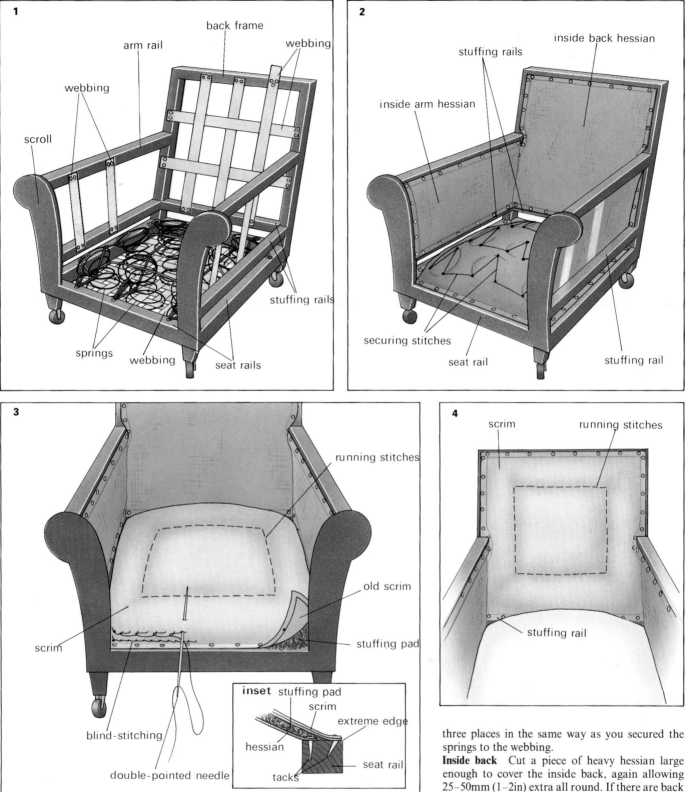

1

2

3

running stitches

old scrim

stuffing pad

scrim

blind-stitching

double-pointed needle

inset stuffing pad
scrim
extreme edge
hessian
tacks
seat rail

4

scrim   running stitches

stuffing rail

1 With the webbing in place refit the springs and lash them in position; if there are back springs, fix these in the same way – but there is no need to lash them
2 Tack hessian to all inner faces of the frame; on the seat, stitch the springs securely to the hessian

Fixing hessian

Cut a piece of heavy hessian to cover the seat, allowing 25–50mm (1–2in) extra all round. Place the hessian on the springs and temporarily tack it to the top edge of the seat with 13mm ($\frac{1}{2}$in) improved tacks; pull the hessian straight and taut, then drive the tacks home. Turn up the 25–50mm (1–2in) allowance on all sides and tack the hessian to the frame between the original tacks. Secure the springs to the hessian with three oversewing stitches in

three places in the same way as you secured the springs to the webbing.
Inside back Cut a piece of heavy hessian large enough to cover the inside back, again allowing 25–50mm (1–2in) extra all round. If there are back springs, bear in mind you will need extra hessian to cover them. Tack the hessian to the face of the inside back frame in the same way as for the seat, attaching the lower edge to the stuffing rail, but use 13mm ($\frac{1}{2}$in) fine tacks. If there are back springs, stitch them to the hessian as before.
Inside arms Cut two pieces of heavy hessian to cover the inside arms, again allowing 25–50mm (1–2in) extra all round. Fix these pieces to the inside face of the frame as before, attaching the lower edge of each to the stuffing rail; leave the hessian unattached at the back.

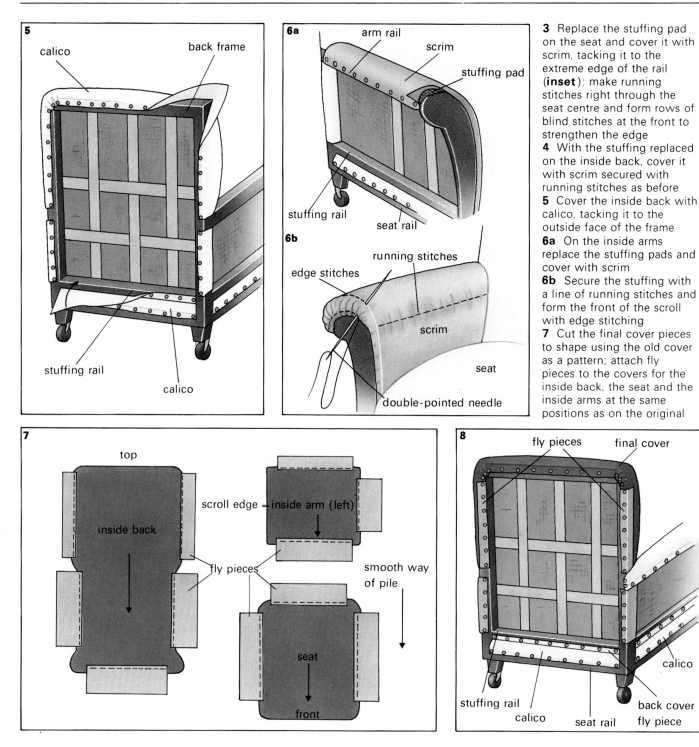

5 calico · back frame · stuffing rail · calico

6a arm rail · scrim · stuffing pad · stuffing rail · seat rail

6b running stitches · edge stitches · scrim · seat · double-pointed needle

7 top · inside back · scroll edge · inside arm (left) · fly pieces · smooth way of pile · seat · front

8 fly pieces · final cover · stuffing rail · calico · seat rail · back cover fly piece · calico

3 Replace the stuffing pad on the seat and cover it with scrim, tacking it to the extreme edge of the rail (**inset**); make running stitches right through the seat centre and form rows of blind stitches at the front to strengthen the edge
4 With the stuffing replaced on the inside back, cover it with scrim secured with running stitches as before
5 Cover the inside back with calico, tacking it to the outside face of the frame
6a On the inside arms replace the stuffing pads and cover with scrim
6b Secure the stuffing with a line of running stitches and form the front of the scroll with edge stitching
7 Cut the final cover pieces to shape using the old cover as a pattern; attach fly pieces to the covers for the inside back, the seat and the inside arms at the same positions as on the original

Replacing stuffing

It is important to disturb the stuffing as little as possible if you are to retain the shape of the chair. To extract the dust from the stuffing, go over each section lightly with a vacuum cleaner attachment.
Seat Replace the stuffing pad on the chair seat and fill in any worn places by adding kerly fibre, coir or horsehair. Cut a piece of scrim to cover the seat, allowing 50–75mm (2–3in) extra all round; turn up the edges and tack the scrim to the top face of the rails all round the seat, using 13mm ($\frac{1}{2}$in) improved tacks and driving them in at a slight angle. Secure the scrim to the stuffing with twine and a double-pointed needle, forming a square of stitches right through the centre of the seat.

Using a regulator and a double-pointed needle and twine, strengthen the front edge of the seat by

working the stuffing forwards and making two rows of stitches to hold it securely in position. It is essential the stuffing and stitching are very firm and tight; bear in mind the stuffing will settle and the cover stretch with use.

Place a thin layer of horsehair or fibre over the scrim to cover the indentations made by the stitching; this should be only a skimming layer to even out the surface. Now cover the whole seat with flock, wadding or cotton linters and a layer of calico; turn up the edges of the calico and tack it to the outside face of the seat rails. If there is no front border, tack the calico under the front rail.
Inside back Treat the inside back in the same way as the seat; replace the stuffing pad and cover it with scrim tacked to the inside face of the frame. Secure the scrim with a square of running stitches right

8 When fixing the final cover to the inside back, pull it over the top rail and tack it to the outside face, pleating it at the corners where necessary. Pull the fly pieces round onto the outside back, passing the lower ones through the gaps at the back of the arms, and tack them to the outside faces as before. Tack the bottom fly to the outside face of the stuffing rail and trim all excess fabric from the fly pieces

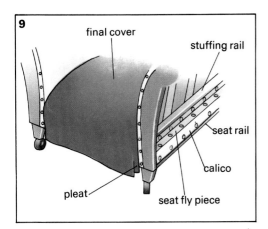

9 final cover / stuffing rail / seat rail / calico / pleat / seat fly piece

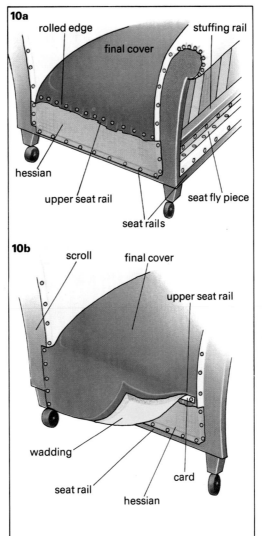

10a rolled edge / final cover / stuffing rail / hessian / upper seat rail / seat fly piece / seat rails

10b scroll / final cover / upper seat rail / wadding / seat rail / card / hessian

through the centre back of the chair. Cover the stitches with a skimming layer of stuffing to even out the surface then top with a layer of wadding, flock or cotton linters. Tack a piece of calico to the outside face of the rails round the top and sides; at the bottom pull the calico through the space between the stuffing rail and the seat frame and tack it to the outside face of the stuffing rail.

Inside arms Replace the stuffing pads on the arms, adding more fibre or hair to form the shape as before. Cover the arms with scrim, fixed with 13mm (½in) improved tacks to the inside face of the stuffing rails and to the outside face of the arm rails; tack the scrim onto the face of the scroll at the front, but leave it unattached at the back.

Using a regulator, work the stuffing forward to form an edge to the scroll at the front of the arms; secure the stuffing with a single line of stitches running across each arm from the scroll to the back. Continue by making rows of edge stitching to form the rolled edge of the scroll. Cover the stitches with a skimming layer of horse hair or fibre, placing a little extra over the edge of the scroll, and top with a layer of wadding or cotton linters to prevent the stuffing coming through.

Fix calico to the inside arms, pulling it through the space at the bottom and tacking it onto the outside face of the stuffing rails at the bottom, onto the outside face of the arm rails at the top and onto the face of the scrolls at the front; leave it unattached at the back.

Fixing final cover
This is where the notes and diagrams you made at the beginning of the job will prove invaluable; follow them closely to ensure you fix the final cover in exactly the right way.

When you look at the old cover you will find fly pieces, usually of strong canvas or hessian, attached at the points where the fabric will be pushed through the frame. These pieces will be invisible when the upholstery is completed and are more economical than using the final cover fabric.

Using the old cover as a pattern and being a little generous in measuring, cut the new cover to size. Make sure any pile on the fabric is running the smooth way down and centre any pattern. Also cut fly pieces to match those on the old cover and machine stitch them in position. When fixing the final cover, always temporarily tack it to the frame and drive the tacks home only when you are sure the fabric is straight and taut.

Inside back Place the cover, which should be large enough to cover the part of the back which will be visible when the chair is finished, on the inside back

9 When fixing the final seat cover on a chair without a front border, pull it down at the front, pleating the fabric at the corners; tack the fabric neatly to the underside of the frame
10a On a chair with a front border there will be two rails at the front of the seat. When replacing the hessian on the seat, also fix hessian to the front border; tack all the various seat layers to the upper seat rail
10b To cover the front border, back tack the fabric and a piece of card to the top edge of the front face of the upper rail, placing soft wadding between the fabric and the hessian; tack the bottom edge underneath the chair and the sides onto the face of the scroll or onto the outside arm frame in the same way as on the original cover
11 When fixing the final cover to each inside arm, take the top fly piece over the arm rail and tack it underneath; the back fly piece is pulled through the gap at the back, round the back frame and tacked to the inside face. Pull the bottom fly under the stuffing rail and tack it up onto the outside face. At the front pleat the fabric and tack it onto the face of the scroll

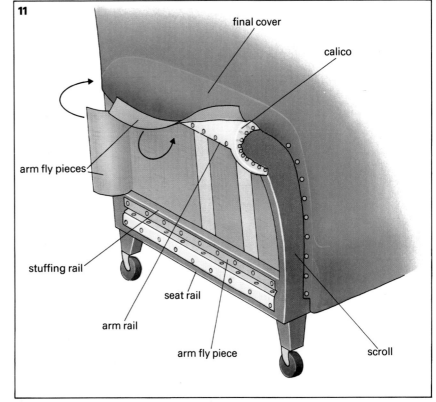

11 final cover / calico / arm fly pieces / stuffing rail / seat rail / arm rail / arm fly piece / scroll

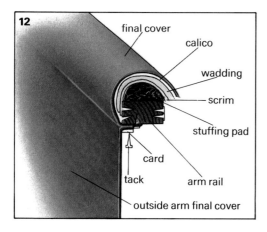

12

final cover

calico

wadding

scrim

stuffing pad

card

tack

arm rail

outside arm final cover

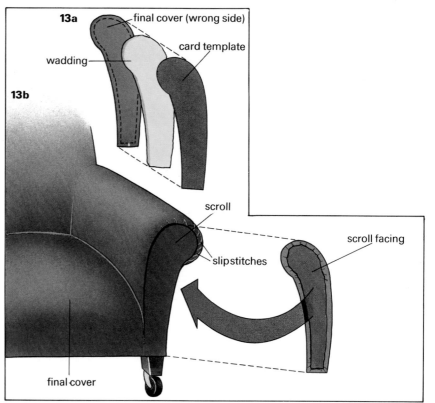

13a

final cover (wrong side)

card template

wadding

13b

scroll

scroll facing

slipstitches

final cover

and tack the top to the outside face of the top rail. Pull the fly pieces round the sides and tack them onto the outside faces of the side rails; the lower fly pieces should be passed through the gaps between the back and arm frames and tacked as before. Pass the bottom fly under the stuffing rail at the back – not the seat rail – and tack it up onto the outside back.

Seat Place the cover on the seat, tuck the fly pieces under the stuffing rail at the arms and back and tack them onto the top face of the seat rails, then tack the front. If there is a front border, the seat front is tacked under the rolled edge of the seat stuffing; if not, pleat the cover on each front corner as described earlier in the book. Tighten the whole cover and tack the sides and back to the top face of the seat rail.

Inside arms In this case the back fly piece is pulled through the gap and round the side rail, then tacked to the inside face of the back frame; the bottom fly should be tacked up onto the outside face of the stuffing rail. The top fly is pulled over the top of the arm rail and tacked underneath. The front edge should be pleated and tacked onto the

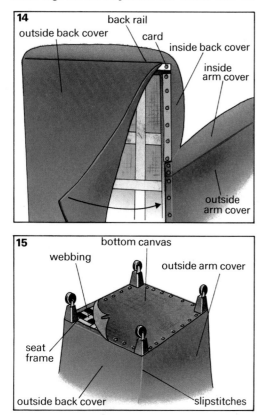

14

back rail

outside back cover

card

inside back cover

inside arm cover

outside arm cover

15

bottom canvas

webbing

outside arm cover

seat frame

outside back cover

slipstitches

front of the scroll in the same way as the original.

Outside arms When dealing with the outside arms, you can back tack the final cover in place using a piece of thin card to give a straight edge. Cut a narrow piece of card to the length of the arm and place it on the top edge of the wrong side of the arm cover. Tack both the card and the cover to the outer edge of the bottom face of the arm rail; pull the cover down and tack it underneath the chair to the bottom face of the seat rail. Tack the back edge of this cover to the outside face of the back frame and the front onto the face of the scroll, pleating it as necessary in the same way as with the inside arm. Repeat for the other arm.

Scrolls Make a paper pattern of the front scroll, transfer the outline onto thin card and cut two templates, one for each arm. Place a thin layer of wadding on one side of each piece of card and cover this with a piece of the top cover; cut the cover 25mm (1in) larger all round and with the pile or pattern running the same way as the seat and back. Turn the surplus material to the wrong side of the card pattern – slashing the fabric where necessary so it lies flat – and secure it to the card with a little adhesive. Place the patterns in position on the chair and slipstitch them to the front of the arms.

Outside back Treat the outside back cover in the same way as the outside arms. If the back rail is straight, back tack a card strip and the top edge of the cover to the outside face of the top rail, turn in the side edges and slipstitch them to the outside arm and inside back covers; tack the bottom under the chair. If the back rail is not straight, turn under all edges and slipstitch them in place; tack the bottom edge under the chair as before.

Bottom canvas Turn the chair upside down and place a piece of black canvas, cut 25–50mm (1–2in) larger all round, over the bottom of the frame. Turn under the allowance on all sides of the hessian and tack it securely in place with 9mm ($\frac{3}{8}$in) fine tacks, fitting it neatly round the legs.

12 To fix the final cover to the outside arm, back tack it with a piece of card to the underside of the arm rail; pull the cover down and tack it to the underside of the frame. If you wish, you can tack heavy hessian to the outside arm before you fix the final cover

13a To cover the face of each scroll, make a card template of the face and place wadding on top; cut a piece of fabric to shape and glue this with the wadding onto the card

13b Place the facing in position and slipstitch it to the front of the arm

14 If the back rail is straight, you can back tack the final cover in place; otherwise slipstitch it to the inside back and outside arm covers. As with the outside arm, you can tack hessian to the outside back frame before fixing the final cover

15 To finish off, turn the chair upside down and cover the underneath with a piece of black hessian; cut the corners to fit neatly round the legs and tack in place

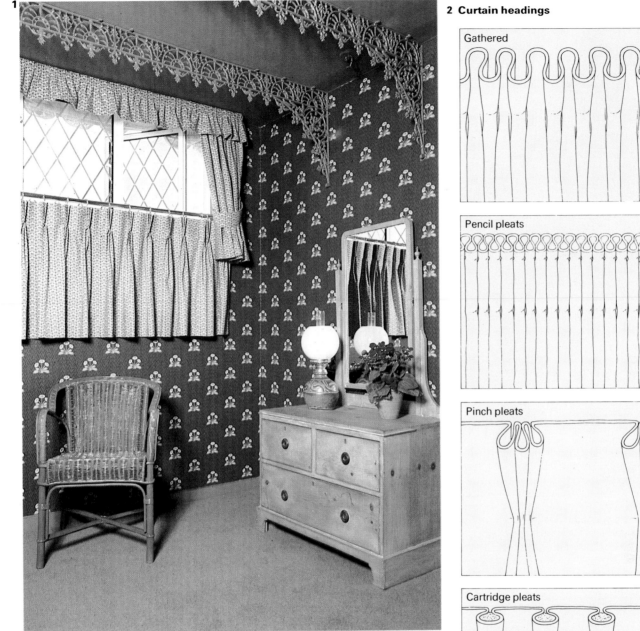

1

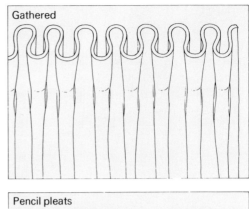
Gathered

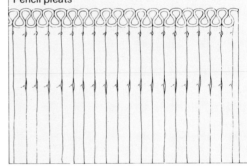
Pencil pleats

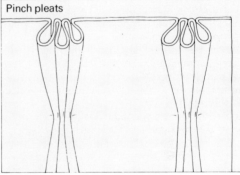
Pinch pleats

Cartridge pleats

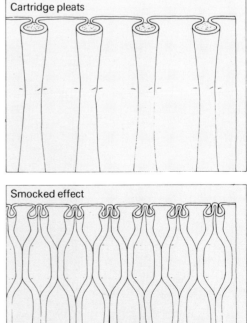
Smocked effect

Choosing curtains

1 Cafe curtains have a pleasant country look and are ideal where you want to shut out an unattractive view without sacrificing too much light
2 Types of curtain heading

Curtains are one of the main design factors in any room and, if the windows are large, they can become its most important feature. To get precisely the effect you want, pay attention to the many details which make one pair of curtains look completely different from another. Make a list of these and go through each point, deciding what suits your taste and your window.

Types of heading
A curtain's heading is the way it is gathered before it is attached to the track and the type of heading you choose will dictate the amount of material you need for the curtain.
Gathered This type is the easiest to make and the cheapest since it requires just one and a half times the width of the track in material. Looking very much like the random gathering on a skirt waistband, it is suitable for curtains where the top

3

4

3 Make a window look larger by fitting the curtain track well beyond it on each side. This arrangement also allows the curtains to be pulled clear of the frame to let in the most light

4 Try not to conceal the shape of unusual windows. These curtains cannot be drawn; but because the room has a sunny aspect, simple tie-backs let in sufficient light

5 With a wide window you will have to accommodate quite a lot of material when the curtains are drawn back. The problem can be eased by using a lightweight material and lining it. The wall recess in this room also helped to house the curtains when drawn back, since the curtain rail was extended into it

5

will be hidden behind a pelmet or for simple, short, unlined curtains.

Pencil pleats Also very easy to do, this heading is more even and formal than the gathered type and needs two to three times the track width in material to look effective.

Pinch pleat A very formal triple pleat which alternates with flat sections of material. The finest pinch pleats are gathered and sewn by hand and take two to two and a half widths of the track.

Cartridge pleats This heading consists of single, cylindrical pleats often stuffed with cotton wadding or tissue paper so they keep their plump shape. Like pinch pleats, they alternate with flat sections of fabric and are still done by hand in curtain workshops, taking about double the track width.

Heading tape Although the best pinch and cartridge pleats are still hand-made, you can buy heading tape for all four types. One company now distributes a slightly different kind of heading tape which gives a smocking effect at the top of the curtain. This tape is sewn with four rows of stitching and requires about twice the width of the track in material.

In theory, all you have to do is sew these tapes to the top of the curtain and pull the cords to get the required heading; but in practice some headings are easier to handle than others. To get the best results, follow the manufacturer's instructions carefully and never skimp on material. It is much better to buy a generous quantity of cheap cotton which will always look luxurious because of its fullness, than to use too little of an expensive fabric which will look mean no matter what it costs.

If you are planning to use one of these tapes, ask your retailer for a cord tidy at the same time. When you pull your curtains up to the required width you will have a length of cord left over which you will need when you want to pull them flat for cleaning - this inexpensive accessory keeps this length of cord out of the way.

Deciding on length

Our grandmothers usually had heavy curtains which trailed on the floor to keep out draughts. Nowadays there are two main lengths: to the sill or to the floor - anything in between will give a very awkward 'half-mast' effect. If your curtains will hang to sill level only, keep them just above the sill or 50-75mm (2-3in) below. Floor length curtains should clear the floor by about 13mm (½in) to protect them from dust and dirt. If they are very long and heavy, allow 50mm (2in) clearance since they are bound to drop after a time.

Sill length curtains are best when there is a radiator under the window since long ones will prevent heat getting into the room. If you need light and privacy at the same time, choose cafe curtains which are usually hung to sill length from a pole fitted halfway down the window.

Whichever style you decide on, special weighted tape sewn into the hem will make your curtains hang more neatly.

Lining and interlining

Unless you particularly want the light to filter in through your curtains, it is almost always better to line them, usually with cotton sateen. Besides helping them to hang more attractively, lining protects curtains from dirt and from the sun which will fade and damage any fabric exposed to it over a long period of time. The lining fabric can be hung

6

7

6 For net curtains, cotton lace is a practical alternative to synthetic fabric

7 To cover the curtain track above this hall window, a pleated valance has been fitted instead of the more usual straight wood or buckram pelmet

8 separately from your curtains so you can take it down for washing, but you will find the curtains look better if the lining and fabric are treated as one.

To give the outside of your house a co-ordinated appearance use the same colour lining throughout. Cream or ecru is usually best unless most of your curtains are white or have a white background, in which case white lining would be more appropriate. There are several special linings on the market which add more to the effectiveness of your curtains than ordinary ones.

Lightproof Available only in cream, this lining costs more than the normal types but is very useful where you want to block out all the sun's rays, such as in a nursery where children could have difficulty sleeping while it is still light.

Milium This has a special aluminium backing which keeps out more light than ordinary sateen and helps to insulate your home against cold in winter and heat in summer. Although the side which faces the curtain fabric has a metallic look, the other side is quite plain and available in a wide range of colours.

Pyrovatex A flame-resistant material often used in public buildings and office blocks. It consists of plain sateen treated with a fireproof substance.

Interlining Interlined curtains, which are especially thick, soft and heavy, have an additional layer between the curtain fabric and the lining. Usually called bump, this is a thick cotton which has its surface brushed up to make it thicker and help it cling to the other two layers. Interlined curtains offer effective insulation and are particularly good in rooms which are subject to cold and daughts.

Pelmets and valances

A pelmet is a piece of buckram (coarse linen or cloth stiffened with gum or paste) or wood which you place over the top of the curtains to conceal the track and heading. If this covering is gathered or pleated, it is called a valance, while a single piece of draped fabric is called a swag. With the advent of plainer, good looking tracks, these are becoming less common; but if you find your track un-attractive, fix a pelmet or valance yourself or buy one ready made.

Curtain trimmings

The most common curtain decoration is a set of tie backs which give the window a formal look and hold the curtains back so as much light as possible is allowed in. If your window is very narrow, make a single curtain and hold it to one side with a tie.

Link your curtains to other design elements in the room by fixing a border decoration or band in fabric which has been used for upholstery, cushions or lampshades.

One particularly fancy curtain is called a festoon and is lifted up by cords running vertically at intervals across it, rather than pulled to each side. A very old fashioned style of curtain, these were often used in restaurants and public houses.

Choosing fabric

Before you buy your fabric measure carefully, calculating the width and length of material required from the track and not from the window itself. There is no such thing as an average window and you will not know what you need unless you take precise measurements.

If you want linen or cotton, always allow a bit extra for shrinkage since even the best quality, pre-

8 Exotically patterned curtains give a dramatic touch to a plain room
9 If you have a narrow window, hang a single curtain and tie it back to one side only

9

shrunk ranges will lose a little in the first few washes. Very thick brocades, velvets and wools are hard for the amateur to handle – if you want your curtains to look heavy, it will be cheaper and easier to interline them. Remember, too, that natural fibres are more prone to rot if they are exposed to direct sunlight.

Think about how you will need to care for your curtains. Kitchen windows might be near the cooker and likely to become dirty very quickly, so choose something light, washable and flameproof.

Pattern and colour will be your final problems. Large motifs and heavy fabrics are best left for long curtains. If the curtains play a very prominent part in the look of the room, you might be wise to play safe and choose a natural or plain coloured fabric which will blend in with many different furnishings styles. If you want to redesign the room later, you can do it without a huge cash outlay by changing smaller or less expensive items like pictures, lights, plants and cushions. Big bold patterns give a striking effect, but they will dominate the room, so keep the rest of it simple.

Net curtains

With cane, wood and pinoleum blinds becoming more popular, net curtains are not so widely used, although many people still prefer them. The most commonly available and least expensive fabrics for nets are synthetics like nylon, but these do tend to become grey in a very short time. If you chose this type, wash them before they look dirty – in warm rather than hot water. Treat white nets alone since the smallest amount of dirt or dye from other fabrics will show. If you never wring them out and always hang them up while they are still damp, net curtains will dry crease-free every time.

This curtaining is often sold so the width of the fabric covers the drop of the window and you buy whatever length you need for the width of your window. You will find a slot at the top for hanging and a hem at the bottom already sewn in.

Cotton lace is a good alternative to synthetic nets. Although it is slightly more expensive, it has a crisp, traditional look and is easier to keep looking fresh than the nylon variety. Wool or cotton fabrics are also sold for this purpose; they have a very open weave which lets you see out in the daytime, without allowing your neighbours to peer in.

10

11

10 If you have a slanted window, you can fix narrow tracks or poles at the top and bottom to keep your curtains in place
11 Make sure curtains hung over a working door do not restrict opening

Making curtains

There are several advantages in making curtains yourself: not only is it much cheaper than buying them ready-made, but it also allows you greater flexibility in design and choice of fabric – and you can be sure of getting them the right width and length for your windows rather than having to accept the sizes available in the shops. Of course you can have your own fabric made into curtains by a professional, but this is expensive and, since curtains are not at all difficult to make up, it pays to do it yourself.

Measuring for width

To calculate the width of your curtains, measure the curtain track, add any overlap and double this figure. This is only a general guide, however, since gathered or pleated curtains require varying amounts of material depending on the type of curtain tape you use.

Measuring for length

Using a steel measuring tape or rule, measure the distance from the top of the track to the bottom of the window sill or to the floor (since some sills and floors tend to slope, it is best to measure in several places to ensure the curtains will hang in line). To this measurement add 20cm (or 9in) to allow for hems top and bottom; if the curtains will have a stand-up heading, double its depth and add this to your measurement.

Divide the width of the finished curtain by the width of your chosen fabric to give the number of fabric widths and multiply the length of each curtain by the number of widths required.

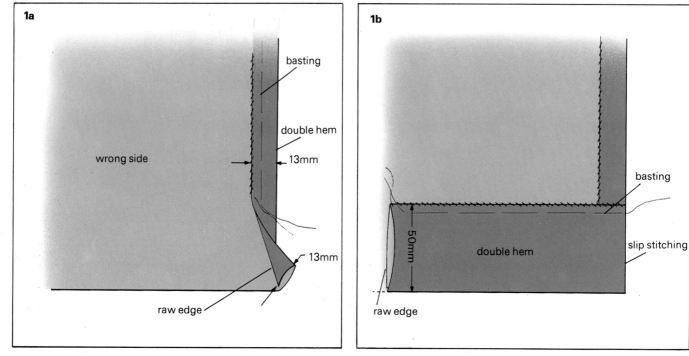

1a basting
double hem
13mm
wrong side
13mm
raw edge

1b basting
50mm
double hem
slip stitching
raw edge

Left If you want to hang this type of curtain, use a pinch pleat tape and a stand-up heading which will conceal the curtain track

1a Turn double hems down the sides of the curtain to the wrong side of the fabric

1b Make a double hem at the lower edge to enclose the side turnings

2 Position the tape flush with the top of the curtain, turn one end under and machine stitch round three sides; turn under the other end of the tape and stitch

3a For a stand-up heading, turn down its depth plus 13mm and baste 13mm from the raw edge

3b Place the top of the curtain tape on the basting line and stitch in place

3c Gather the curtain by drawing up the cords; knot the ends of the cord to secure the width

For example, suppose you require a finished length of 180cm (or 72in), add 20cm (or 9in) to this figure, giving a total length of 200cm (or 81in). If the track is 240cm (or 96in) wide, including overlap, double this figure to give the finished curtain width: 240 × 2 = 480cm (or 96 × 2 = 192in). Divide the finished width by the fabric width, for example 120cm (or 48in): 480 ÷ 120 = 4 (or 192 ÷ 48 = 4); this is the number of widths of fabric required. Multiply the required length by the number of widths: 200 × 4 = 800cm/8m (or 81 × 4 = 324in/9yd); this is the total length of fabric required.

Patterned material You will need to buy extra fabric in order to match the patterns at the seams on each curtain and to ensure the pattern falls in the same place on both curtains. Divide the length of the curtain by the depth of the pattern repeat and take the nearest whole number above. For example, if your curtains will be 180cm (or 72in) long and the pattern repeat is 25cm (or 10in) deep, you will need to buy a length of fabric with eight pattern repeats.

Unlined curtains

These are obviously the simplest and cheapest to make. If the fabric is not pre-shrunk, either wash it before you cut it to length or allow for a generous temporary hem so you can lengthen the curtains if necessary after the first wash.

Making up Make sure the fabric is square: at one end pull a thread at right-angles to the selvedge or margin of the fabric and cut along this line. Measure the required length, pull a thread at this point and cut along the line as before. If it is not possible to pull threads, fold the material back at right-angles to the selvedge at both ends and use the folds as your cutting lines. Cut the other lengths in the same way, matching the pattern if necessary.

Join the widths for each curtain by placing the right sides of the fabric together, selvedge to selvedge, and machine stitch, using a long stitch and a loose tension. Press the seams open and make several snips at intervals along the selvedge to relieve puckering.

Turn double hems along the sides of the curtain to prevent the edges curling: fold over the edge 13mm (½in) to the wrong side of the material and fold this over another 13mm (½in) so the raw edge is no longer visible. Pin and baste this into position, then stitch: you can use a machine but hand sewing the side hems does give a better finish. Press the seams and remove basting stitches.

Making the hem Measure the required finished length and mark this point with a row of pins. Turn up 50mm (2in) double hems and hand stitch; slip stitch the ends and press lightly.

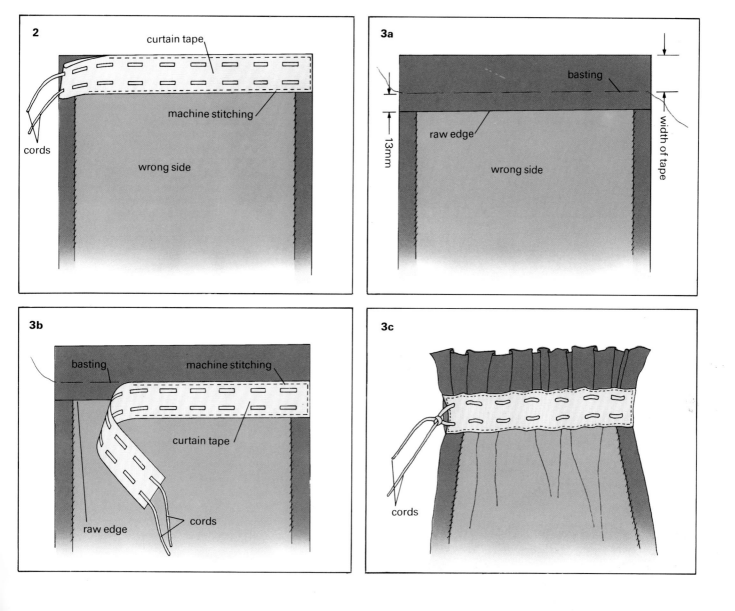

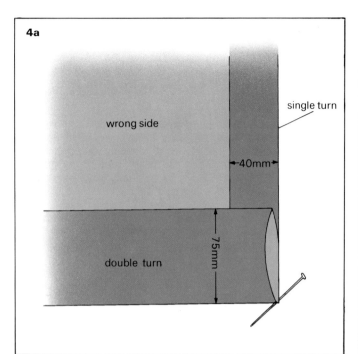

4a

wrong side

single turn

←40mm→

75mm

double turn

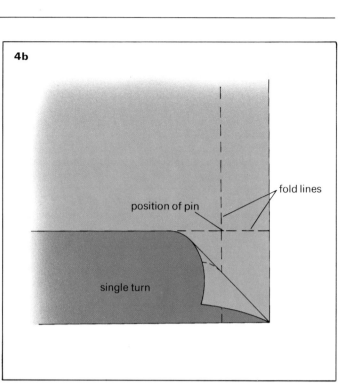

4b

position of pin

fold lines

single turn

Weighting the curtains To help the curtains to hang well insert a length of lead-weighted tape in the bottom hem before stitching down the ends.

Attaching curtain tape At the top of the curtain, turn down the raw edge 13mm ($\frac{1}{2}$in) to the wrong side of the fabric and baste. If the curtain will have a stand up heading, turn the top edge down to the depth of the heading, plus 13mm ($\frac{1}{2}$in). Baste 13mm ($\frac{1}{2}$in) in from the raw edge to act as a guide for positioning the tape. Cut a length of tape to the width of the curtain, plus 50mm (2in) for turnings. Pull out and knot the ends of the cords, then turn the tape under 25mm (1in) at one end, tucking in the knotted ends of the cords. Place the tape on the curtain so it covers the raw edges and baste and machine stitch along the top and bottom edges of the tape and the end you turned under. Pull out the cords at the other end and leave these free. Turn under the tape 25mm (1in) and stitch this to itself, lifting the cords out of the way; remove all basting stitches and press lightly.

Draw up the cord to the required width, adjust the gathers evenly and tie the ends of the cords to secure the width. Push the ends of the cords between the tape and the curtain and slip stitch this end of the tape to the curtain. When the curtain needs laundering you can easily release the gathers by unpicking the stitches and undoing the cords.

Finishing Arrange the curtains in even folds along their length and tie a remnant of fabric loosely round the bottom of the folds; leave the curtains for two to three days so they will hang evenly.

4a To mitre the lower corners of lined curtains, mark each corner with a pin
4b Open out the material and fold back one turn on the lower edge. **4c** Fold up the material diagonally. **4d** Turn in the side and bottom edges and stitch. **5** Place the lining on the curtain and sew the two together with locking stitches
Left Here pinch pleats are used to help full length curtains hang well; the curtains are made without a heading to expose the decorative brass pole

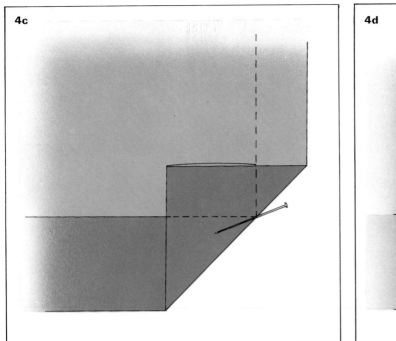

4c

4d

45° mitre

slip stitching

Lined curtains

For the best results you should sew the lining to the fabric; although you can have separate lining, the curtains will not hang so well.

Lining attached Cut the required lengths for the curtains and the lining (the lining should be the same size as the curtains). On both fabrics, join widths and half widths in the same way as for unlined curtains and press seams flat. Press single 40mm (or 1½in) turnings down both sides of the curtain, then press a 75mm (3in) double hem at the bottom. To mitre the corners of the lower edges, mark each corner with a pin, open out the material and fold back one turn on the lower edge. Fold up the material diagonally, then turn in the side and bottom edges to form the mitre. Slip stitch the mitre seam, then stitch the side and bottom hems.

Along the bottom edge of the lining, machine a double hem at the same depth as that on the curtain. Place the lining on top of the curtain, wrong sides together, with the lower edge of the lining 25mm (1in) above the lower edge of the curtain. Pin the two together down the centre and turn back a third width of the lining. Now join the fabrics together with locking stitches, starting about 150mm (6in) from the bottom. Make the stitches about 100mm (4in) apart, keeping the thread fairly loose so as not to pucker the material. Make another row of stitches on the other half of the lining or, if the curtains are very wide, make several rows 450mm (18in) apart.

Smooth the lining flat and turn the side edges under to leave 25mm (1in) of curtain showing. Baste the side and bottom edges of the lining to the curtain and sew the top edges together with a diagonal stitch. Slip stitch the lining to the curtain down the sides and 25mm (1in) along the bottom edge near the corners so the lining hangs free at the lower edge. Attach tape as for unlined curtains.

Detachable lining Make up the curtains and the lining separately as for unlined curtains, but have the lining 25mm (1in) shorter and 50mm (2in) narrower than the curtain. Attach ordinary tape to the curtains, but use special lining tape for the lining. Bring them together with hooks through both tapes.

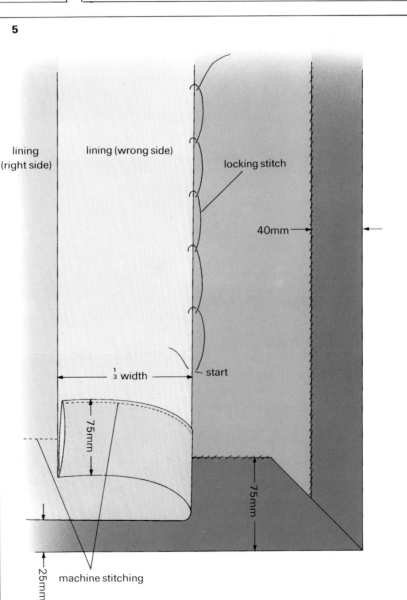

5

lining (right side)

lining (wrong side)

locking stitch

40mm

⅓ width

start

75mm

75mm

25mm

machine stitching

Curtain tracks

The extensive range of curtain tracks enables you to choose the type which best suits your room and the curtains you wish to hang. Make sure the track is strong enough to take the weight of the curtains; some plastic track will not be sufficiently sturdy to hold full length curtains, which may have to be hung on metal track. If the track will be visible when the curtains are hung, choose either a decorative track which blends with the room, or a plain, unobtrusive one which you can paint or leave white. Alternatively hide the rail by fitting a pelmet or valance in front of it.

Pelmet tracks

The traditional and still popular I-section track is not very attractive and therefore is mostly used with a pelmet or valance. It can be made from brass, aluminium, plastic or plastic-covered steel. Brackets, which clip into the top section of the track, hold the rail to the wall, window frame or ceiling. The curtain hooks are attached to double-wheel runners (on metal rails) or to nylon gliders (on plastic tracks). Strong enough to support heavy curtains. I-section rail is sufficiently flexible to be bent into fairly tight curves (useful for fitting square bay windows or for forming overlaps).

You can buy ready-made wood pelmets (finished in dark walnut, other timber or gilt) with the curtain track already fitted and corded on a track board; this is attached by metal clips to the front and side assembly.

Above right Flexible track is useful for taking curtains round corners as well as for fitting in bow and bay windows
Right I-section rail can be bent to enable curtains to overlap or to fit into tight corners
Inset Section of fixing bracket
Below You can conceal unattractive curtain track by fitting a valance rail
Below right You can buy ready-made pelmets which come fitted with curtain track and cording mechanism

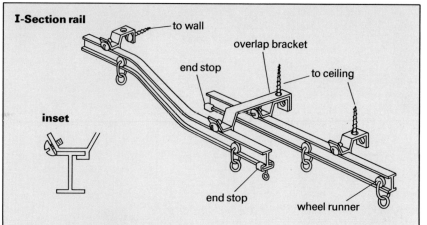

I-Section rail

to wall
overlap bracket
end stop
to ceiling
inset
end stop
wheel runner

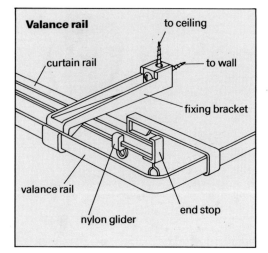

Valance rail

to ceiling
curtain rail
to wall
fixing bracket
valance rail
nylon glider
end stop

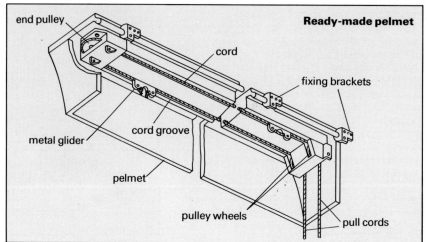

end pulley
cord
Ready-made pelmet
fixing brackets
metal glider
cord groove
pelmet
pulley wheels
pull cords

Non-pelmet tracks

Most modern tracks are designed for use without pelmets or valances. Some of these have the runners concealed in a box section or clipped over a flat rail. Box rails are normally flexible enough to be used in bay windows and recesses and can be bent to a radius as small as 50mm (2in). But if you have to bend the track as tight as this, check with your supplier that the track is suitable.

Tracks for use without pelmets are normally made from plastic or aluminium. Apart from a plain track, various finishes are available such as silver or gold coating, wood grain and carved wood. And you can buy ornamental finials (end pieces) which clip onto the track. You can also buy a fluted trim to clip over straight lengths of track to give the impression of a cornice pole.

Another type of non-pelmet track is the neat, inconspicuous U-shaped channel, in which gliders slide. Ideal in recessed windows, it blends well with the clean lines of modern decor. Made from plastic or coated aluminium, it can be mounted on the wall or ceiling but is only suitable for straight runs. It is often used with a second track for hanging nets behind heavier curtains.

Cording sets Available as optional extras with many tracks, these prevent wear and tear on the curtains caused by hand-pulling; even long curtains can be drawn with ease. Many cording sets have a device included in the kit to assist in the overlapping of curtains. You can fit any good corded curtain track with an electric curtain motor and connect it via a conveniently placed two-way control switch to a socket outlet or fused connection unit.

Curtain poles

For straight runs only, the old style curtain or cornice poles are again popular. The simplest design is a stout pole (of wood, plastic or metal with a brass finish) with plain or ornate turned ends mounted on matching brackets.

Many modern curtain poles are made in the same styles as the old brass ones, but with easy-running false rings which slide in channels hidden behind the poles. Some poles are telescopic, fitting a range of widths, and they are often supplied with integral cording sets.

Hanging nets

Net or café-style half-pane curtains are usually hung on plastic-covered wires pushed through the top hem of the curtains. You can adjust the gathers as required, but it is almost impossible to open the

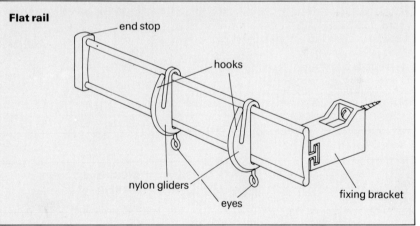

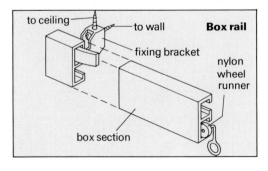

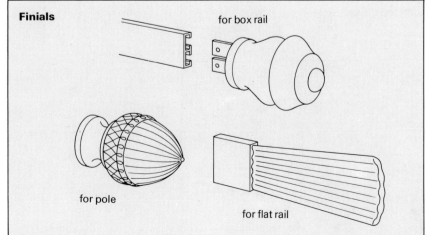

Above Box rail, designed for use without a pelmet or valance
Top right Aluminium cornice pole giving a traditional brass appearance
Centre right Simple flat rail
Right Types of finial

curtains completely; so this method of hanging is really only suitable for curtains which will be left undisturbed.

The neat and simple way of fixing plastic-covered curtain wire is by using rings and hooks. The ring screws into the end of the wire and the hook is screwed into the window frame. This can be done by hand, but if the wood is too hard or you want to put the fixing into the wall (if the window frames are metal) you can use a small round head screw instead. With wall fixing you will have to drill a hole and plug it before inserting the screw. Make sure you leave a 6mm ($\frac{1}{4}$in) clearance between the screw head and the wall to allow for the ring to be hooked over the screw. Trim the curtain wire with pliers so it is slightly shorter than the width required. This ensures the wire is really tight when hung and

the curtain does not sag. Screw the rings into each end of the wire, thread the wire through the top hem of the curtain and stretch the wire across the window, hanging it over the hooks or screws already fixed at each end.

The curtain wire does tend to sag, so hang only lightweight curtains. (If you are hanging floor-to-ceiling nets, use the neat U-channel track.)

An alternative method of hanging fixed net curtains is to use lightweight curtain rods (wood dowels are ideal) although you will not be able to open the curtains completely. The rods are fixed near the top of the window frame using curtain rod brackets; the cranked version is screwed to the window frame and the straight version is fixed to each side of the window recess (useful for metal window frames).

Below left Box rail with fluted trim
Centre left U-shaped rail
Bottom left Double U-shaped rail for hanging two sets of curtains
Below centre Simple wood cornice poles are fairly inexpensive and make a plain window more interesting
Below Plain white track is unobtrusive enough to blend with any style of decoration
Bottom Cording sets make drawing curtains easier; most corded curtain tracks can be fitted with a motor

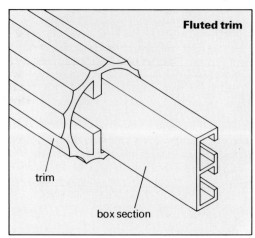

Fluted trim

trim

box section

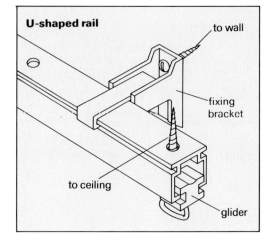

U-shaped rail

to wall

fixing bracket

to ceiling

glider

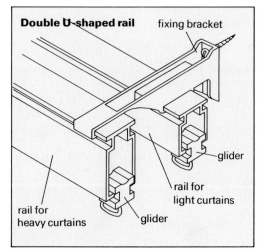

Double U-shaped rail   fixing bracket

glider

rail for light curtains

rail for heavy curtains   glider

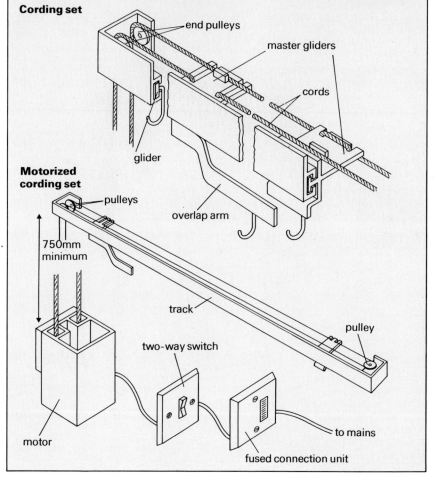

Cording set

end pulleys

master gliders

cords

glider

Motorized cording set

pulleys

overlap arm

750mm minimum

track

two-way switch

pulley

motor

fused connection unit

to mains

Below Some cornice poles are pre-corded and will extend to fit a range of window widths
Below centre Traditional curtain pole
Bottom Curtain pole with false rings
Below right Plastic wire for hanging net curtains
Bottom right You can use lightweight curtain rod instead of wire to hang nets; in this case you will need either cranked brackets for frame fitting or straight ones for recess fitting

Fixing curtain tracks

Unless you are fitting the track in the recess above a window, or you want wall-to-wall curtains, the track should extend either side of the window so the open curtains will hang neatly to the side without cutting out any light. If, however, you have a wide window which you would like to look narrower, you can fit the track just to the end of the window so when the curtains are drawn back they cover the frame and part of the window itself.

The easiest way to put up a track is to screw the fixing brackets to the top of the window frame. Fixing instructions are usually supplied with new track. Always fit the number of brackets recommended by the manufacturer for the length of track used and make sure there is a bracket close to each end to support the weight of the curtains when drawn back. For sill length curtains fit the brackets at equal heights from the sill (or from the floor for floor length curtains) to ensure the bottom hems of the curtains hang in line with the sill (or floor).

Fix the end brackets at each side of the window, then stretch taught a length of string between them and use this to align the other brackets, spacing them at equal intervals. If you have to fix the brackets directly to the wall, make the fixing holes with a masonry drill bit, which has a specially hardened tip for drilling walls. The masonry bit can be used with a hand wheel brace, but it is much easier to use an electric drill set at slow speed.

You can make the holes with a cheap, easy-to-use tool called a jumping bit, which you tap into the wall with a hammer and twist occasionally to clear the dust from the hole.

Many houses have concrete lintels above the windows and you may find it difficult to make the

Even with a hammer drill the going can be slow. To reduce the number of fixings in the lintel you can screw the appropriate length of 12mm ($\frac{1}{2}$in) thick timber above the window and fix the track brackets to this. Alternatively, fit a long curtain pole which will extend far enough on each side of the window to avoid the lintel.

When you have made your holes in the wall above the window, it is vital the fixing is secure since the weight of the curtains will otherwise quickly loosen it. A guide to the right fixings is given in the Appendix. Having inserted suitable wall plugs, secure the brackets to the wall with screws.

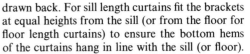

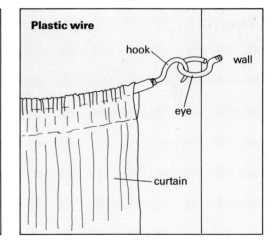

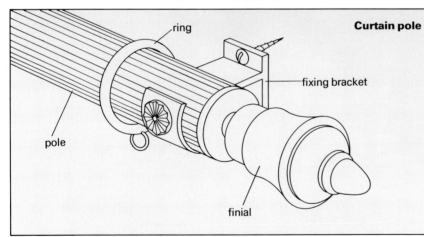

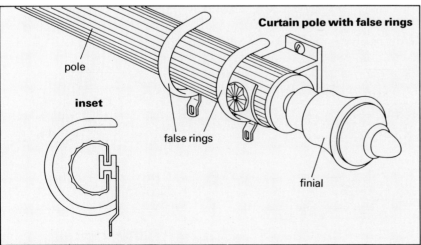

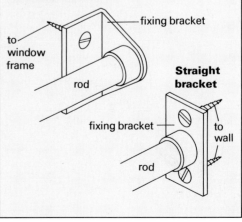

Jobs around the home

Minor repairs are needed in even the best-run home and you should find it quicker and cheaper to tackle them yourself. You will also find those odd jobs need doing to keep the home tidy and running efficiently. This section shows you the way to stop a dripping tap, repair a faulty cistern or mend a leaking gutter. Other plumbing problems can be prevented by protecting the system, particularly in cold weather; this is also explained. You can create more space in a room by rehanging the door to open the other way and build shelves for storage. Unsightly pipes can be boxed in, too.

Repairing taps & washers

Pillar taps

To rewasher the conventional pillar tap (**see 1**), you must cut off the water supply to the tap. If the fault is in the cold water tap over the kitchen sink (which should be supplied direct from the mains) you will need to turn off the main stopcock. Other taps may have a stopcock or gate valve on the distribution pipe serving them; if so, turn off this valve. If there is no such valve, tie up the arm of the ball valve serving the main cold water storage cistern and open all bathroom taps and the kitchen hot tap to drain the cistern and distribution pipes.

Unscrew the protective cover of the tap (**see 2a**). You should be able to do this by hand, but if not you can use a pipe wrench (**see below**), although you must pad the jaws to avoid damaging the chromium plating on the tap.

Insert an adjustable spanner (**see below**) under the base of the cover (**see 2b**), unscrew the head-gear nut and remove the headgear. The jumper (or valve) of the cold water tap over the kitchen sink will usually be resting on the valve seating in the body of the tap (**see 2c**). Remove it, unscrew the small retaining nut (**see 2d**) and replace the washer. If the nut proves difficult to unscrew you can replace the jumper and washer complete.

Some taps may have the jumper pegged into the headgear. Although it will turn, it may not be easy to remove. You may have to unscrew the retaining nut with the help of a little penetrating oil. If the retaining nut will not move, insert the blade of a screwdriver between the plate of the jumper and the base of the headgear and break the pegging. Replace the jumper and washer complete, but burr the stem of the jumper with a coarse file to ensure a tight fit. Reassemble the tap and turn on water.

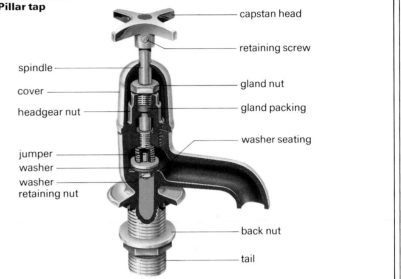

1 Pillar tap

- capstan head
- spindle
- retaining screw
- cover
- gland nut
- headgear nut
- gland packing
- washer seating
- jumper
- washer
- washer retaining nut
- back nut
- tail

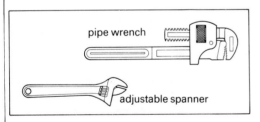

pipe wrench

adjustable spanner

2a

2b headgear nut

2c jumper / washer

2d washer retaining nut

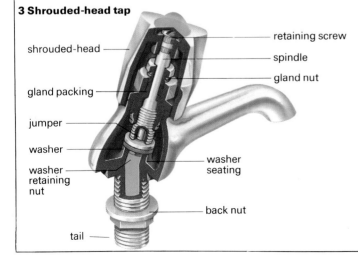

3 Shrouded-head tap

- shrouded-head
- retaining screw
- spindle
- gland nut
- gland packing
- jumper
- washer
- washer seating
- washer retaining nut
- back nut
- tail

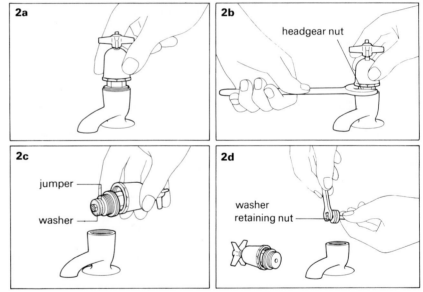

Shrouded-head taps

To expose the inside of a shrouded-head tap (**see 3**), remove the head. This is normally done by prising off the plastic 'hot' or 'cold' label, under which there is a retaining screw. Undo the screw and lift off the shrouded-head.

A few shrouded-head taps have the head retained by a tiny grub screw in the side, similar to the grub screw retaining the capstan or crutch head of a conventional tap. Others may have no retaining screw at all, in which case after they are fully opened you must give a final turn that allows the head to be pulled off.

Supataps

Rewashering a Supatap is a quick job that avoids cutting off the water supply. Open the tap slightly and with a spanner unscrew and release the retaining nut at the top of the nozzle (**see 4a**). Start turning the tap; there will be an increasing flow of water, but this will cease as the check valve falls into position. The nozzle will then come off in your hand (**see 4b**).

Tap the nozzle on a hard surface (not one that will chip) to loosen the anti-splash device in which the washer and jumper are fixed. Turn the nozzle upside down and the anti-splash will drop out (**see 4c**). Remove the washer and jumper by inserting a blade between the plate and the anti-splash (**see 4d**) and insert a new set. Replace the anti-splash in the nozzle (**see 4e**) and reassemble the tap, remembering the nozzle screws back on with a left-hand thread (**see 4f**).

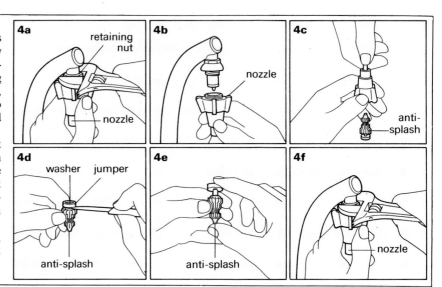

Continued dripping

Occasionally a tap will continue to drip even after being fitted with a new washer. This indicates the valve seating has been scratched and scored by grit in the water supply and no longer gives a watertight connection.

There are reseating tools available, but the simplest way to deal with this problem when it affects a conventional tap is to use a new nylon washer and seating kit (**see 5**). The nylon seating is placed squarely on the brass seating of the tap. Put the new washer and jumper in the headgear of the tap and screw them down hard into the tap body, forcing the nylon valve seating into position. This method cannot be used on Supataps, but the manufacturers of these taps make and supply a reseating tool for the purpose.

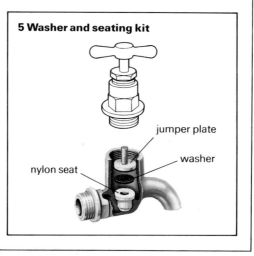

5 Washer and seating kit

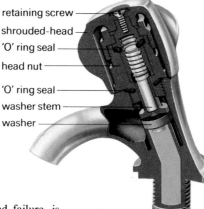

6 Removing tap head

7 Shrouded-head tap with 'O' ring

Gland failure

Another common fault in taps, gland failure, is indicated by water escaping up the spindle when the tap is turned on. The tap can also be turned on and off very easily, with just a spin of the fingers, which often causes water hammer (the effect of shock waves in the pipes produced by the sudden cessation of flowing water). Causes of gland failure may be back pressure resulting from the connection of a hose or detergent-charged water running down the spindle and washing grease from the gland packing.

To adjust or renew the gland of a conventional tap, remove the capstan or crutch head by unscrew-

ing and removing the tiny retaining grub screw. If taking off the head proves difficult, open up the tap and unscrew and raise the protective cover as high as possible. Insert two pieces of wood (at back and front) between the base of the raised cover and the body of the tap. Then close the tap down again and the upward pressure of the cover will force off the head or handle (**see 6**).

The gland-adjusting nut is the first nut through which the spindle of the tap passes. To tighten, turn in a clockwise direction. Eventually all the allowance for adjustment will be taken up and the gland packing will have to be renewed. To do this, unscrew and remove the gland packing nut. Existing gland packing material can be removed with the point of a penknife. Repack with strands of wool steeped in vaseline, press down hard and re-assemble the tap.

Some modern taps have a rubber 'O' ring seal instead of a conventional gland (**see 7**). These are less likely to give trouble, but if they do simply renew the ring.

Fitting new taps

Before you renew a tap the existing one has to be taken out and this can be the most difficult part of the job. The back nut, which secures the tap underneath, is likely to be inaccessible and may well be firmly fixed by scale and corrosion.

Cut off the water supply to the tap and then unscrew the 'cap and lining' nut that connects the tail of the tap to the water supply pipe. With a basin or sink it may be necessary to disconnect the waste pipe, take the appliance off its mounting and turn it upside down on the floor in order to get a better purchase on the back nut. A cranked 'basin spanner' will help do this.

Removal of old bath taps can be particularly difficult because of the cramped and badly lit space in which you will have to work. It may prove better to disconnect the water supply and waste pipes and pull the bath forward to give yourself more room to work.

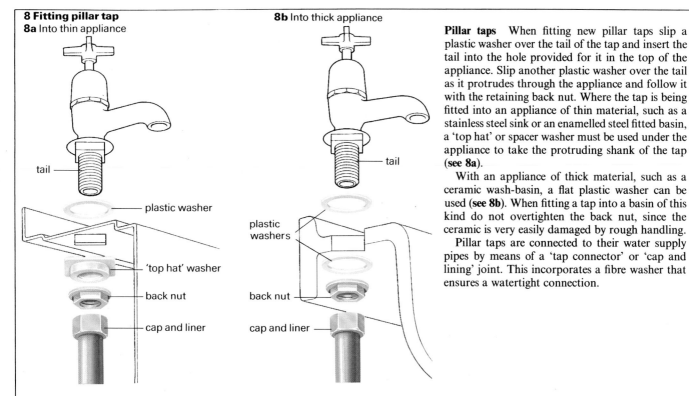

8 Fitting pillar tap
8a Into thin appliance

tail

plastic washer

'top hat' washer

back nut

cap and liner

8b Into thick appliance

tail

plastic washers

back nut

cap and liner

Pillar taps When fitting new pillar taps slip a plastic washer over the tail of the tap and insert the tail into the hole provided for it in the top of the appliance. Slip another plastic washer over the tail as it protrudes through the appliance and follow it with the retaining back nut. Where the tap is being fitted into an appliance of thin material, such as a stainless steel sink or an enamelled steel fitted basin, a 'top hat' or spacer washer must be used under the appliance to take the protruding shank of the tap (**see 8a**).

With an appliance of thick material, such as a ceramic wash-basin, a flat plastic washer can be used (**see 8b**). When fitting a tap into a basin of this kind do not overtighten the back nut, since the ceramic is very easily damaged by rough handling.

Pillar taps are connected to their water supply pipes by means of a 'tap connector' or 'cap and lining' joint. This incorporates a fibre washer that ensures a watertight connection.

equipment

pipe wrench
adjustable spanner
cranked basin spanner
screwdriver, penknife
coarse file
penetrating oil
wool, vaseline
PTFE plastic thread
  sealing tape
jumper, washer and
  seating parts (as
  needed)

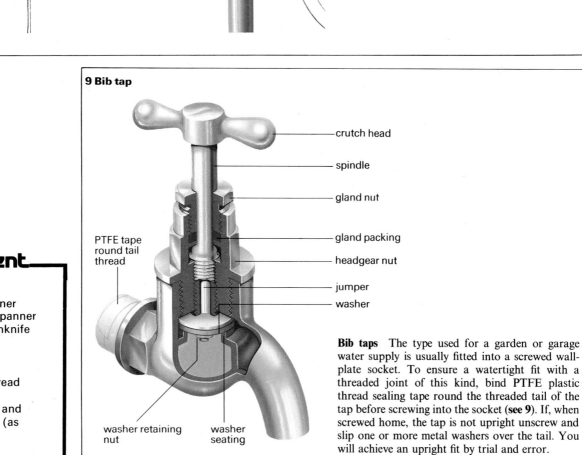

9 Bib tap

crutch head

spindle

gland nut

gland packing

headgear nut

jumper

washer

PTFE tape
round tail
thread

washer retaining
nut

washer
seating

Bib taps The type used for a garden or garage water supply is usually fitted into a screwed wall-plate socket. To ensure a watertight fit with a threaded joint of this kind, bind PTFE plastic thread sealing tape round the threaded tail of the tap before screwing into the socket (**see 9**). If, when screwed home, the tap is not upright unscrew and slip one or more metal washers over the tail. You will achieve an upright fit by trial and error.

Ball valves

Ball valves are vital parts of the plumbing system in the home, since they control the amount of water in your cold water storage and WC cisterns. They must operate efficiently, otherwise the cisterns will overflow – or not fill up correctly.

The purpose of the ball, or float, valve is to maintain water at a constant level in cold water storage and WC flushing cisterns. All ball valves have a metal or plastic arm terminating in a float (not necessarily a ball) that rises or falls with the level of the water in the cistern. As the water level falls the movement of the float arm opens the valve to allow water to flow through it; as the level rises the arm closes the valve.

The older types of ball valve – the Croydon and the Portsmouth – control the flow of water by a washered metal plug. The main disadvantage of these is that failure of the washer or dirt or corrosion on the parts can cause leaks. Modern ball valves, which have a rubber diaphragm instead of a washered plug, are designed to overcome these problems.

Croydon and Portsmouth valves

On both these valves a washered metal plug is forced tightly against the valve seating to prevent a flow of water when the cistern is full. The plug of a Croydon moves vertically within the valve body. When the valve is open, water splashes into the cistern via two channels built into either side of the body of the valve. Croydon valves are always noisy in action and, for this reason, are now rarely, if ever, installed in homes.

The Portsmouth valve is the one now most likely to be found in installations, particularly new ones. Its plug moves horizontally within the valve body and the end of the float arm is bent over to fit within a slot built into the plug. The noise of these valves used to be reduced by fitting a silencer tube into the valve outlet. This is a plastic or metal tube that delivers incoming water below the level of the water already in the cistern; it eliminates splashing and reduces the ripple formation that is a common cause of noise and vibration in ball valves. Unfortunately water authorities no longer permit the use of these silencer tubes, since in the event of water pressure failure they could cause water from storage and flushing cisterns to siphon back into the main.

Dealing with leaks A steady drip from the cistern's warning pipe indicates a worn washer – a common fault on the Croydon and Portsmouth valves. It may be possible to cure the leak, at least temporarily, without changing the washer simply by lowering the level of the water in the cistern. There is no need to cut off the water supply to do this: remove the cover from the cistern, unscrew and remove the float from the end of the float arm. Take the arm firmly in both hands and bend the float end downwards, then reassemble. This will keep the water below the normal level, which is about 25mm (1in) below the warning pipe in a cold water storage cistern and 13mm ($\frac{1}{2}$in) below the warning pipe in a flushing cistern. (If you need to raise the water level in a cistern, bend up the float end of the arm.)

Changing the washer If lowering the level of the water does not cure the leak, you will need to change the ball valve washer. First cut off the water supply at the nearest stopcock. Some Portsmouth valves have a screw-on cap at the end of the valve body: this must be removed.

Straighten and pull out the split pin on which the float arm pivots and remove the float arm; insert the blade of a screwdriver in the slot in the base of the valve body from which the float arm has been removed and push out the plug.

The plug has two parts: a body and a cap retaining the washer, but it may be difficult to see the division between these parts in a plug that has been in use for some time. To replace the washer you will need to remove the retaining plug: insert the blade of a screwdriver through the slot in the body and turn the cap with a pair of pliers. This can be very difficult, so don't risk damaging the plug. If the cap will not unscrew easily, pick out the old washer with the point of a penknife and force a new washer under the flange of the cap, making sure the washer lies flat on its seating.

Cleaning It is important to remove any dirt or scaling on the metal parts as this can also cause leaks. Before reassembling the plug, clean it with fine abrasive paper and smear with petroleum jelly.

When to replace the valve Continued leaking after renewal of the washer may indicate the valve seating of the plug has been scored by grit from the main or

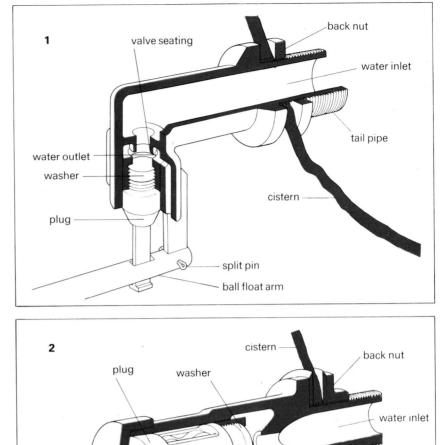

a low pressure valve has been fitted where a high pressure one is required. In either case, a new valve will be needed.

Ball valves are classified as high pressure (HP) or low pressure (LP) depending on the diameter of the valve seating and are usually stamped accordingly on the valve body. High pressure valves are usually installed where the water supply is direct from the main and low pressure valves where the water supply is from another storage cistern, as is usually the case with WC flushing cisterns.

Using the wrong kind of valve will result in either constant leaks or a long delay in the refilling of the cistern. Where a WC flushing cistern is supplied from a cold water storage cistern only a metre (or 3ft) above the level of the WC suite, it may be necessary to fit a full-way valve – which has a wider orifice – to ensure the cistern refills rapidly after it has been flushed.

Equilibrium valve

In some areas water pressure may fluctuate considerably throughout a 24-hour period. In such cases, the provision of an equilibrium valve is

Opposite page Types of ball valve: Torbeck (**top left**), diaphragm (**top right**), Croydon (**centre left**), Portsmouth (**centre right**) and equilibrium (**bottom**).

1 The Croydon ball valve: the plug moves vertically in the valve body and water enters through channels on either side
2 The Portsmouth ball valve: the plug moves horizontally and water enters through a single channel

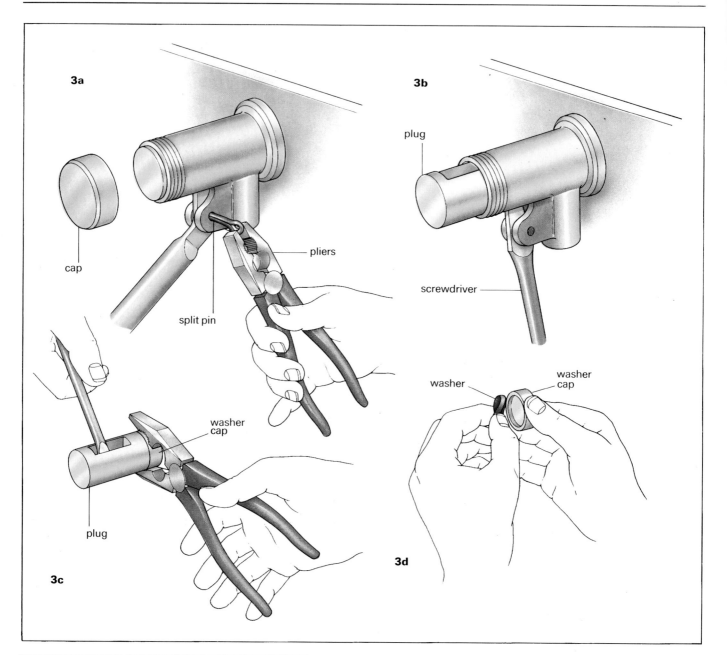

3a

cap

pliers

split pin

3c

washer
cap

plug

3b

plug

screwdriver

washer   washer
                cap

3d

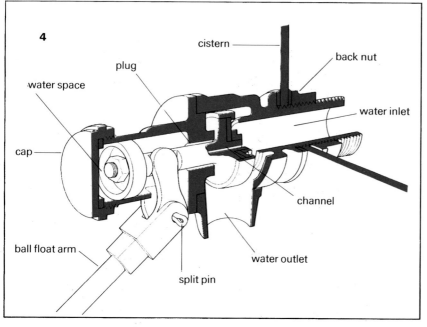

4

cistern

plug   back nut

water space

water inlet

cap

channel

ball float arm

split pin

water outlet

recommended. This valve has a wide nozzle orifice but is closed by a special plug with a channel bored through its centre: this allows water to pass through to a sealed chamber behind the valve. The plug is therefore in a state of equilibrium: water pressure is equal on each side of the plug and the valve opens only at the prompting of the float arm – not partly as a result of the pressure of water in the rising main trying to force the valve open.

An equilibrium valve is also useful in preventing water hammer – shock waves produced when the conflict between water pressure in the rising main and the buoyancy of the float result in the valve bouncing on its seating.

Diaphragm valves

A new type of ball valve – the diaphragm valve (also known as the Garston or BRS as it was developed at the Government's Building Research Station at Garston) – has been designed to reduce noise and eliminate other common ball valve problems. It may be made of brass or plastic and has a tough, score-resistant nylon nozzle that is closed, when the cistern is full, by a large rubber or plastic dia-

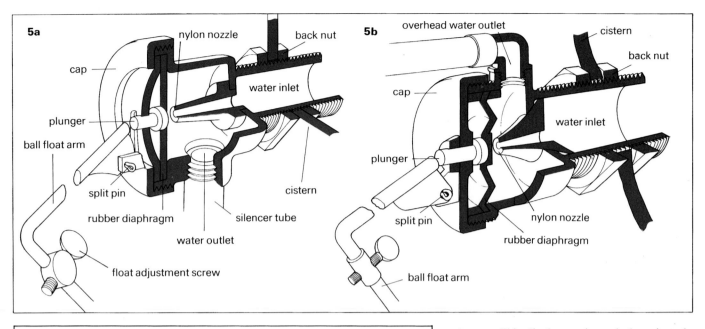

5a

cap

nylon nozzle

back nut

water inlet

plunger

ball float arm

split pin

rubber diaphragm

silencer tube

cistern

water outlet

float adjustment screw

5b

overhead water outlet

cistern

back nut

cap

water inlet

plunger

split pin

nylon nozzle

rubber diaphragm

ball float arm

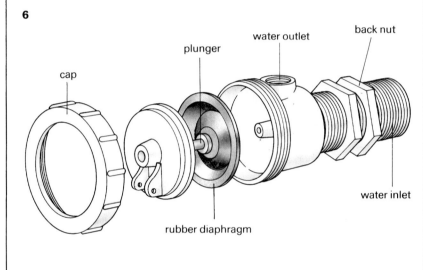

6

cap

plunger

water outlet

back nut

water inlet

rubber diaphragm

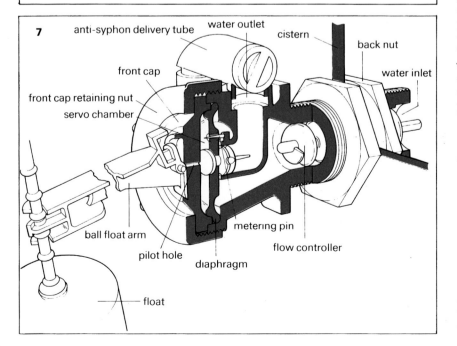

7

anti-syphon delivery tube

water outlet

cistern

back nut

water inlet

front cap

front cap retaining nut

servo chamber

ball float arm

pilot hole

diaphragm

metering pin

flow controller

float

phragm. This diaphragm is pushed against the nozzle by a small plunger actuated by the float arm. All diaphragm pattern valves have some means of adjusting water level without having to bend the float arm.

An important feature of this kind of valve is that it has few moving parts. These are anyway protected from the water by the rubber diaphragm, so the valves cannot jam as a result of scale or corrosion.

Early models of diaphragm valves were fitted with silencer tubes, but since these have fallen out of favour, manufacturers have developed overhead outlets with a distributing device that can be directed at the side of the cistern to ensure silent action. Modern diaphragm valves also have a detachable nozzle which allows them to be changed quickly from high pressure to low pressure.

Poor flow from a diaphragm valve is usually due to the diaphragm jamming against the nozzle or, more likely, to debris from the rising main accumulating between nozzle and diaphragm. The valve can be easily dismantled for cleaning and servicing: to release the nozzle simply turn by hand the large knurled retaining cap – but remember to cut off the water supply first.

Torbeck A more recent development is the Torbeck valve, which has some of the features of the diaphragm valve and some of the conventional equilibrium valve. It operates solely by water pressure acting on both sides of the diaphragm and has been found to be very efficient. It is also silent in action, unlike the other types of valve.

3a To change washer on Portsmouth or Croydon valve, pull out split pin holding ball arm (having cut off water supply). **3b** Push out plug with screwdriver. **3c** Insert screwdriver through slot in plug body and turn washer cap with pliers. **3d** Remove washer and fit new one. **4** Equilibrium ball valve. **5a** Early diaphragm valve fitted with silencer. **5b** Modern diaphragm valve with overhead outlet; spray delivery ensures silent action. **6** To dismantle diaphragm valve, unscrew cap and remove components. **7** Torbeck valve includes features from diaphragm and equilibrium ones

Guarding against corrosion

Some plumbing fittings are subject to corrosion. When this occurs, they are weakened and eventually leaks develop. There are several ways of preventing this happening in your system.

Modern galvanized steel water storage cisterns frequently show signs of rust within a few months of being installed. Older plumbing systems, which were constructed entirely of lead or galvanized steel, could generally be expected to last, without this kind of deterioration, for 50 years or more. In modern systems the use of copper, which itself virtually never corrodes, has greatly increased the risk of corrosion to any galvanized iron or steel fittings incorporated in the system.

The process which gives rise to this corrosion is known as electrolytic action. This is the same principle on which the simple electric battery cell is based; where rods of zinc and copper are in electrical contact with each other and are immersed in a weak acid solution which is able to conduct an electric current (an electrolyte), electricity will pass between the rods, bubbles of oxygen will be produced and the zinc rod will slowly dissolve away. A plumbing system in which copper water supply and distribution pipes are connected to a galvanized steel cold water storage cistern or hot water storage tank, may reproduce these conditions; the copper tubing and the zinc coating of the galvanized steel are in direct contact and the water in the cistern or tank, if very mildly acidic, will act as an electrolyte. This results in rapid failure of the protective galvanized coating, allowing aerated water to penetrate to the vulnerable steel underneath; eventually rust will form.

A particular form of electrolytic corrosion may result in damage to brass plumbing fittings, such as compression joints and stop valves. Brass is an alloy of copper and zinc; electrolytic action may result in the zinc in the fittings dissolving away to leave them unchanged in appearance but totally without structural strength. Where these fittings in your plumbing system are showing signs of leakage, it would be worth checking with a local plumber if the type of water in your area is likely to create a situation favourable to electrolytic corrosion. If so, you should replace brass fittings with fittings made of gun-metal (an alloy of copper and tin), which is not susceptible to this kind of damage.

Warning Corrosion as a result of electrolytic action is also likely to occur in pipework if a new length of copper tubing is fitted into an existing galvanized steel hot or cold water system. Always use stainless steel tubing instead – this is not liable to the same risk.

Protecting cisterns and tanks
There are steps you can take to prevent corrosion in galvanized steel cisterns and tanks. For example, when you are installing a new cistern or tank, it is important to make sure you remove every trace of metal dust or shaving resulting from drilling holes for tappings. The least fragment remaining will become a focus for corrosion.

One way of protecting a cold water storage cistern is to ensure the metal of the cistern does not come into direct contact with the water it contains. This can be done by painting the internal surfaces with two coats of a taste and odour-free bituminous paint to prevent these surfaces from rusting. Before applying this treatment to a new tank, cut holes for the pipe connections; when you are painting, pay particular attention to the areas in the immediate vicinity of these holes.

Warning Galvanized steel hot water storage tanks, which can still be found in many older homes, cannot be protected by this paint treatment.

Cathodic protection A sacrificial magnesium anode which dissolves instead of the zinc coating will protect both galvanized steel cold water storage cisterns and hot water tanks. With a cold water storage cistern, clamp the copper wire attached to the anode to the side of the cistern using a G-clamp

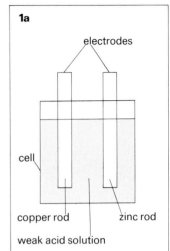

1a

electrodes

cell

copper rod   zinc rod

weak acid solution

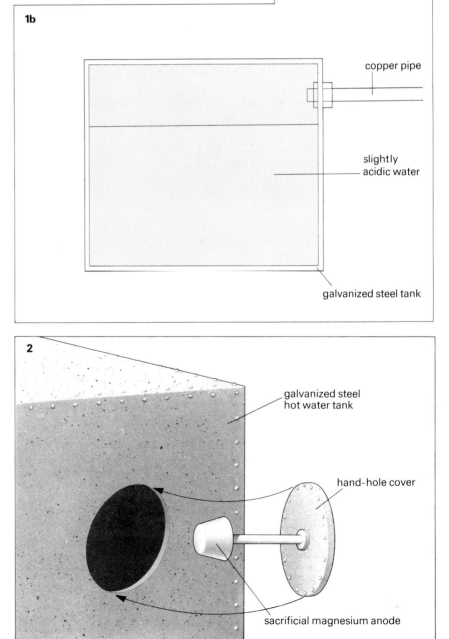

1b

copper pipe

slightly acidic water

galvanized steel tank

2

galvanized steel hot water tank

hand-hole cover

sacrificial magnesium anode

1a & b The process which causes corrosion in plumbing systems with copper and galvanized iron or steel fittings is principally the same as the process which takes place in a battery cell
2 Fit a sacrificial magnesium anode into a galvanized steel hot water tank to prevent corrosion
3 When venting a radiator check for the presence of hydrogen – which indicates internal corrosion – by holding a lighted taper to the escaping air
To remove magnetite sludge from a central heating system, drain the system (**4a**) and introduce a special solvent into the feed and expansion tank (**4b**)

and suspend the wire over a timber batten into the water in the middle of the cistern. Make sure you replace the anode before it dissolves completely. When protecting a hot water tank, fit the anode to the hand-hole cover of the tank. Turn off the water supply and drain the system from the draincock beside the boiler; unscrew the bolts retaining the hand-hole cover and remove it. Drill a hole in the centre of the cover, use abrasive paper to rub down the area of metal around the hole and screw in the anode before replacing the cover.

Protecting central heating systems
A form of electrolytic corrosion can take place in a central heating system where copper tubing is used in conjunction with pressed steel radiators. Some air – a prerequisite of corrosion – will always be present in the system; it dissolves into the surface of the water in the feed and expansion tank and may also enter through minute leaks too small to permit water to escape.

Electrolytic corrosion within a central heating system results in the formation of black iron oxide

sludge (magnetite) and hydrogen gas. This leads to impeded water flow and radiators will need continual venting to release airlocks to keep up the required heat level. The iron oxide sludge is drawn towards the magnetic field of the circulating pump and its abrasive qualities contribute towards early pump failure. Also the metal of the radiators, from which the magnetite and hydrogen are produced, becomes thinner until leaks eventually develop in the radiators.

Removing airlocks by venting the radiator is a simple process. A key supplied for this purpose is inserted in the radiator when the water is warm and turned anti-clockwise to open the vent valve. Hold a container underneath the key since some water may escape when the valve is opened. Air will come out of the radiator – when it stops doing so and water begins to flow you should tighten the valve. If a radiator in your heating system needs to be continually vented, it is worth testing for internal corrosion while you are carrying out this operation. Apply a lighted taper to the gas escaping from the radiator; hydrogen gas burns with a blue flame and indicates the presence of corrosion.

Protection treatment A chemical corrosion-proofer can be introduced into the feed and expansion tank to protect the system against corrosion. It is best to do this when the system is first installed, but it can be carried out with an existing system; it will not, however, undo damage already done. Before introducing a corrosion-proofer into an existing system you should get rid of any magnetite sludge with a special solvent. Like the corrosion-proofer, this is introduced into the feed and expansion tank and you should drain the system first. Disconnect the fuel supply to the boiler and switch off the ignition system several hours before draining to give the water time to cool. Tie up the ball float arm of the feed and expansion tank and fit a hose to the draincock near the boiler, running the hose to a drain outside. Undo the draincock, empty the system and, when you have closed the draincock, free the ball float arm in the feed and expansion tank. Allow the system to refill, introducing the solvent at the same time. Follow the manufacturer's instructions for the length of time you should allow for the solvent to complete its work before carrying out treatment with the corrosion-proofer.

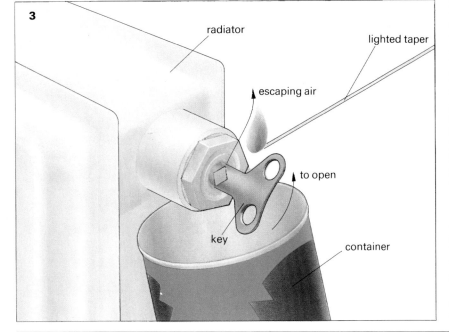

3

radiator
lighted taper
escaping air
to open
key
container

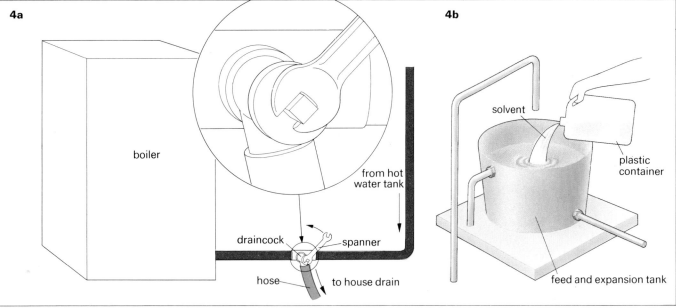

4a

boiler
from hot water tank
draincock — spanner
hose — to house drain

4b

solvent
plastic container
feed and expansion tank

Cold weather protection

If the plumbing system in your home is not adequately protected, severe weather can cause water to freeze in the pipes, producing blockages and burst pipes. You can deal with these yourself, but it is better to prevent any damage by checking your anti-frost defences every autumn.

Protecting plumbing

Frost protection is built into the structure of a well-designed, modern home and the important design points are explained below.

Service pipe This pipe conveys water from the water authority's communication pipe to the house and should be covered by at least 750mm (or 30in) of earth throughout its length. If it enters the house by a hollow, boarded floor, it should be thoroughly protected from draughts. The pipe should be taken up into the roof space – to supply the cold water storage cistern – against an internal wall.

Storage cistern The cold water storage cistern is best situated against a flue which is in constant use.

To prevent icy draughts blowing up the warning pipe leading from the cistern, you can fit a hinged copper flap over the outlet; there is, however, a risk that this will jam in the open or closed position. A better method is to extend the pipe within the cistern and bend it over so its outlet is about 38mm (1½in) below the surface of the water. There are gadgets, such as the frostguard, which make it easy to extend internally the warning pipe from a storage or flushing cistern.

The boiler, hot water storage cylinder and cold water storage cistern are best installed in a vertical column so the vulnerable cold water cistern receives the benefit of the rising warm air.

All lengths of water pipe within the roof space should be kept short and well away from the eaves.

Lagging Efficient lagging of storage tanks and pipes reduces the rate at which water loses its warmth and protects pipes exposed to cold air; but it cannot make up for a bad plumbing design and it will not add heat to the system.

Pipes to lag are those against external walls, under the ground floor and in the roof space. Don't omit the vent pipe of the hot water system since the water in this pipe is not as hot as that in the rest of the system and, if it freezes, it can create a vacuum which could damage the cylinder.

There are several types of pipe lagging available and it is best to use inorganic materials. These include wrap-round glass fibre; moulded polystyrene (which comes in rigid sections which fit round the pipe) and flexible moulded foam plastic (which you split open to fit round the pipe). Polystyrene is rather awkward to use, but is good for underground pipes since it does not absorb water. The moulded types of lagging come in a variety of sizes to fit different pipes, so make sure you buy the appropriate size.

Whichever type you use, make sure you lag behind pipes against external walls to protect them from the cold wall. Cover the tails of ball valves and all but the handles of stopcocks and gate valves; if you are using rigid lagging sections, you will need some of the wrap-round type for these areas.

Bind wrap-round insulation round the pipe like a bandage, overlapping it to prevent gaps, and secure it with string or adhesive tape. Where a pipe joins a cistern, make a full turn and tie it to hold the end in place. When joining two lengths overlap them and tie securely.

Secure moulded sections with plastic adhesive tape, starting at the cistern. Where the sections join along a length of pipe, seal the joint with tape. Open up flexible moulding along one side, slip it round the pipe and seal the opening with adhesive tape, taking particular care at any elbows. If you lag the pipes before fitting them, there is of course no need to slit the lagging; you can slide the pipe length through it. Where pipes go through a wall, make sure the insulation goes right up to the wall.

You also need to protect the cold water cistern. The easiest way to cover a square cistern is to use expanded polystyrene slabs. For a circular cistern use glass fibre tank wrap. If you have insulating material between the floor joists in the loft, make sure the area immediately below the tank is left uncovered so warm air is allowed to reach the tank.

Dealing with frozen pipes

If, in spite of your precautions, a freeze-up does occur, it is essential to deal with it immediately. If there is any delay the plug of ice will spread along the pipe and increase the risk of damage.

You can gauge the position of the freeze-up from the situation of the plumbing fittings which have stopped working. If, for instance, water is not flowing into the main cold water storage cistern but is running from the cold tap over the kitchen sink, the plug of ice must be in the rising main between the branch to the kitchen sink and the cistern.

Strip off the lagging from the affected pipe and apply heat – either with cloths soaked in hot water and wrung dry or a filled hot water bottle. If a pipe is inaccessible, direct a jet of warm air towards it from a hair dryer or the outlet of a vacuum cleaner. Fortunately modern copper tubing conducts very well and a small plug of ice can often be melted by applying heat to the pipe about a metre from the actual location of the ice.

Burst pipe If the freeze-up results in a burst pipe the first indication will probably be water dripping through a ceiling, since pipes in the loft are most likely to burst; wherever the leak, immediate action is vital. Turn off the main stopcock and open up every tap in the house. This will drain the cistern and pipes and reduce the damage. When the system is completely drained, find the position of the leak.

Damaged copper piping If you have copper piping, you will probably find a compression or soldered capillary joint will have been forced open by the expansion of ice. All you need to do in this case is fit a new joint. Copper piping does sometimes split under pressure. If that happens, you will have to cut out the defective length and insert a new length. An easy way of doing this is to insert a repair coupling.

Cut out the damaged section of pipe with a fine tooth hacksaw, leaving a gap of not more than 89mm (3½in) between the pipe ends. Remove the burr from the tube ends with a small file. One end of the coupling has a tube stop, the other is free to

Right Efficient lagging will protect pipes against freezing conditions

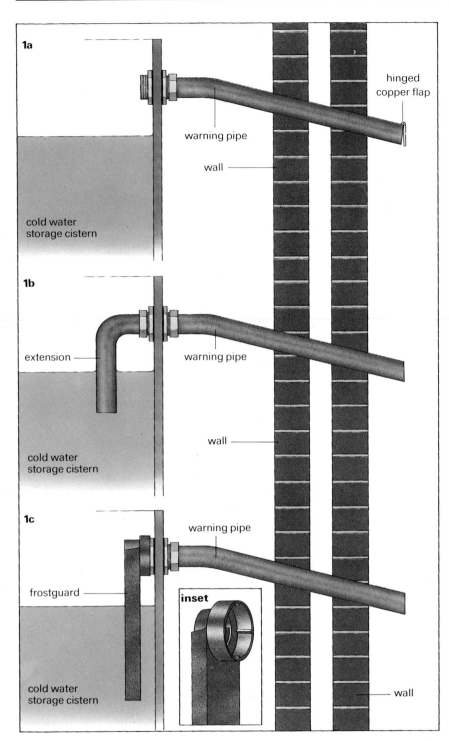

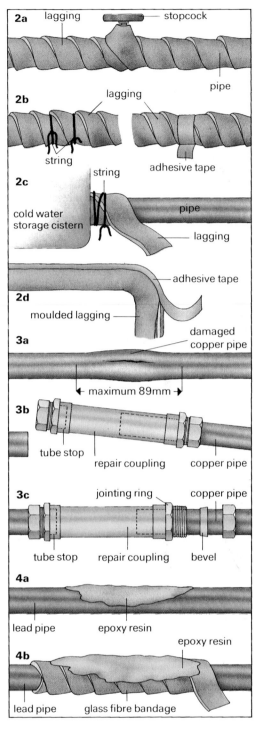

1a-c Ways of protecting cold water cistern from severe external conditions. **2a** Lagging pipe but leaving handle of stopcock clear; **2b** Secure lagging with tape or string; **2c** Where pipe meets cistern, make full turn and bind lagging firmly; **2d** Cut moulded lagging along one side, place round pipe and seal join with tape. Removing damaged section of copper pipe and fitting repair coupling. Making temporary repair to lead pipe with epoxy resin and bandage

slide along the pipe. Slacken the nuts of the coupling, spring one end of the pipe out just enough to allow you to slide the repair coupling over it. Line it up with the other pipe end and push the coupling on to it until the tube stop is reached. Unscrew the nuts and slide them and the copper jointing rings along the pipe. Apply jointing compound or gloss paint into the bevels of the fitting and around the leading edge of the jointing rings. Tighten the nuts with a spanner so the tube is lightly gripped; make another turn, or a turn and a quarter, making sure you do not overtighten.

Burst lead pipe The orthodox and approved method of repairing a burst lead pipe is to cut out the affected length and replace it with a new length of pipe; this job is best left to an expert.

You can, however, make a temporary repair with

one of the epoxy resin repair kits available. Dry the affected length of pipe thoroughly and knock the edges of the split together with a hammer. Rub down with abrasive paper. Make up the resin filler according to the manufacturer's instructions and apply it round the pipe to cover the split and the surrounding area. While the filler is still plastic, bind round it with a glass fibre bandage and 'butter' a further layer of resin filler over the bandage. When thoroughly set, rub down with abrasive paper to make an unobtrusive joint. You will be able to use the pipe again within a few hours.

Repairing plaster

Few homes escape damage to plaster – caused by wear and tear, settlement of the main structure or through damp or excessive heat. Not only does it look unsightly, but it can become a major problem. So tackle the job early and save yourself time and trouble.

The thought of having to repair damaged or flaking plaster may be fairly daunting to some people, but tackled in the right way with the right materials it is a relatively straightforward operation. Obviously it is quite a different matter if you have to replaster an entire wall or ceiling, in which case this is probably best left to the professional. But most of the small repairs normally required in the home are well within the capabilities of the DIY enthusiast.

Ceiling cracks These are caused by the movement in roofing and flooring joists, leading to the plasterboard (where fitted) parting at the joints. Hairline cracks can easily be filled. With larger gaps you should seek professional advice.

Wall cracks These are more likely to occur in new houses and are caused by the settlement of the main structure. The area most likely to be affected is the angle between the wall and the ceiling. Apart from filling in these cracks, which are likely to reopen later, one of the most effective methods is to cover over the gaps round the room. This can be done simply by fitting cove.

Unsightly cracks across the wall may also be caused by settlement and normally only affect the plaster. If, however, you get a wide diagonal crack appearing not only in the plaster but also in the wall, this could be a major problem and professional advice should be sought immediately. When this happens it is usually on external walls and is clearly visible from the outside as well.

Filling cracks

Common hairline cracks can be repaired simply and quickly. Rake out the affected area with a sharp knife or the edge of a paint scraper. Cut a 'V' shape into the wall along the crack so that it is widest at the deepest point of the crack. This allows you to push the filler into the cavity dovetail fashion to prevent it falling out on drying. Apply cellulose filler with a flexible steel filling knife. Use either a 75 or 100mm (3 or 4in) filling knife, the larger size being preferred since you can work quickly over large areas. Don't confuse this knife with a paint stripping knife, which looks similar, but must not be used as a substitute. The blade, which will bend about 90 degrees, should be perfectly straight and undamaged. Correctly used the knife can be used to give a smooth finish and make the job of rubbing down later unnecessary. Otherwise rub down with medium fine, then fine, glasspaper when the filler has completely dried, before redecorating.

Replacing loose plaster

Plaster often comes away from the surface around fireplaces. It can work loose due to vibration such as excessive hammering near the affected area – possibly when fitting a door or window frame. One simple test for loose plaster is to tap the suspect surface with the handle of a knife or a small blunt instrument. A hollow sound indicates poor adhesion between the plaster and substrate. Lift all the loose pieces with a broad knife and clean the surface beneath with a soft brush.

Filling cracks
sharp knife or paint scraper
cellulose filler
flexible filling knife
medium fine and fine glasspaper

Replacing loose plaster
knife or blunt instrument
broad knife and soft brush
undercoat plaster
finishing plaster
wood float, plasterer's trowel
cellulose filler and flexible filling
   knife (if needed)

Repairing external corners
cellulose filler, flexible filling
   knife and medium fine
   glasspaper (if needed)
undercoat plaster
finishing plaster
soft brush, timber batten
plasterer's trowel or wood float

Recessing fittings and cables
cold chisel
brick bolster
plaster or cellulose filler

equipment

Filling deep cavity

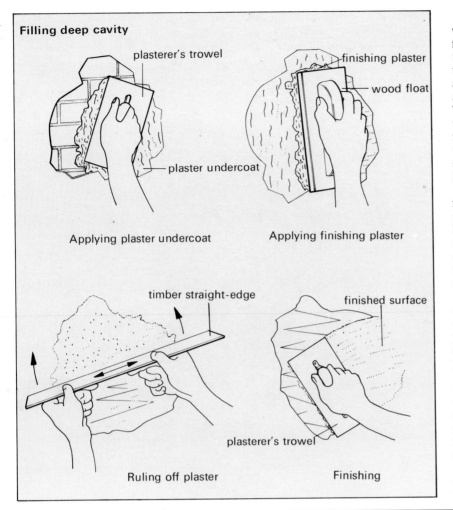

Applying plaster undercoat

Applying finishing plaster

Ruling off plaster

Finishing

If you are dealing with only a small cavity you will probably get away with filling the area with fresh finishing plaster. In the case of a deep cavity, first apply a plaster undercoat. Wet the wall thoroughly, then roughly fill the cavity to within about 3mm ($\frac{1}{8}$in) of the original plaster surface, applying the undercoat with a plasterer's trowel. The undercoat will dry with a rough texture which will provide a key for the finishing plaster. You will find a small 'hawk' useful to carry the plaster to the wall area after mixing it; make one by nailing a square of plywood to a short length of broom handle.

When the undercoat is quite dry, mix up enough finishing plaster to a creamy consistency to complete the job. In powder form it does not keep that long and old plaster will often set too quickly to enable you to spread it properly; in this case the application will just crack and fall away. If you find the plaster is hardening before you have a chance to use it, take it back to your supplier for replacement.

To complete filling, go over the undercoat surface with a dampened brush, put a generous amount of plaster onto the bottom of a wood float or plasterer's trowel and apply it into the remaining cavity. When the cavity is filled you can rule off the plaster. Using a timber straight-edge, which must be longer than the area being repaired, start from the bottom and work upwards over the new plaster with a sawing action, making sure both ends of the timber keep in contact with the surface of the existing plaster. This method ensures high spots are removed and low spots are built up as excess plaster is pushed up the wall, giving a level finish. When the plaster has almost set, rub a plasterer's trowel over the new surface to give a smooth, polished finish. Lift the front edge of the trowel away from the wall

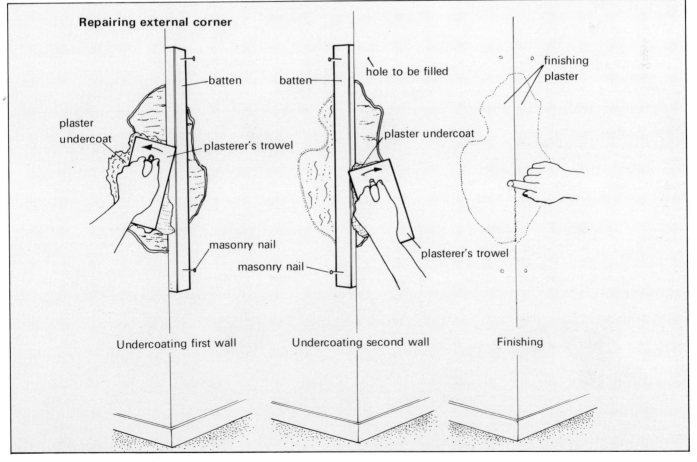

Repairing external corner

Undercoating first wall

Undercoating second wall

Finishing

so only the back edge is in contact; this will prevent the trowel cutting into the new plaster. Alternatively wait until the plaster has set completely and apply a layer of cellulose filler over the fresh plaster using a filling knife.

Repairing external corners

In any room it is the plaster on external corners that is the most vulnerable to damage. You can repair small holes and chips with cellulose filler as described earlier. When making good these small areas, apply the filler with a flexible filling knife working in each direction away from the corner. When dry the filler can be rubbed down lightly to form an edge to match the rest of that corner.

With a badly damaged corner you will make the best repair by building up the corner with a plaster undercoat, then applying a layer of finishing plaster. Remove any loose plaster and clean back the area with a soft brush. Fix a batten, which must be longer than the affected area, to the wall so its edge is in line with the existing front wall plaster – and flush to the corner. Either hold the batten in position as you work or tack it lightly to the wall with masonry nails, knocking the points of the nails through the batten before fixing. You can screw it into position by drilling the necessary holes in the batten and the wall, plugging the wall and inserting screws through the batten. Make sure you fix the batten well clear of the affected area or you may cause further damage.

Build up the level by applying the undercoat plaster with a trowel or float, always working away from the corner. On one side, plaster the area to within about 3mm ($\frac{1}{8}$in) of the original surface, then move the batten to the other wall to complete the undercoating. When this is dry, complete the repair with finishing plaster, using the batten on each wall as before.

If you nailed or screwed the batten to the wall, fill the holes with any plaster you have left over or with cellulose filler. Before the plaster sets hard, round off the corner by rubbing your fingers over the plaster to form an edge to match that on the rest of the corner. Use glasspaper if the plaster has set really hard.

Recessing fittings and cables

When new socket outlets have to be fitted or wiring extended along walls or ceilings, you will have to cut a channel in the plaster to conceal the cable. You will also have to chop out some of the brickwork to house the steel box for the socket.

Cut through the plaster cleanly with a sharp cold chisel (or fit a specially designed router to an electric drill and work at slow speed), making the grooves and openings as wide as necessary. Chop through the brickwork with a sharp brick bolster, making the hole deep enough for the front edge of the box to lie flush with the wall surface. Screw the box into position, feed in the cable and fill any surrounding gaps with plaster or cellulose filler, finishing the surface as before. When you have made the necessary repairs you can then connect up the socket and screw it onto the box.

Plastering large areas is physically demanding work best left to a skilled professional, who can apply large amounts of plaster before the mixture begins to harden. If you employ a contractor to insert a new damp proof course, an estimate for replastering internal walls should be included if hacking away old plaster is involved.

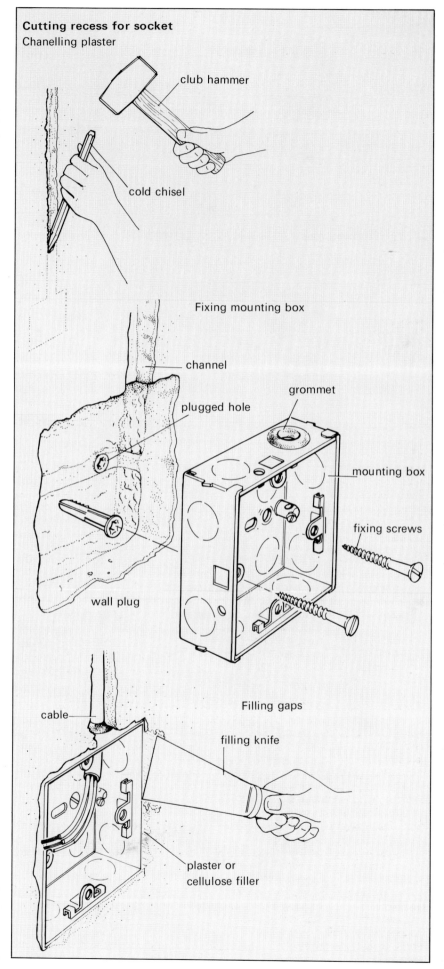

Cutting recess for socket
Chanelling plaster

club hammer

cold chisel

Fixing mounting box

channel

grommet

plugged hole

mounting box

wall plug

fixing screws

cable

Filling gaps

filling knife

plaster or cellulose filler

Plastic or cast iron guttering comes in three shapes
1 Half-round, to rest in brackets fixed to fascia board, rafters or brickwork
2 Square, fixed as above
3 Ogee, to be screwed direct to fascia, or rest on brackets as shown here

Repairing gutters

Defective rainwater systems cause all sorts of damp problems in the house structure. Water constantly pouring down an outside wall will eventually penetrate inside, ruining the decoration and causing mould growth. So it is important to keep your guttering in good repair. If you are prompted now to check your guttering for the first time, you may have a fair amount of work on hand to get it into shape. But once the repair work has been done, maintenance is a simple yearly task.

If you need an extra incentive to start immediately, remember if you allow things to deteriorate you may have to call in a professional to repair the guttering or even to replace the complete system and this would prove expensive. The best time to check the gutters is in the late autumn, once all the leaves have fallen. If you have already noticed leaks or damp patches, make the job a priority.

Working at height is not to everyone's liking. Use a secure ladder or make the job easier with a scaffolding system (available from hire shops). When working on metal gutters, wear an old pair of gloves to guard against cuts from sharp edges.

Types of gutter
In the past cast iron was the most common material for guttering, but plastic is now widely used. Today you cannot easily obtain a complete cast iron system, although you can buy replacement parts. Cast iron guttering comes in three shapes: half-round, square and ogee (a cross between half-round and square section). Half-round and square types rest in brackets fixed to the fascia board, rafters or brickwork. Ogee section can either be screwed direct to the fascia or be supported on brackets. The joints are sealed together with red lead, putty or other suitable jointing mastic and secured with bolts.

Plastic rainwater systems have a distinct advantage over cast iron ones since plastic is light, durable and needs little or no decoration. Plastic guttering is made in half-round, ogee and square sections which fit into special brackets. The lengths are joined together with clips housing rubber seals, or gaskets, to make them waterproof; a jointing cement is sometimes used instead of, or in addition to, the gasket.

Gutter blockages
Scoop out the rubbish with a trowel or a piece of card shaped to the profile of the gutter. Don't use the downpipe as a rubbish chute as it may become blocked or the rubbish sink into the drain.

Flush out the gutter with water; it should flow steadily towards the downpipe. If it overflows at the entrance then the downpipe is blocked and needs to be cleared.

If the downpipe gets blocked tie a small bundle of rags to the end of a pole and use this as a plunger to push away any obstruction. Place a bowl at the outlet on the ground to prevent rubbish sinking into the drain. If there is a 'swan neck' between the gutter and the downpipe, use a length of stiff wire to clear it of debris. To prevent further blockages, fit a cage into the entrance of the downpipe. You

---

Basic items
drill, hammer and screwdriver

For clearing blockages
trowel or piece of card
pole or stiff wire, rags and bowl
wire or plastic netting (to prevent blockages)

For realigning
string line, spirit level (if used)
nails 150mm (6in) long
No 8 chrome-plated round head screws 37mm (1½in) long
wall plugs

For treating rust
wire brush or electric drill with wire cup brush
rust killer, rust-resistant primer

aluminium bridge, non-hardening mastic, fine glasspaper

For repairing joints
epoxy repair material
medium glasspaper
mastic sealer or replacement gasket

For replacing a section
nails (to locate bolt holes)
rust killer
penetrating oil or hacksaw (to remove bolts)
old chisel (to scrape off)
metal putty
rust-resistant primer
aluminium primer (over bituminous coatings)
undercoat and top coat paint

equipment

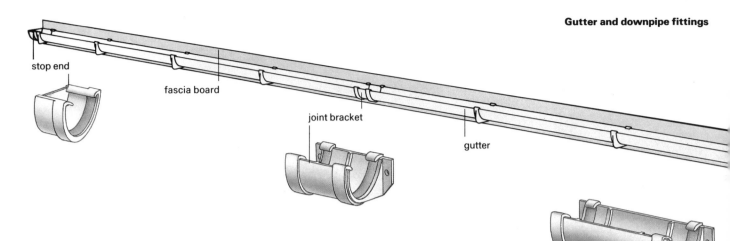

stop end

fascia board

joint bracket

gutter

running outlet

112° bend

Below Three bracket types: rafter top, rafter side, fascia
Bottom If necessary, remove roof tiles to gain access to rafter top brackets. Wedge up tiles in row above that concealing bracket. Raise each tile to release holding nibs from roof battens and lift out tile. If roofing felt is nailed to rafter top bracket, break off old bracket and fit rafter side bracket

can easily make one of these by rolling a piece of wire or plastic netting into a ball the same size as the downpipe.

Realigning sagging gutters

Gutters are normally fixed on a slight slope, from 5–25mm in 3m ($\frac{1}{4}$–1in in 10ft), to ensure a good flow of water to the downpipe. If pools of water collect in the gutter then it is sagging and needs to be realigned by replacing the fixing screws and re-fitting the brackets.

Fix a string line along the top of the gutter to mark the required slope. Drive a couple of strong

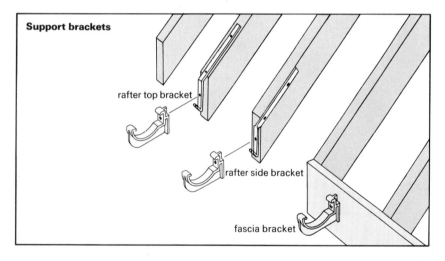

Support brackets

rafter top bracket

rafter side bracket

fascia bracket

nails into the fascia about 25mm (1in) below the gutter for support while it is being refitted. Take out the old fixing screws (if these are in the edges of the rafters you may have to remove a tile from the roof to gain access to them). Now release the brackets so the gutter rests on the support nails; tap wall plugs into the old screw holes and refix the brackets using new screws. Pack the gutter up to the required height with bits of timber placed between it and the support nails. Finally remove nails and string line.

Rust and cracks

Inspect metal systems for any signs of rust and clean back with a wire brush or, if you have an extension lead, with an electric drill fitted with a wire cup brush – this saves a lot of hard work. Now treat the cleaned areas with a rust killer.

Fill hairline cracks with two coats of rust-resistant primer. Fill definite cracks or holes with an aluminium bridge fixed in place with non-hardening mastic. Rub down with fine glasspaper.

Corrosion is always worst at the back edge of the gutter and to repair this you will have to dismantle the system and treat each section separately.

Leaking joints

Seal leaking joints in metal gutters with an epoxy repair material and rub down. If a leak develops at the joints of a plastic system, release the affected section by squeezing it at one end and lifting it clear of the adjoining length. If the gasket in the joint is sound, simply replace the section making sure the spigot end butts tightly against the socket of the adjoining piece. If the gasket is worn, scrape away all the old material and insert a replacement gasket or apply three good strips of mastic sealer in its place. Then press the two sections together again.

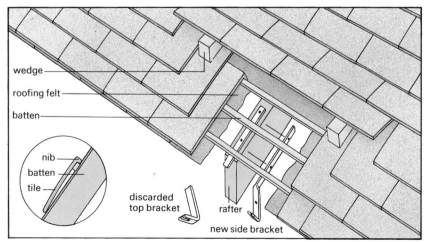

wedge

roofing felt

batten

nib

batten

tile

discarded top bracket

rafter

new side bracket

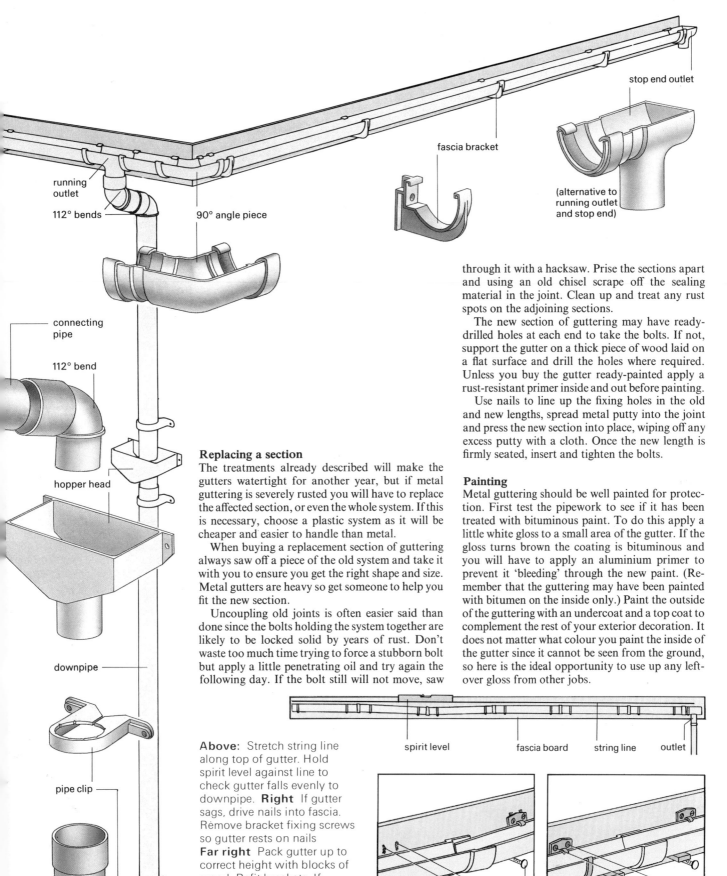

running outlet

112° bends

90° angle piece

fascia bracket

stop end outlet

(alternative to running outlet and stop end)

connecting pipe

112° bend

hopper head

downpipe

pipe clip

shoe

spirit level

fascia board

string line

outlet

wall plugs

support nails

packing

bracket fixing screws

Replacing a section

The treatments already described will make the gutters watertight for another year, but if metal guttering is severely rusted you will have to replace the affected section, or even the whole system. If this is necessary, choose a plastic system as it will be cheaper and easier to handle than metal.

When buying a replacement section of guttering always saw off a piece of the old system and take it with you to ensure you get the right shape and size. Metal gutters are heavy so get someone to help you fit the new section.

Uncoupling old joints is often easier said than done since the bolts holding the system together are likely to be locked solid by years of rust. Don't waste too much time trying to force a stubborn bolt but apply a little penetrating oil and try again the following day. If the bolt still will not move, saw through it with a hacksaw. Prise the sections apart and using an old chisel scrape off the sealing material in the joint. Clean up and treat any rust spots on the adjoining sections.

The new section of guttering may have ready-drilled holes at each end to take the bolts. If not, support the gutter on a thick piece of wood laid on a flat surface and drill the holes where required. Unless you buy the gutter ready-painted apply a rust-resistant primer inside and out before painting.

Use nails to line up the fixing holes in the old and new lengths, spread metal putty into the joint and press the new section into place, wiping off any excess putty with a cloth. Once the new length is firmly seated, insert and tighten the bolts.

Painting

Metal guttering should be well painted for protection. First test the pipework to see if it has been treated with bituminous paint. To do this apply a little white gloss to a small area of the gutter. If the gloss turns brown the coating is bituminous and you will have to apply an aluminium primer to prevent it 'bleeding' through the new paint. (Remember that the guttering may have been painted with bitumen on the inside only.) Paint the outside of the guttering with an undercoat and a top coat to complement the rest of your exterior decoration. It does not matter what colour you paint the inside of the gutter since it cannot be seen from the ground, so here is the ideal opportunity to use up any left-over gloss from other jobs.

Above: Stretch string line along top of gutter. Hold spirit level against line to check gutter falls evenly to downpipe. **Right** If gutter sags, drive nails into fascia. Remove bracket fixing screws so gutter rests on nails
Far right Pack gutter up to correct height with blocks of wood. Refit brackets. If bracket screw holes are not accessible with gutter in place, follow procedure as for replacing section

Rehanging internal doors

The way a door opens can play an important part in a successful room layout and often builders fail to pay enough attention to this fact when the doors are originally positioned. You may, for example, decide you want a door to open out of a room rather than into it – or that it is more convenient to have the door opening from left to right and not the other way round. There are also occasions when you may have to adjust the position of the door frame, particularly if you are insulating the walls of a room with boards or panels fixed to battens. Rehanging a door or repositioning it is not a difficult job – and one you can do yourself.

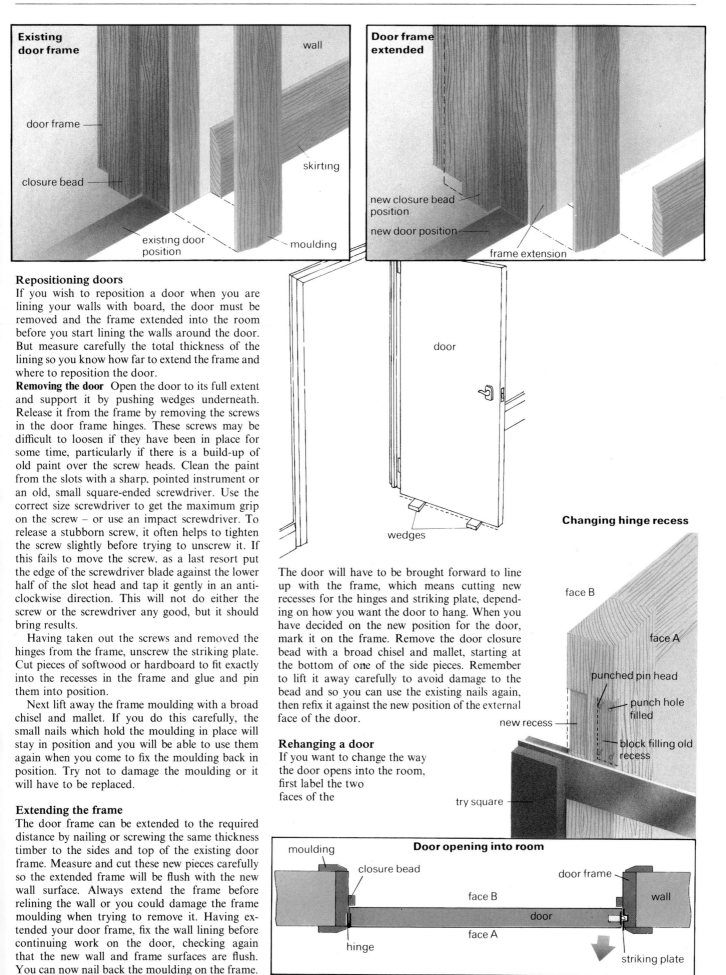

Repositioning doors
If you wish to reposition a door when you are lining your walls with board, the door must be removed and the frame extended into the room before you start lining the walls around the door. But measure carefully the total thickness of the lining so you know how far to extend the frame and where to reposition the door.

Removing the door Open the door to its full extent and support it by pushing wedges underneath. Release it from the frame by removing the screws in the door frame hinges. These screws may be difficult to loosen if they have been in place for some time, particularly if there is a build-up of old paint over the screw heads. Clean the paint from the slots with a sharp, pointed instrument or an old, small square-ended screwdriver. Use the correct size screwdriver to get the maximum grip on the screw – or use an impact screwdriver. To release a stubborn screw, it often helps to tighten the screw slightly before trying to unscrew it. If this fails to move the screw, as a last resort put the edge of the screwdriver blade against the lower half of the slot head and tap it gently in an anti-clockwise direction. This will not do either the screw or the screwdriver any good, but it should bring results.

Having taken out the screws and removed the hinges from the frame, unscrew the striking plate. Cut pieces of softwood or hardboard to fit exactly into the recesses in the frame and glue and pin them into position.

Next lift away the frame moulding with a broad chisel and mallet. If you do this carefully, the small nails which hold the moulding in place will stay in position and you will be able to use them again when you come to fix the moulding back in position. Try not to damage the moulding or it will have to be replaced.

Extending the frame
The door frame can be extended to the required distance by nailing or screwing the same thickness timber to the sides and top of the existing door frame. Measure and cut these new pieces carefully so the extended frame will be flush with the new wall surface. Always extend the frame before relining the wall or you could damage the frame moulding when trying to remove it. Having extended your door frame, fix the wall lining before continuing work on the door, checking again that the new wall and frame surfaces are flush. You can now nail back the moulding on the frame.

The door will have to be brought forward to line up with the frame, which means cutting new recesses for the hinges and striking plate, depending on how you want the door to hang. When you have decided on the new position for the door, mark it on the frame. Remove the door closure bead with a broad chisel and mallet, starting at the bottom of one of the side pieces. Remember to lift it away carefully to avoid damage to the bead and so you can use the existing nails again, then refix it against the new position of the external face of the door.

Rehanging a door
If you want to change the way the door opens into the room, first label the two faces of the

door A and B. A will be the face of the existing door on the room side and B the external face.

Changing sides If you are moving the hinges so the door still opens into the room but from the opposite side of the frame, you must patch the old hinge recesses on the door. If your door has a natural finish which you want to keep, you will have to match up the wood carefully. If you are going to paint over the door, any softwood will do.

Cut the filling pieces slightly larger than the recesses and glue and pin them firmly into place, driving the pin heads below the surface with a nail punch. Fill the punch holes with cellulose filler or matching plastic wood, depending on whether you are painting the door or leaving a natural finish. For a really flush surface, plane down the filled edge and face A of the door and rub smooth with medium glasspaper.

With a try square and pencil continue the top and bottom lines of the old hinge positions across the edge of the door and mark out the new hinge positions from the B side of the door, then cut out the recesses with a sharp chisel and mallet. Unscrew the striking plate from the door frame; this must be placed on the opposite side later.

Fill the plate recess in the frame with softwood or hardboard in the same way as before if the frame is to be painted; match the wood carefully if you want to keep a natural finish. Complete the patching up by filling the hinge recesses on the other side of the frame. Then screw the hinges into the new recesses in the edge of the door.

Turn the door round so the side B faces into the room. Push it tightly into the frame, using the wedges to raise the door to its original clearance height above the ground. Mark the top and bottom positions of the new hinges onto the door frame and then take away the door from the frame. Cut out these recesses and screw in the unattached leaves.

You will now have to reverse the spring-loaded door catch, since this will be facing the wrong way to engage the striking plate. (If the door has a ball catch, there is no need to transpose its position.) Remove the door handles and cover plates from either side, pull out the connecting rod and remove the catch assembly fixing screws. Using a screwdriver ease out the catch assembly housing, replace it upside down and screw back all the fittings.

To find the correct position for the striking plate, dab paint on the catch and push the door closed. The paint mark left on the door frame will indicate the area for the striking plate. Position the plate to fit correctly over this mark and trace the outline of the plate on the frame. Chisel out the recess to the required depth and screw the striking plate into position.

Changing direction After removing the door, lift the closure bead away from the frame and patch the existing hinge recesses, cutting new ones on the same edge of the door but flush to the B face, as described before. Patch up the hinge and striking plate recesses on the frame in the same way. Reverse the catch assembly housing as before, cut out new recesses for the hinges on the outer side of the frame and also a new striking plate cavity. Tack back the door closure bead close to the A face of the door on the room side. If the door closure bead is formed as a solid recess, as it is in some older properties, you will have to cut about 13mm ($\frac{1}{2}$in) from each side of the door with

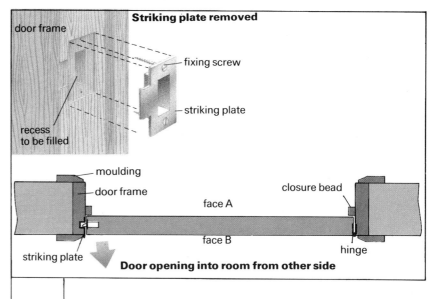

Striking plate removed

door frame — fixing screw — striking plate — recess to be filled

moulding — door frame — face A — face B — closure bead — hinge — striking plate

Door opening into room from other side

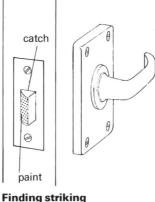

catch — paint

Finding striking plate position

a panel saw and tack on a new closure bead.

Changing sides and direction Remove the door closure bead, door and striking plate, leaving the hinges on the door and patch up the recesses on the frame. Reverse the door so face A is on the outside, mark and cut out new hinge and striking plate recesses on the door frame and screw the striking plate into its new position. Fix the door in place and tack the closure bead down close to face B of the door, now on the room side.

Warning Whenever you reposition and hang a door, to fix the hinges always insert the centre screw only into each hinge and check the door opens and closes properly before inserting the remaining screws. This saves a lot of time and trouble drilling unnecessary holes in the door frame. If the screws do not tighten, plug the holes and insert the screws again.

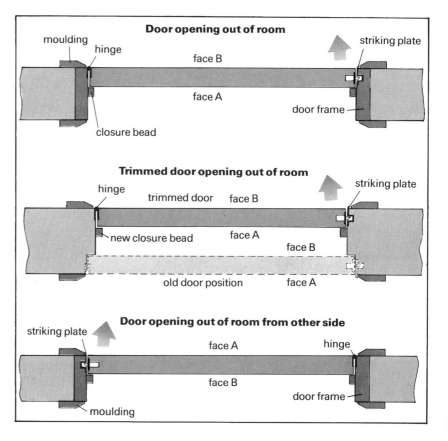

Door opening out of room

moulding — hinge — face B — face A — closure bead — striking plate — door frame

Trimmed door opening out of room

hinge — trimmed door — face B — new closure bead — face A — face B — striking plate — old door position — face A

Door opening out of room from other side

striking plate — face A — face B — hinge — moulding — door frame

Boxing in pipes

Plumbing means pipes, which can be unsightly if left exposed. Boxing them in will tidy up the look of the home.

Whichever method you choose to conceal pipes, the first task is to strip the wall around the pipes so a supporting frame can be securely fixed. Make sure the pipes are in good condition and that the joints are well made. Check compression joints for tightness and, if there is any corrosion, remake the joints. Before boxing in make sure the pipes are fixed securely to the wall with pipe clips. Where pipes come through the floor from a room below, seal the gap between the pipes and the floor with a shaped piece of 12 or 18mm ($\frac{1}{2}$ or $\frac{3}{4}$in) chipboard to reduce the risk of fire spreading. Pipes on an outside wall should be insulated with a glass fibre blanket or with shaped foam secured with tape.

Making the box

Using plugs and screws fix 25×19mm ($1 \times \frac{3}{4}$in) timber battens vertically to the wall on each side of the pipes; check with a plumb line to ensure accurate positioning. Where the pipes are on an open wall, glue and screw or pin 12mm ($\frac{1}{2}$in) thick plywood or chipboard to the sides of the battens (the width of the timber side pieces depends on the depth required for the box). Where the pipes are in a corner you will need only one side piece and, if the pipes protrude less than 50mm (2in) from the wall, you may not need side pieces at all. In this case use 25mm (1in) battens, wide enough to clear the pipes, as side pieces.

Front panel Cover the pipes with 3 or 5mm ($\frac{1}{8}$ or $\frac{3}{16}$in) hardboard or plywood; if you want a more solid panel, use 12mm ($\frac{1}{2}$in) chipboard. Don't glue the front panels in place because you must have access to the pipes in case of leaks. Fix hardboard or plywood with panel or hardboard pins and

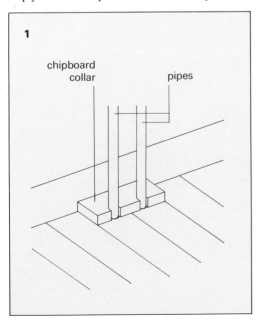

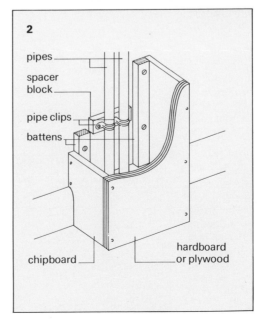

Above You can conceal awkward fittings such as this by building an L-shaped frame; simply follow the principles for boxing in straight runs of pipe
1 If pipes come through the floor from the room below, fit a piece of chipboard round them to seal the gap in the floorboards
2 Boxing in pipes on an open wall: shape the sides of the box so they fit neatly over the skirting

secure chipboard with countersunk screws. You will achieve a better finish if you cut your front panel slightly oversize and trim it back with a plane once it is fixed in position.

Use a cellulose filler to fill any cracks and countersunk screw heads, except where these provide access. Give the box a coat of primer before decorating as required. When decorating, make sure you do not cover the join or your decorations will be spoiled when you need to remove the box.

Stopcocks and draincocks Where there are stopcocks or draincocks in the pipe runs you must cut holes in the front panel to allow the handles to protrude, unless you fit access covers in the boxes. Alternatively construct a box which can be easily removed. Make up a hardboard box of the required size, using 25mm (1in) square battens at the front corners to give it form. On the inside face of the front panel glue 19mm ($\frac{3}{4}$in) wide battens at approximately 1m (or 3ft) intervals and secure them with panel pins hammered through from the outside. Screw Terry clips of the required size,

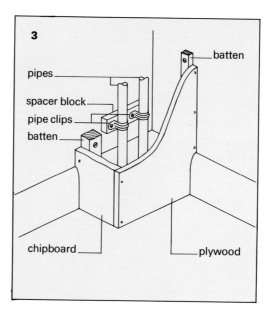

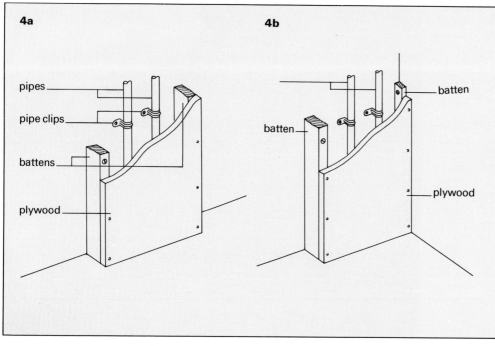

3 Where the pipes are in a corner, you will need only one side piece
4a With small diameter pipes you may be able to use timber battens as side pieces
4b If the pipes are against a corner, you can use a thinner batten on the side wall
5 If you need to gain access to the pipes, make a box which can be easily removed: screw battens to the inside face of the front panel and fix Terry clips to the battens; the clips fit over the pipes and hold the panel in place (**inset**)

according to the pipe dimensions, to the battens; these will snap over the pipes and secure the panel.

Disappearing pipes

Where pipes disappear into a wall, the bottom or top (as applicable) of the box can be finished at an angle. Cut the side pieces and/or battens at 45 degrees, pin a small piece of hardboard or plywood to the sloping part and plane across the front panel until it forms a neat joint.

Alcove pipes

When you wish to conceal pipes in an alcove it is often best to cover the entire wall area with a full width panel; this robs you of little space and does not affect the look of the wall line. Fix timber battens on each side of the pipes, as previously explained. Plug and screw a piece of batten on each side of the alcove level with the front of the battens on each side of the pipes. Use 9mm ($\frac{3}{8}$in) chipboard, fixed with countersunk screws, to conceal the pipes and to provide easy access and nail 9.5mm ($\frac{3}{8}$in) plasterboard either side of the chipboard.

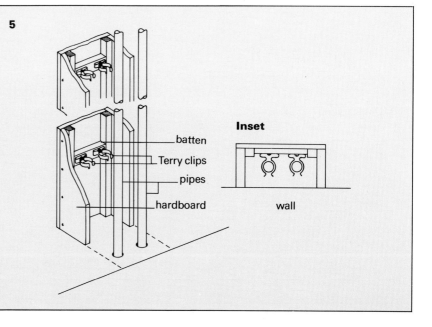

You can use the same method, but with a stronger framework, to conceal cisterns and soil and water pipes.

Skirting board pipes

Nail a 25 × 19mm (1 × ¾in) batten to the floor with its face just in front of the maximum projection of the pipes. Glue and nail a 12mm (½in) facing board to the batten, then glue and nail scotia moulding to the top of the facing board. Finally glue and pin a strip of hardboard or plywood between the moulding and the top of the skirting.

If you want a round edge finish, use a facing board of the same height as the skirting; glue and pin a length of 12mm (½in) board to the top of the facing board and skirting and round the front edge with a plane.

Although a certain amount of time, effort and money is involved, you will be surprised how much neater rooms will look when the pipes have been boxed in. You can paint or wallpaper the covering.

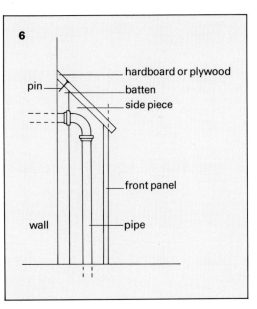

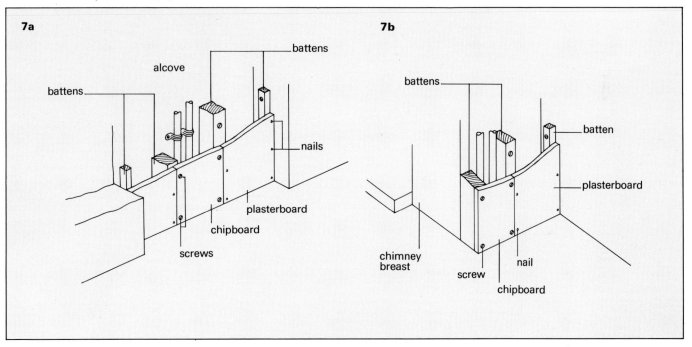

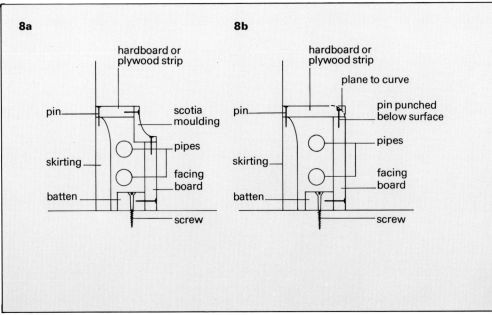

6 Making an angled box to conceal pipes which disappear into a wall: plane the top flush with the front panel for a smooth finish
7a Where the pipes are in an alcove, fit panels across the whole width of the recess to make it look neater
7b If the pipes are beside the chimney-breast, make the box the full depth of the projecting wall and flush with the front edge to avoid awkward corners
8a When concealing pipes running along the skirting, you can give shape to the box by using scotia moulding
8b Alternatively use facing board the same height as the skirting and round off the front edge with a plane

Putting up shelves

Shelves can solve many storage problems in any room in the house and enable you to make use of odd corners and unused space in cupboards and alcoves. Very few tools are needed and the materials are widely available. The methods described here are for permanently fixed shelves, using battens, brackets or angled metal strips.

Shelf loads

The load a shelf can safely carry depends on the thickness of the shelf material, the strength of the supports and the distance between them. If you overload a shelf, it will begin to sag and may eventually loosen the supports. When planning your shelving, take into account the size and weight of the items you want to store and overestimate your needs to allow for future acquisitions. The chart below gives a guide to the maximum span for different shelf materials for medium to heavy loads. If you want to exceed the span given, use intermediate supports. Extra support can be given in a recess by fixing a batten to the back wall.

Recommended maximum distance between supports

Material	Thickness	Maximum span
Blockboard	12mm ($\frac{1}{2}$in)	450mm (1ft 6in)
Chipboard	12mm ($\frac{1}{2}$in)	400mm (1ft 4in)
	18mm ($\frac{3}{4}$in)	600mm (2ft)
	25mm (1in)	750mm (2ft 6in)
Plywood	18mm ($\frac{3}{4}$in)	800mm (2ft 8in)
	25mm (1in)	1000mm (3ft 3in)
Timber	16mm ($\frac{5}{8}$in)	500mm (1ft 8in)
	22mm ($\frac{7}{8}$in)	900mm (3ft)
	28mm ($1\frac{1}{8}$in)	1050mm (3ft 6in)

Shelf material

Natural timber (hardwood or softwood) makes attractive shelves, but you may find the cost prohibitive if you want several shelves. Man-made boards in chipboard, blockboard and plywood are available in a wide range of standard shelf sizes, some of which are wider than the wood normally stocked by timber yards.

Chipboard is popular for shelving since it is light in weight and is available veneered in a wood grain finish or melamine-faced: this is much stronger than unfaced chipboard, which tends to sag under heavy weights.

Shelf supports

Your choice of shelf supports may depend on where you wish to put the shelves. Timber battens and angled metal strips can be used only in recesses since they are fixed to side walls. Metal and timber angle brackets can be used in a recess or on an open wall.

Fixing shelves

The methods of fixing the different types of support vary slightly, but the general principles are the same.

Remember to check, when deciding where to place the shelves, that you will not be drilling into electric cables or water pipes. Cables to socket outlets normally run up from the floor, while those for light switches normally run down from the ceiling; but to be safe, don't drill holes in the wall either vertically above or below these fittings.

Plan the position of the shelves, taking into account the height of objects to be stored and allowing a little extra space above. Also check you will be able to reach the top shelf easily. Lightly mark with a pencil the position of each shelf on the wall. When fixing the shelves in position, use these

1 Timber battens used as shelf supports in recess
2 Angled metal strips used to support shelf in recess

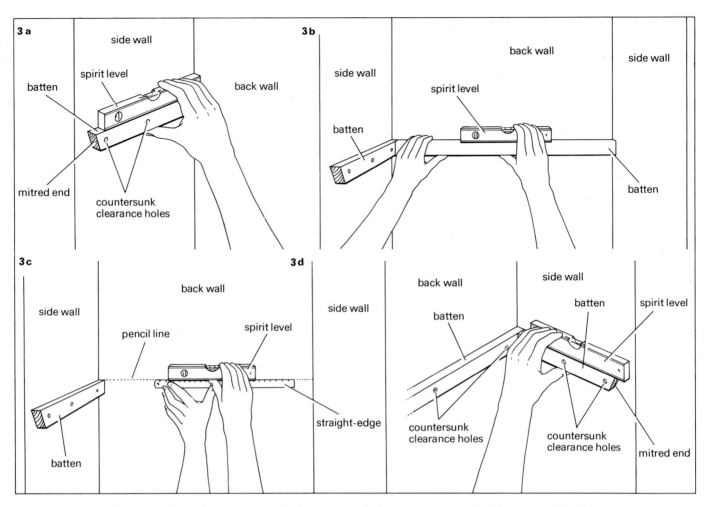

3a batten / side wall / spirit level / back wall / mitred end / countersunk clearance holes

3b side wall / back wall / side wall / spirit level / batten / batten

3c side wall / back wall / pencil line / spirit level / straight-edge / batten

3d back wall / side wall / side wall / batten / batten / spirit level / countersunk clearance holes / countersunk clearance holes / mitred end

marks only as a preliminary guide; always check with a spirit level to ensure they are truly horizontal.

Using battens

This traditional system is probably the simplest of all. A timber batten is screwed to each side wall of a recess and the shelf is laid across. For extra support across a long span, fix a batten to the back wall too.

To make the battens you can use softwood or offcuts of the shelf material, such as chipboard. For a lightweight shelf intended to display a few ornaments, you could use 25 × 12mm (1 × ½in) battens. For large books or heavy kitchen utensils, use 50 × 25mm (2 × 1in) battens. For medium loads, use timber between these two sizes.

Screws Use 50mm (2in) No 6 screws for a lightweight job, 63mm (2½in) No 8 screws for medium weight shelves and 75mm (3in) No 10 for a sturdy assembly.

Fixing method Cut out both side wall support battens a little shorter than the width of the shelf. Drill a countersunk clearance hole 25–50mm (1–2in) from each end of the batten, depending on the length of the batten and mitre or bevel the front edges of the battens so they will be less noticeable.

If using a back batten, cut it to the width of the recess minus the thickness of one of the side battens; cut the thickness of the back batten off the straight end of the other side batten. Drill holes at not more than 300mm (or 12in) intervals.

Position the first side wall batten at the required height. Rest a spirit level on top to check the batten is horizontal and mark with a bradawl or nail the positions of the holes onto the wall. Remove the batten and drill the holes in the wall to the required

depth. Insert wallplugs or cavity wall fixings, depending on the type of wall involved. Place the batten in position again and partly drive in the fixing screws. Check the horizontal again with the spirit level before finally driving the screws home.

If you are using a back batten, line it up so its top edge is level with the top of the side wall batten already fixed. Place the spirit level on top to check the batten is horizontal. Get someone to hold it in place while you mark the screw positions on the wall as before. Drill the holes, insert plugs (or other wall fixings) and drive in the screws, checking again the batten is horizontal.

If a back batten is not being fixed, use a straight-edge and pencil a line across the back wall level with the top edge of the side batten; use a spirit level to check the straight-edge is horizontal. Line up the second side wall batten with the pencil mark, checking the horizontal with the spirit level. Fix the second side wall batten in the same way as the first, making sure its top edge is aligned with the back batten or pencil line.

Position a squarely cut scrap piece of shelving on the battens in both corners of the recess to check the side walls are square. If there is a gap between the end of the shelving and the side walls, you will have to cut the shelf to fit. The back of the shelf may also need shaping and this must be done first. Pin a length of card or stiff paper onto the back wall batten so it fits exactly into each corner. Using a small block of wood and a pencil trace the outline of the back wall onto the template. Cut along this line carefully, tape the template onto your piece of shelving and transfer the outline. Then use two smaller pieces of card and mark on them the out-

3a To fit battens in recess, position first side batten and check horizontal with spirit level. **3b** Position back batten flush with side batten. **3c** If you are not using back batten, place straight-edge level with top of first side batten and mark across back of alcove to other wall; this will give position for second side batten. **3d** Fit second side batten flush with top edge of back batten.

4a Position card on back batten and use block and pencil to trace outline of back wall onto card; transfer outline onto shelving.

4b Following same procedure, make templates for side walls. **4c** Measure diagonally from each corner to proposed front edge of shelf on opposite side wall; use string cut to length of diagonals. **4d** Tape string in position on shelving and place side templates on back template; angle of template is found when front corner coincides with diagonal from opposite corner. **4e** Transfer side wall outline onto shelving to give shelf shape

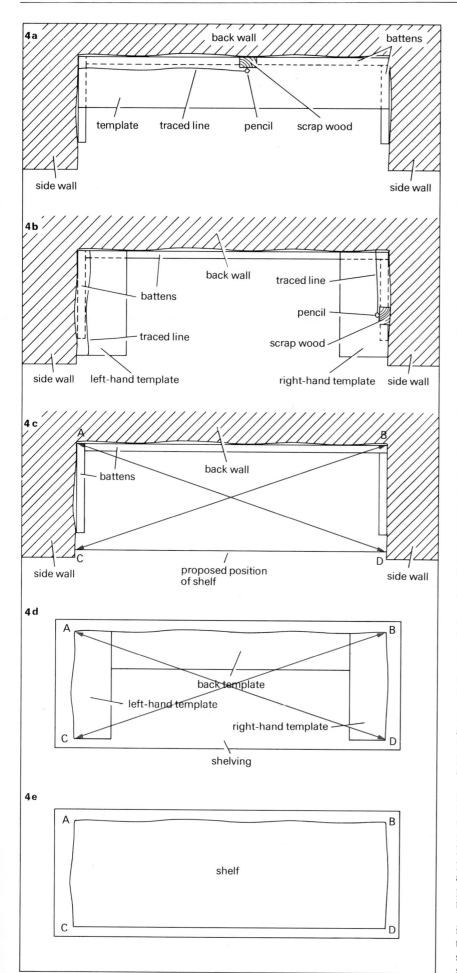

4a back wall · battens · template · traced line · pencil · scrap wood · side wall · side wall

4b back wall · traced line · battens · pencil · traced line · scrap wood · side wall · left-hand template · right-hand template · side wall

4c A · B · battens · back wall · C · D · side wall · proposed position of shelf · side wall

4d A · B · back template · left-hand template · right-hand template · C · D · shelving

4e A · B · shelf · C · D

line of each side wall in turn, following the same procedure. Measure from each corner diagonally across to the proposed front edge of the shelf on the opposite side wall, making a small allowance for the trimmed back edge of the shelf before determining the width of the shelf.

Position each side wall template carefully in turn on your piece of shelving. Starting with the left-hand side wall, place the back left-hand corner of the template to coincide with the left-hand end of the already marked shelf. The angle of the template will be determined when the front left-hand corner of the template coincides with the length of the diagonal from the opposite corner.

Tape the template onto the shelf in this position and transfer the side wall outline onto the shelf. Working from the opposite end, repeat this procedure for the right-hand side wall. This will give you the correct outline for your shelf, which can then be cut to shape. Place the shelf on the battens; it can be loose-laid, screwed or glued and pinned in position.

Using angled metal strips

These serve the same purpose as battens, supporting the shelves against the side walls of an alcove. Screw holes are often provided, so you just need to mark the position of the screws on the wall with a pencil. Place a spirit level on the horizontal part of the strip to check the strip is level. Screw in place as for battens, using a screw size to match the pre-drilled holes and ensuring at least 38mm (1½in) of the screw will be in the wall.

If you wish, you can make a recess in the edge of the shelf so the top of the metal strip will be invisible when the shelf is in position. Place a bracket on the shelf side edge and draw round it with a pencil to mark the cutting lines. Chisel out to the required depth with a paring chisel, grooving plane or electric router. Stop the recess just before the front edge of the shelf, so the bracket will be concealed. Recess the other end of the shelf in the same way, fit the angled strips to the side walls of the alcove and slide the shelf on to them.

Using L-shaped metal angle brackets

These can be bought in various sizes; the arm of the bracket should extend almost to the front edge of the shelf to give full support. Some brackets have one arm longer than the other, in which case you must fix the longer arms to the wall.

To fix the brackets, place a straight-edge in the required position, check with a spirit level and draw a line along the lower edge where you want the shelf to be. Measure and mark off the intervals at which you want to place the brackets, putting the end ones a short distance in from the ends of the shelf.

Fix the two end brackets in place first. Hold the first bracket in place on the wall, checking the horizontal and vertical with a spirit level, and mark the screw positions with a pencil. Screw in place as for battens, using screws to match the pre-drilled holes. Before fixing the second bracket, hold it in position and check it is level with the first by placing a straight-edge on top of the two brackets and putting a spirit level on it. Do the same with intermediate brackets.

When all the brackets are in place, lay the shelf in position and mark the screw positions through the holes in the brackets onto the underside of the shelf. Drill pilot holes to take the screws, replace the shelf on the brackets and screw it in place.

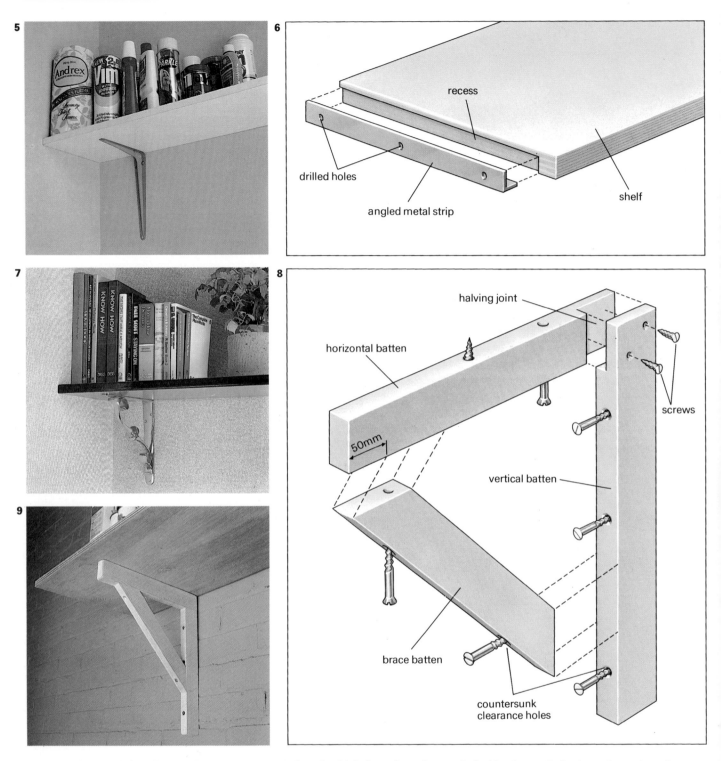

5 *(photograph of shelf with household products supported by L-shaped bracket)*

6
recess
drilled holes
angled metal strip
shelf

7 *(photograph of book shelf supported by decorative L-shaped metal brackets)*

8
halving joint
horizontal batten
50mm
vertical batten
screws
brace batten
countersunk clearance holes

9 *(photograph of timber angle bracket on open wall)*

Using timber angle brackets

Strong, home-made brackets are ideal for a garage or workshop where strength is more important than appearance. The brackets are made by fixing two pieces of wood at right-angles and inserting a brace between them to form a triangle.

Use 25 × 12mm (1 × ½in) softwood for medium loads and 50 × 25mm (2 × 1in) for heavier loads. Cut one length a little shorter than the width of the shelf and another length about 50mm (2in) longer than the first; this will be fixed vertically to the wall. Fit the lengths together at right-angles using a halving joint and glue; screw through the joint. Position another length of wood across the right-angled piece so it forms a triangle, placing it about 50mm (2in) from the end of the horizontal. Mark

where the third piece of wood meets the inside edges of the other two sides of the triangle; mark the two sides and join up these marks across the top and bottom to give you your cutting lines. Cut the brace timber to the exact length, checking the brace fits exactly when you place it inside the right-angle.

Drill three countersunk clearance holes in the vertical batten and two in the horizontal batten; the size of the holes should correspond to the recommended screw sizes. Screw the bracket to the wall and fit the shelf in place, drilling pilot holes for the shelf fixing screws. Finally glue and screw the angled piece in position with countersunk screws.

5 L-shaped metal angle bracket used to support shelf in recess
6 With angled metal strip, you can recess edge of shelf so strip will be invisible when shelf is in position
7 Decorative L-shaped metal angle brackets are available
8 Timber angle bracket; vertical batten should be longer than horizontal one
9 Timber angle bracket on open wall; ideal where strength is more important than appearance

Adjustable shelving systems

You have probably found however much storage space you have, you always fill it. One way to keep up with growing plants, varying book heights, additional equipment and children's changing interests is to install adjustable shelving; this is easy to put up and can just as easily be taken down if you move house. The shelves may be fitted onto brackets which slot into strips or uprights screwed to the wall, so you can move them about and fit additional or wider shelves; alternatively there are free-standing units with adjustable shelves.

Before buying a shelving system decide where you want to put it, what items you need to store and how much flexibility you want; for example, some systems have a variety of special-purpose brackets so you can use a shelf as a desk or work top. Check the length of the brackets available, since some manufacturers do not make brackets for very wide shelves. Some systems have matching shelves you can buy or you can use shelves of your choice.

Wall shelving

Adjustable shelving systems are available in a variety of materials and finishes so you should be able to find one which will fit in with its surroundings. Hardened aluminium is commonly used for uprights and brackets and often for shelves as well; systems manufactured from this material are available in a silver satin finish or a matt anodized finish in gold, silver or black. Units are also made in painted steel. One system, which can be used for commercial or domestic purposes, has matching steel shelves but can also be used with wood or glass shelves. For a living room you may want a wood unit and you can buy teak uprights and brackets with matching teak finished shelves.

Uprights There are two main types of metal upright: those with slots into which the brackets are fitted and those with a continuous channel into which the shelves are slid and clicked or locked into place at the required position. Brackets of the slotted type can be moved at 25mm (1in) intervals; the sliding type is easier to adjust, but more care is needed in lining up the brackets to ensure the shelves are straight. It is easier to fix the sliding-type uprights to the wall since there are no slots to be lined up; with the slotted type you need to line up the slots exactly or the shelves will not be level. Wood uprights have threaded holes into which the brackets are screwed.

Some shelving systems have uprights which will hold hardboard panels, hessian or cork-covered boards or mirrors. For walls which are uneven, there are uprights which hold 3mm (or ⅛in) hardboard panels at a slight distance from the wall.

Uprights are available in two or more lengths, the exact dimensions varying with the make of the system; some are in Imperial and some in metric

measure, but most manufacturers supply supports in the region of 500 and 1000mm (or 20 and 39in). You can butt two lengths together or cut them if necessary for in-between sizes.

Wiring and lighting One system has built-in facilities for an adjustable spotlight, which can be fitted at any height on the upright. Cables for lights or hi-fi equipment can be run inside the uprights and hidden with a cover strip. A switch is available which can be fitted on an upright for connection to a lamp or other appliance.

Brackets These come in 150–600mm (or 6–24in) sizes to fit standard shelf widths, although not all manufacturers make the larger sizes. You should allow for the shelf to overlap the bracket slightly unless the bracket has a lipped edge, in which case it should fit exactly. Wood brackets have rubber grip pads to hold the shelving, while the other type are screw-fixed or have a hooked edge which fits into a groove in the shelf or a lipped end which holds the edge of the shelf. Some systems have special brackets to hold glass shelves.

Some manufacturers make brackets for taking coat hangers for use in a cupboard or alcove wardrobe. To house items which might roll off a

1 Types of upright used in adjustable shelving systems: (**from left**) wood with bookend and screw-in bracket, matt silver and matt black continuous metal channel
2 These brackets, for use with continuous metal channel uprights, come in a range of finishes

3 Metal shelving system used for simple dining room display
4 Metal shelving system used to house hi-fi equipment
5 Metal shelving system used as work area
6 Metal shelving system used for storage in bathroom
7 Metal shelving system used to take range of kitchen items
8 Free-standing metal shelving system used for central display
9 Metal shelving system with cork panels used for general storage in living room
10 Teak shelving system offering natural finish

straight slope, you can use a shelf supported by brackets which slope slightly towards the wall. This type of bracket is also useful for a worktop shelf since it will not tilt downwards when pressure is put on the front edge of the shelf. Brackets which slope away from the wall can be used for shelves on which magazines can be displayed or used to hold a child's desk or a drawing board; you will, however, need to add raised lipping to the shelf to stop items sliding off and to provide a ledge for pens and pencils. Brackets for fixing pelmets and canopies are also available; these are particularly useful if you want to install concealed strip lighting.

End-pieces For a shelf on an open wall you can fit an end-piece to hold books in place. One system has an end-piece which screws into the shelf to serve as a bracket as well. Some systems include metal shelves and trays with end supports; although intended mainly for commercial use, these could be useful in a kitchen or workshop.

Loads The load a shelf can take depends on the strength of the support and the distance between the supports. Most systems allow for normal domestic loads, but it is advisable to follow the manufacturer's recommendations.

Fixing wall shelving

When fixing the uprights make sure they are vertical and parallel to each other and with slotted supports ensure the slots are correctly lined up; check with a straight-edge and a spirit level. Follow the manufacturer's instructions for spacing between supports, which will be dictated by the load the shelves will carry, and check whether you need to buy

screws; some manufacturers supply screws while others just specify the size of screw required.

Draw a pencil line where the top fixing hole of each upright is to be placed, using a straight-edge and a spirit level to make sure it is horizontal. Make a cross on the line where the top screw of each support is to be placed, making sure the supports are the required distance apart. At each marked point drill a hole of the correct diameter for the wall fixings you are using and insert the fixings. Fix each support at the top with a screw, leaving the screw slightly slack at this stage. Use a plumb line to check the first upright is vertical and mark the positions of the remaining screws. Swivel the support aside while you drill and plug the fixing holes; fix the bottom screw, followed by the intermediate ones, and finally tighten the top screw. Fix the remaining uprights in the same way, checking they are parallel to each other by using a batten cut to the exact distance between the supports.

Place the brackets in position according to the manufacturer's instructions, checking they are level by using a straight-edge and a spirit level. Place the shelves in position and screw them in place or cut grooves as required.

Free-standing shelving

This type of unit provides a storage system which does not need to be fixed to the wall and can be used, if you wish, as a room divider. There is a variety of makes available and you should follow the manufacturer's instructions for assembly. One

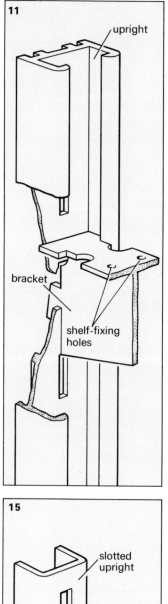

11
upright
bracket
shelf-fixing holes

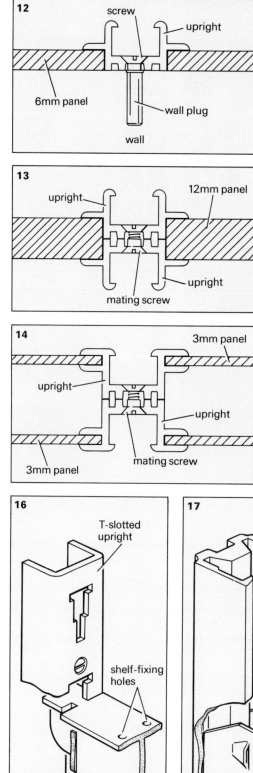

12
screw
upright
6mm panel
wall plug
wall

13
upright
12mm panel
upright
mating screw

14
3mm panel
upright
upright
mating screw
3mm panel

type, which is made of plastic-coated steel, is strong and durable and would be useful in a kitchen or workshop. It has angled uprights from 914 to 2440mm (3–8ft) high and shelves of 864 × 229–610mm (34 × 9–24in). The shelves are adjustable to 50mm (2in) intervals, but changing their position is not as easy as with other systems because the shelves are bolted in place. To assemble the unit, lay two of the angled uprights flat on the ground and loosely bolt the shelves vertically in the required positions. Place the remaining two uprights along the front of the shelves and bolt them loosely in place. Then stand the unit upright, check it is square and tighten all the nuts and bolts.

Stud supports An inexpensive method of providing support for shelves in a free-standing adjustable unit is to use studs screwed into bushes. To take the shelf bush, drill a 10mm (or $\frac{3}{8}$in) diameter hole in the upright to a depth of 10mm (or $\frac{3}{8}$in). Press a bush into the hole and insert the shelf stud; the stud clips into the bush for fast holding. Fit two parallel rows of bushes on the uprights at each side and place studs into the required bushes.

11 Section through continuous metal channel upright. **12** Plan of continuous metal channel with panels, fixed to wall. **13** Plan of free-standing metal channel — with panels — joined with mating screw. **14** Plan of free-standing metal channel with panels, used as room divider. **15** Section through slotted metal upright. **16** Section through T-slotted metal upright. **17** Section through continuous metal channel with squeeze and slide bracket. **18** Section through wood upright and screw-in bracket. **19** Wood upright with bookend

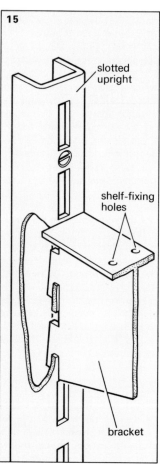

15
slotted upright
shelf-fixing holes
bracket

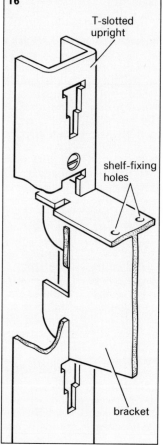

16
T-slotted upright
shelf-fixing holes
bracket

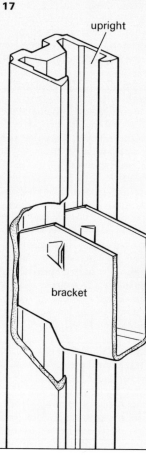

17
upright
bracket

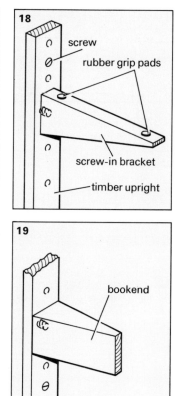

18
screw
rubber grip pads
screw-in bracket
timber upright

19
bookend
timber upright

Keeping the home warm

One of the greatest money-wasters is heat loss, caused by poor insulation and ill-fitting doors and windows. This section describes the way in which you can solve these problems and cut down on your heating bills. Check with the heat-loss guide to see where your money is going and follow the steps necessary to keep the warmth where it belongs – inside. Preventitive measures including double glazing and insulating the loft are both tasks you can do yourself. Broken windows should be replaced as soon as possible. Condensation can lead to the greater problem of damp; advice is given on how to eliminate it.

Replacing glass in windows

If you break a window and cannot get replacement glass immediately, as a temporary measure fix a sheet of polythene to the inside of the window.

With a wood frame either fix the polythene with adhesive tape or, for a stronger fixing, secure the top of the polythene to the window with drawing pins, nail a batten along the top and then secure each side and bottom edge with battens (**see 1**). Stretch the polythene to smooth out wrinkles as you work. Use heavy duty polythene secured with strong adhesive tape for a metal frame.

Wood frames

Clear up the glass left on the ground and remove the fragments in the frame. These should pull away easily; you may have to remove the holding material.

Take out the glass from the top of the frame, then work down the sides and along the bottom edge. To remove stubborn pieces run a glass-cutter round the perimeter of the glass and close to the rebates (**see 2**). Tap out the pieces with the handle of a light hammer, holding each piece until it is free.

If the holding material is putty chop away with a hacking knife or old chisel (**see 3**). This will reveal a series of small headless nails (sprigs) which do the real job of holding the glass. Carefully remove the sprigs with pincers (**see 4**). If they are still straight, you can re-use them; if not, buy new ones 16mm ($\frac{5}{8}$in) long.

Sometimes the glass will have been secured by wood beading fixed with panel pins. Prise away the beading and remove the pins (**see 5**). Take care when removing since the beading will have mitred

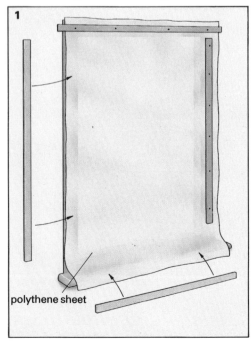

polythene sheet

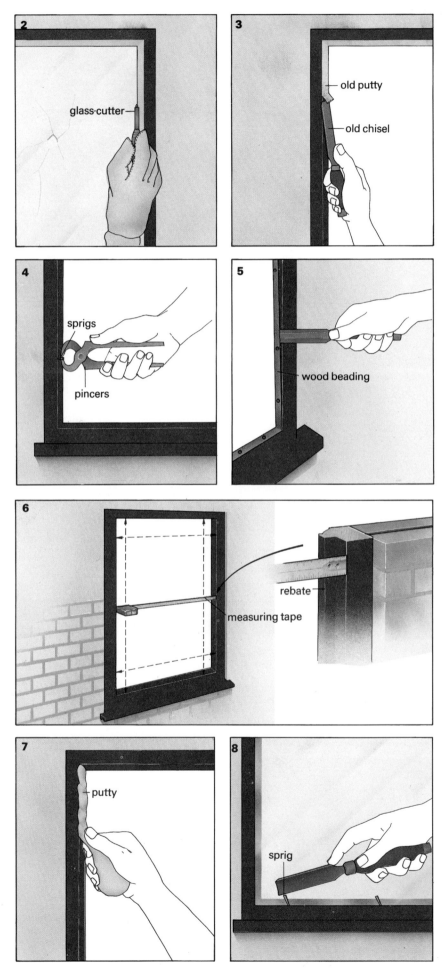

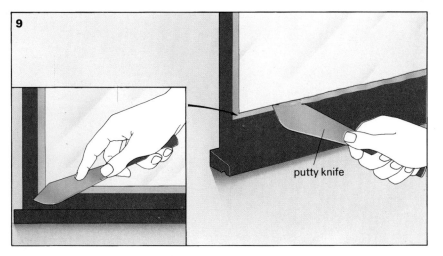

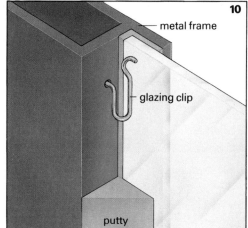

1 Make a temporary repair to a broken window by covering it with polythene sheet
2 Use a glass-cutter close to the rebates to remove every piece of glass from the frame
3 Hack out all the old putty from the rebates
4 Remove the holding sprigs with pincers
5 If wood beading holds the glass in place, prise it away with old chisel
6 To find the dimensions for the new glass always take three measurements across the width and over the length of the frame to ensure accuracy
7 Press soft putty in a continuous layer round the rebates
8 Refit the sprigs, tapping them in flush with the glass
9 Smooth out the final layer of putty shaping it to form mitres at the corners
10 When fitting glass in a metal frame use glazing clips and metal casement putty

ends to form neat corner joints and if you damage these you will have to buy more beading and shape the mitres yourself.

Brush out all the dust from the rebates and rub the timber smooth with medium coarse glasspaper. Apply a coat of wood primer and leave to dry.

Measuring up
Accurate measuring for the new sheet of glass is vital. Measure the full width of the opening between the side rebates at the top, centre and bottom of the frame (**see 6**). These should be the same, but if there is a slight difference work on the smallest measurement. Next measure between the other two rebates, top to bottom, again if necessary noting the smallest measurements. Deduct 3mm ($\frac{1}{8}$in) from these dimensions (this is to allow for the glass expanding and contracting in the frame). These are the dimensions to use when ordering your glass.

If your window frame is badly out of square or an awkward shape, such as curved, make a template (pattern) of the frame from card or stiff paper so the glass can be cut to the exact size.

For normal domestic use you will need 3mm ($\frac{1}{8}$in) sheet glass. Take some old newspapers to wrap round the glass or wear gloves to protect your hands from the edges when carrying it.

Fitting the glass
Hold the new glass up to the frame to check it is the right size. Knead some linseed oil putty into a ball in your hands to make it soft and pliable and if necessary add a little linseed oil to make the putty more workable. (Putty has an irritating habit of clinging to dry surfaces when you do not want it to, so keep both hands and the putty knife wet.)

Run a continuous layer of putty about 3mm ($\frac{1}{8}$in) thick round the rebates and press well in with your thumb (**see 7**). Carefully lift the glass into position, allowing for the 3mm expansion gap, and press it into the layer of putty pushing only on the edge of the glass, never in the middle.

Refit the sprigs, spacing them at intervals of about 150mm (6in) around the glass. They must be flat against the glass to hold it securely, so tap them in carefully. The flat edge of a wide chisel could be used for this (**see 8**). Run another layer of putty around the front of the glass, pressing it in with your thumb. With a putty knife smooth out the layer, shaping it to match the angle on your other windows, and form mitres at the corners (**see 9**). Use the edge of the knife to trim off surplus putty from the glass.

Run over the putty with a paint brush dampened with water to make sure it adheres firmly to the glass to give a tight, water-resistant seal. Leave the putty for one to two weeks to dry out before painting or the paint surface will crack.

Metal frames
To fit a new pane of glass into a metal frame adopt basically the same method as for a wood one except you must use metal casement putty, since linseed oil putty is not suitable for metal. The glass is held in place by special glazing clips rather than sprigs – one arm of the clip slots into a hole in the rebate, while the other arm of the clip clamps onto the face of the glass (**see 10**).

Hack away the old putty and note the positions of the glazing clips so you will know where to refit them. Remove the clips from the frame (if you do this carefully, you will be able to use them again). Brush the rebates clean, apply a coat of metal primer and leave to dry for a few hours.

Spread a layer of putty in the rebates and fit the new pane of glass into the frame on the putty. Replace the clips in their original positions and finish off as for a wood frame.

Basic items
protective spectacles and old leather gloves
glass-cutter, light hammer
hacking knife or old chisel
putty knife, small paint brush
measuring tape
card or stiff paper (for template)

For emergency repair
polythene sheet
adhesive tape or drawing pins
four 25 × 12mm (1 × $\frac{1}{2}$in) battens and
    round wire nails, 25mm (1in) long
    (for wood frames)

For wood frames
pincers
medium coarse glasspaper
wood primer
linseed oil putty
linseed oil (to soften hard putty)

For metal frames
metal primer
metal casement putty

equipment

Coping with condensation

For most people condensation conjures up pictures of bathroom walls running with moisture, windows steamed up and water on the window sills. These more easily recognizable forms of condensation can be temporarily cleared up with a little time and effort devoted to mopping up. But there are ways of helping to prevent condensation forming in the first place.

Condensation is caused when moisture in warm air comes into contact with a cold surface and turns to water. Kitchens and bathrooms are the obvious places to suffer, but condensation will often occur in patches on walls or ceilings in living areas too.

Windows
Single glass windows are undoubtedly one of the worst offenders in causing condensation. In damp winter conditions few homes escape the problem – and bedrooms in particular suffer from its effects. This is the result of lower night temperatures reacting with the warm air we breathe out or warm air circulated by heating equipment.

The problem is made worse by the introduction of new moist air into a room by cooking, using hand basins or running baths. Probably the worst effect of condensation is the damage it can do in a short time to window frames and paintwork. Even when frames are correctly painted 3mm ($\frac{1}{8}$in) in on the glass pane, the lower beading quickly breaks down

Above Condensation on window will break down paint surface and attack wood or metal frame

Far left When lining walls with expanded polstyrene, hang first length and over-lap second length by about 13mm ($\frac{1}{2}$in). Check with your supplier on suitable adhesive
Left Trim halfway across overlap through both thicknesses of polystyrene

Far left Peel away both trimmed edges
Left Stick back edges, having applied more adhesive to wall, to give flush finish to join

To test for damp floor, place piece of glass on ring of plasticine over affected area
Left Moisture on underside of glass indicates penetrating damp
Below left Moisture forming on top of glass indicates condensation present

and allows moisture to attack the timber or metal beneath.

One remedy is the installation of good quality double-glazing. Although condensation may not be completely eliminated, the build-up is reduced sufficiently to prevent moisture being a problem.

Bathrooms

Decorative materials with cold surfaces, such as ceramic tiles, are renowned for the rapid formation of condensation. The build-up can be quickly dispersed by opening the windows. An extractor fan set into the window or mounted on (or ducted to) an exterior wall will also help remove vapour quickly. You can reduce condensation in cold bathrooms by heating the room for a short time before running the bath water. But remember you must use wall or ceiling-mounted heaters of the type recommended for bathrooms. Try running a little cold water into the bath before you turn on the hot tap, as this will also help reduce condensation.

Other wall surfaces

The real problem areas are patches of condensation which sometimes appear in odd corners of the home. Often these go unnoticed until a patch of mould appears. Poor circulation of air is one of the prime causes and on a damp day a short burst of warm air from a fan heater, or a hair dryer, will help to check condensation.

If mould persists – and the surface is not wallpapered – rinse the wall with a strong solution of bleach. If the surface is wallpapered you will have to remove the paper and line the wall with rolls of expanded polystyrene which you can then wallpaper over or paint with emulsion. In severe cases this may not be completely successful and a painted wall, which can be treated with bleach from time to time, is preferable.

Damp walls

Patchy wall condensation is often confused with penetrating damp. Removal of a small area of plaster should tell you which it is. If it is condensation, the brick area behind will be perfectly dry; if it is damp, try to find the cause. At ground floor level it could be a faulty damp proof course; upstairs it may be a faulty gutter or down pipe or driving rain on porous solid brickwork might be the reason. Try to increase the circulation by warm, dry air in the affected area, but remedy the cause of the problem as soon as possible otherwise the trouble will recur.

Ceilings

Those with a high gloss finish are most susceptible to condensation and covering the area with expanded polystyrene, cork or fibre tiles will help solve the problem.

Damp floors

These are often caused by damp from the outside and not by condensation. You can make a simple test to see which condition is present with a piece of glass on a ring of Plasticine, as shown above.

Condensation on floors usually occurs with cold-surfaced materials on concrete, such as tiles in the kitchen. The most effective remedy is to substitute cork or a similar warm-surfaced flooring.

Double glazing

While heat losses vary depending on the nature of a building and its aspect, in a typical uninsulated house about 15 percent of house heat is lost through the windows. If all the windows in such a house are double-glazed, this heat loss will be halved to give a seven and a half percent saving on fuel bills. There are many factors which can affect this figure – for example, the type of system used and how well it is fitted. Installing double glazing in an old cottage with just a few small windows would not obtain this saving, whereas there will be higher savings in a modern 'goldfish bowl' type of property.

Double glazing is not a money saver on the scale of other forms of insulation such as glass fibre laid in the loft or cavity wall infill; however, there are a number of reasons why you will find the necessary expenditure worthwhile to add to the comfort of your home. An efficient system will eliminate cold, draughty areas round windows, making the whole floor area of a room usable on cold days, and rooms will seem larger without the need for occupants to cluster round the fire or radiators.

Preventing condensation
When rooms are properly heated and ventilated, condensation will be reduced and possibly eliminated by double-glazed windows, since the inner panes of glass will be warmer and less susceptible to misting. With some double glazing systems, interpane misting may occur; this is usually slight and can be wiped away provided the new window is hinged or sliding. Alternatively you can place silica gel crystals between the panes of glass; these absorb moisture and, when saturated, should be temporarily removed and dried in a warm oven.

Misting on the room side of the window indicates the temperature of the glass is too low, given the water content of the room's atmosphere; by a process of trial and error, you should carry out adjustment until there is a proper balance between heat and ventilation in the room.

Condensation on the cavity surface of the outer glass is usually a sign that moist air is leaking into the cavity from the room. Make the seal round the new double glazing as airtight as possible, using a

1 Sachets of silica gel crystals placed between the two panes of glass can help reduce interpane misting; when saturated, the sachets should be removed, dried in a warm oven and replaced
2 To cure condensation on the cavity surface of the outer glass, drill ventilation holes right through the primary frame
3 Drill the ventilation holes 10mm deep and pack them with glass fibre to act as a filter

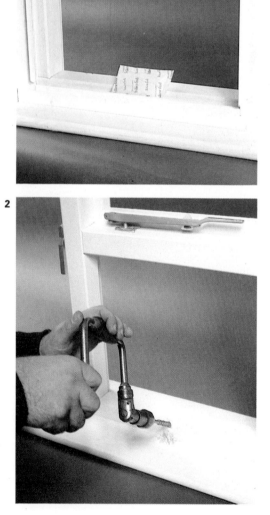

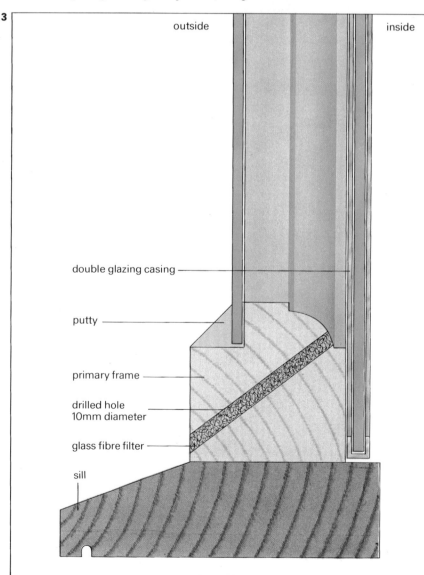

outside   inside

double glazing casing

putty

primary frame

drilled hole
10mm diameter

glass fibre filter

sill

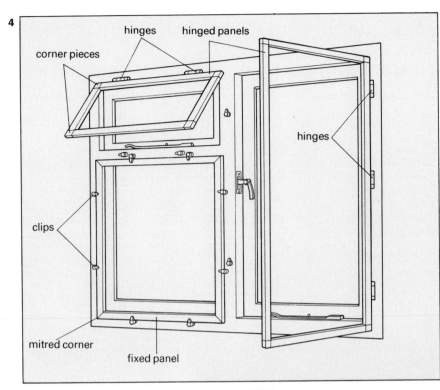

4

corner pieces

hinges   hinged panels

hinges

clips

mitred corner

fixed panel

4 Installing fixed or hinged double glazing. The new panes are fitted in aluminium or plastic U-shaped channel, joined at the corners by mitring or by using special corner pieces; use hinges to fix the panels to opening windows and clips for fixed windows
5 Using plastic film as double glazing; cut the film to size and fix it to the frame with double-sided adhesive tape

5

tape form of draught excluder, and seal any gaps in the joints of a timber framework with a matching wood filler, making sure the filler penetrates through to the full depth of the joint.

If this fails to cure the problem, drill ventilation holes through the primary frame to the drier air outside. In a 1m (39in) wide window, two 10mm (or $\frac{3}{8}$in) diameter holes set 500mm (or 20in) apart should be sufficient. More will be needed for larger windows; you can decide the exact number by a process of trial and error – drilling an extra hole and waiting to see if this cures the problem. Pack the holes with glass fibre to act as an air filter.

With hermetically sealed units (see below) the air in the cavity is dried, so condensation between the panes is not possible as long as the seals remain sound; failure of the seals is a rare occurrence, but reputable manufacturers give long-term guarantees to cover the possibility.

Sound insulation
Installing a good quality double glazing system will give a substantial reduction in the decibel level of noise permeating through windows from typical town traffic or a local playground. However, if your noise problem is more acute, noise prevention is a more extensive technical matter – the actual source of the noise, the location of the house, the type of glass thickness needed, the distance the two panes are set apart and any additional insulation around windows or between the double glazing should all be considered. Professional advice should be sought on other methods of sound insulation.

Remember Government grants to install double glazing can be given to people living in certain heavy traffic areas or where there is an airport nearby. Your local authority will be able to supply details and advice.

In normal noise level situations the two sheets of glass in a double glazing system should be at least 100mm (or 4in) apart to provide adequate sound insulation. To provide effective thermal insulation, the optimum gap should be of 19mm ($\frac{3}{4}$in). If you want both sound and thermal insulation, you should select a wider gap of up to 200mm (or 8in); you will find thermal insulation is not greatly reduced in this case.

Buying double glazing
Certain double glazing firms do not cater for the DIY market, others cater for both professional and DIY work and some solely for the DIY market. If you choose a professional installation, a representative from the company will call on you, discuss your requirements, measure up and arrange for the work to be carried out by company operatives. If you choose to install double glazing yourself, you will find local retail outlets stock at least one kind of kit for the framework. Measure up your requirements and buy the correct size; then read the instructions carefully to find out the thickness of glass required – 3 or 4mm (or $\frac{1}{8}$ or $\frac{1}{6}$ in) – and the height and width of glass. Glass can vary in price, so it is well worth shopping around.

One or two companies offer a mail order service whereby you measure up, send the firm the dimensions and they return a kit – in one case at least the glass also is supplied. At least one company offers the best of both worlds – a company representative will call and measure up and you will then receive a tailor-made kit complete with glass. The advantage of this method of buying double glazing is the company takes responsibility for any errors in measuring and making the framework; also, since you are dealing directly with a company and not through a middle man, this system is often less expensive than other systems.

Costs Depending on the house style and the system chosen, to double glaze all the windows in a house could be a costly business. You could reduce the amount by completing only selected windows – perhaps those in the living room, hall and landing or a particularly draughty bedroom. A little-used dining room or spare bedroom might not be worth the expense; it would probably be better to keep the doors of these rooms closed and well sealed in cold weather to prevent the house heat drifting into them. When they are in use, heavy curtains pulled across would be as effective as double glazing, as long as the windows have been effectively draught-proofed.

Factors which can drastically affect the price of double glazing one window, let alone all the windows in the house, are obviously the cost of the glass and the retail price of the kit you choose, which again can differ from shop to shop.

Types of double glazing

There are four types of double glazing in common use: insulating glass, secondary sashes, coupled windows and plastic film.

Insulating (hermetically sealed) glass These units look like a single pane of glass and consist of two pieces of glass joined together and hermetically sealed in the factory – a process in which the air space between the panes is dried to prevent misting when installed. The pieces of glass are sealed with edge spacers of metal, alloy or plastic. The units are tailor-made and replace a single pane, enabling a window to open and close normally.

There are two types – standard and stepped. The stepped units are ideal where there are shallow rebates since installation can be carried out without having to alter the existing frame to accept the new units. The existing frame must be well fitting and sound enough to take the extra weight which will be imposed by the units.

Secondary sashes This is the most popular DIY method of installing double glazing. A second pane of glass in its own frame is secured to the existing frame or to the inner or outer sill and reveal; in some circumstances it is possible to fit the new window outside the existing frame. The existing window remains unaltered to form the other half of the double glazing. Manufacturers supply frames of aluminium or plastic; other types consist of plastic extrusions which are cut to length and joined with corner fittings to enable a frame for the glass to be made up. Hinges or clips are then used to secure the secondary sash to the existing window. The secondary sash is movable for cleaning, ventilation or summer storage and can be fixed, hinged or sliding.

Coupled windows These are usually specified only for new buildings or where entire frames are being replaced during conversion. One single-glazed window has an auxiliary window coupled to it, allowing both to move together. They are fitted with hinges and fasteners so the frames can be separated for cleaning purposes.

Plastic film This is not double glazing in the traditional sense, although at least one proprietary system is available. Plastic film is cut to size and applied to the window frame with double-sided adhesive tape. If you use this method, make sure that where windows are to be opened they are double-glazed separately from fixed panes; if a complete film was stretched across the entire window it would not be possible to open the window without first removing the film.

If you are restricted to a very small budget, you can use kitchen self-clinging plastic to make a form of double glazing for small panes. For larger panes, you will have to break up the pane space with a thin timber framework to create the effect of smaller panes and fix the film inside these smaller areas.

Installing double glazing

If you are going to install your own double glazing, it is likely you will choose a secondary sash type since kits for these are widely available and are relatively easy to install.

There are, however, a number of problems you may come across when fitting them. For example,

they can be fitted to existing timber or metal window frames; but if metal frames are fixed directly into masonry, you will have to drill and tap the frame to provide screw-fixing points or fit a secondary timber frame to accept the double glazing, particularly if the frame is too narrow. However, most metal windows are set in a timber surround and this can be treated as the window.

If you want to fix the double glazing frame to the reveal, you may come across the problem of an out-of-square reveal; to deal with this you will have to pack the out-of-square area with timber wedges or choose a system which fits directly to the window. Again, certain types of kit require the channels in which the new glazing is fitted to be mitred at the corners and joined. If you think you will find this too much of a problem, choose a type which is supplied with corner pieces. Remember to cut the channel lengths squarely at the ends or you will find it difficult to fit on the corner pieces and the final appearance of the glazing will be marred. Also, don't expect the glass to be a push-fit into the channel; it might slide in, but often you will need to encourage this by tapping gently with a mallet or with a hammer and a block of wood placed to protect the glass.

Warning If you are going to double glaze bay windows, remember to treat each window as a separate unit.

There are many makes of secondary sash double glazing available and the manufacturers supply

6 Fitting sliding secondary sashes; this type may be fixed to the face of the window or to the reveal

7 Fitting shatterproof panels into self-adhesive plastic track; mark the sill trim where it reaches the edge of the frame

8 Cut the side channel to length, remove the adhesive backing and press the strip onto the wall

9 Fit the top channel along the top of the frame

10 To shape the panels, score with a sharp knife and break over the edge of a firm surface

11 Fit the first panel, slit the top channel at the end of the panel and clip in place

12 Fix a panel divider and continue fitting the panels

13 Fit the final panel, ensuring the side channel is pressed firmly along its length

14 The finished installation; separate panels can be removed by opening the channel at the top and side

6

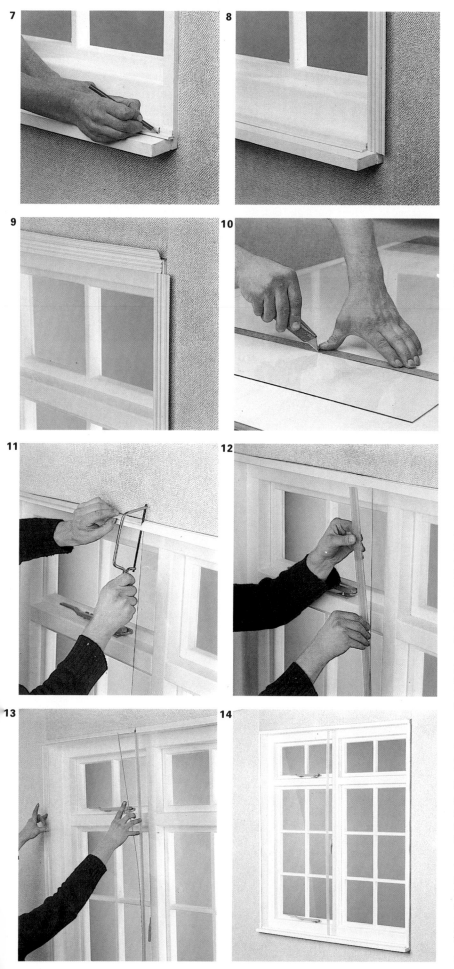

detailed instructions for installation. There are, however, three basic types of system: plastic channel, fixed or hinged, and sliding secondary sashes.

Plastic channel With this type, each pane of glass is fitted into a frame made by cutting lengths of U-shaped plastic channel to size; remove any sharp edges from the glass with a carborundum stone. The corners of the channel have to be mitred. Using a sharp knife and a mitre guide, cut the first mitre corner and then fit the channel to the glass to determine the position of the second corner. Remove the channel and mitre-cut at this position; repeat this process until all four corners have been cut. Secure the channel to the glass; some kits require the use of adhesive to form a rigid frame. Hold this assembly up to the window and fix it in place on the frame with the plastic clips supplied with the kit.

With this type of double glazing, out-of-square reveals will not cause problems since the channel is always fixed to the frame.

Fixed or hinged Usually this type consists of plastic or aluminium channel cut to shape and joined at the corners by mitring or by using special corner pieces. Fixing is either by clips to non-opening windows or by hinges to opening windows (the new windows can be hinged to open sideways or upwards). You could, of course, use hinges with fixed windows to make them easier to clean. This type of double glazing will, if correctly assembled, eliminate draughts and the new windows can be removed for summer storage.

Before you buy this type of system, read the manufacturer's instructions carefully to check the frame around your window is wide enough to take the double glazing and that it is made of the right material to take this particular system. With some systems the manufacturer recommends fixing only to wood rather than metal frames. Again, your existing window catches or handles may protrude in such a way they will interfere with the installation of the new system. You can usually solve these problems by fitting a secondary timber frame to take the double glazing; butt-join the corners of the frame, fill in any gaps with wood filler and apply a wood primer followed by two coats of paint, allowing the first coat to dry before applying the second.

There is one system which uses PVC shatterproof panels instead of glass. These are fitted into self-adhesive plastic tracks which are cut and pressed into place to the wall outside the reveal. The panels can be easily removed, but you may consider this too much trouble with opening windows.

Sliding Usually this type is fitted in the reveal. An outer frame is fixed in the reveal to square up the opening; use pieces of wood as packing if necessary. The glass is fixed in a separate frame which is fitted inside the outer frame to enable the glass and its separate frame to slide. The framed glass is removable and horizontal and vertical sliders are available. Depending on the size of the window, two or more sliding panels will be needed.

One system can be fixed to the face of the window frame so you will avoid the problems of squaring up a reveal, although it can be reveal-fixed as well. In this case the company offers a kit specially designed to suit your windows; it comprises plastic channelling cut to size and ready to be joined on site so no cutting or mitring is required. The glass comes complete in its tailor-made frame ready to be installed in the channelling.

Insulating the loft

Heating costs rise with the warm air if heat is allowed to escape through the roof. By insulating the loft area you can keep down the bills and hold heat where it belongs – in the house

A loft that is not insulated accounts for a heat loss of about 25 percent in the average size house. Several forms of insulation are available and fall into two categories: loose-fill materials such as vermiculite granules, and the mat type made from glass fibre or mineral wool. The materials we mention are all resistant to fire and you must check on the fire-resistance of any alternative product you consider buying. As a precaution, first treat all timber for woodworm.

joists in most houses, and can be cut quite easily with a large pair of scissors or a sharp knife. Even handled carefully, glass fibre can irritate the skin, so always wear gloves when working with it.
Mineral wool (Rocksil) Another mat type, this is made from rock fibre and is handled in the same way as glass fibre.
Laying rolls Place the roll of material between the joists and tuck the end under the eaves. Working backwards, unroll the material until you reach the other end of the roof. Cut it and tuck the end under the eaves as before. Lay the strip flat between the joists or, if it is a little wider, turn the sides up against the sides of the joists. Continue in this way until the whole loft area has been covered. If you have to join two strips in the middle of the roof, butt them together.

Below left To lay granules, pour them between joists and level them with T-shaped piece of timber
Below If your insulating roll is wider than space between joists turn up each side against joists
Below centre Don't lay insulation under cold water cistern; leave area uncovered so warm air from below can stop water freezing
Bottom Use latex adhesive to glue piece of glass fibre on loft flap

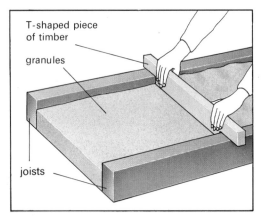

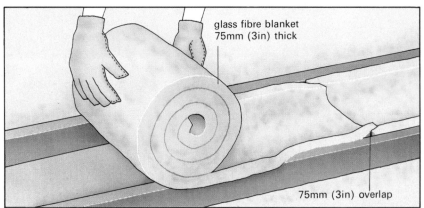

Granule insulation
One advantage of using granules to insulate your loft is that they flow easily and smoothly and will fill any awkward spaces. They are also safe to handle since they do not contain any splinters or loose fibres.
Vermiculite Expanded mica in granule form, this is supplied in easy-to-handle bags. The manufacturer's instructions will give you a guide to the number of bags needed for specific areas.
   You should wear a mask and some form of eye protection when using vermiculite since it is a dusty material that easily gets into the atmosphere.
Laying granules Pour vermiculite between the joists to a depth of about 100mm (4in), which will bring it almost to the level of the joists. Level the granules to the required depth by dragging a T-shaped piece of timber along the top of the joists. This can be made from any piece of scrap wood at least 150mm (or 6in) wide and 500mm (or 20in) long. You must cut the base of the 'T' to fit the gaps between the joists. Use a broom or rake for awkward corners.

Mat insulation
This form of insulation does not need to be laid as thickly as granules and should be used in lofts where there are gaps around the eaves, since wind might blow the granules about.
Glass fibre The most economical form of mat insulation for loft spaces. It comes in 80 or 100mm (3 or 4in) thick rolls and is available in 400mm (16in) widths, equivalent to the space between roof

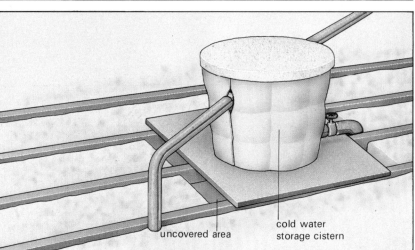

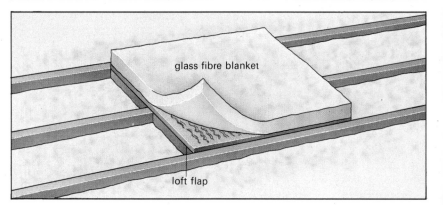

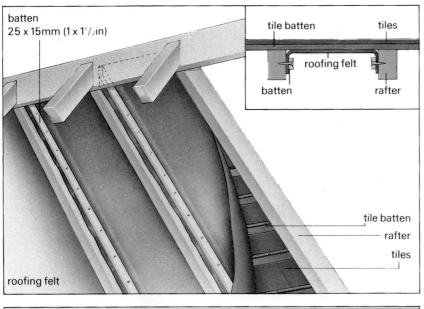

batten
25 x 15mm (1 x 1¹/₂in)

tile batten   tiles

roofing felt

batten   rafter

roofing felt

tile batten
rafter
tiles

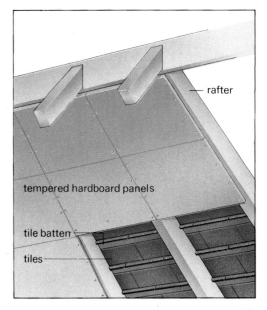

rafter

tempered hardboard panels

tile batten

tiles

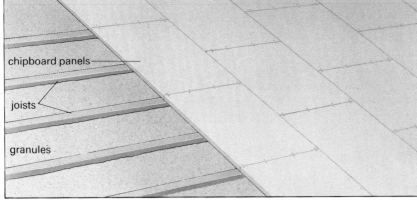

chipboard panels

joists

granules

Top When fixing felt between rafters, allow enough width to turn onto rafters and hold felt in place by screwing through battens and felt into rafters. **Inset** Cross-section of felt and batten fixing

Top right When insulating with tempered hardboard, butt-join panels and fix to rafters with countersunk screws

Above Improve insulation by laying floor using chipboard panels, staggering joins and screwing through sides of each panel into joists. Cut panels so they butt-join each other in middle of each joist

Insulating awkward areas You will find it easier to cover awkwardly shaped or inaccessible areas with granules. A 100mm (4in) thickness of granules is equivalent to 80mm (3in) of blanket materials in terms of effective insulation.

Warning Whichever method of insulation you use, don't insulate under the cold water tank. You must allow a warm air current to flow from below to prevent the tank from freezing in cold weather. But don't forget to insulate the loft flap or cover. Cut a piece of mat material to the size of the cover and stick it down with a latex adhesive. And when working in the loft, remember to tread only on the joists or on a board placed across them.

Other forms of insulation

Even more insulation can be provided if you make a floor to the loft by fixing panels of chipboard or planks of timber to the joists above the insulating material. This will also give you extra storage space, but you may have to strengthen the joists by spanning the load-bearing walls with large timbers before laying the floor if you want to put heavy items on it. Seek advice from a builder or your local authority.

Heat loss through the roof space can be further reduced by lining the ceilings immediately below the loft with an insulating-type material such as expanded polystyrene or acoustic tiles. It should be emphasized, however, that this is not a substitute for loft insulation.

Effective insulation of the floor will make the loft colder, so it is vitally important to ensure the

cold water tank (except beneath it) and all pipes are thoroughly protected, otherwise they will be susceptible to frost damage.

Protection from frost

The type of loft most likely to suffer from frost damage is one with an unboarded tile-hung roof. If your roof has no close-boarding or roofing felt – as is the case with many older houses – it is worth insulating it.

Cut lengths of roofing felt about 200mm (8in) wider than the distance between the rafters. Lay one long edge onto the inside edge of one rafter, lay a 25 × 15mm (1 × ½in) batten onto the felt and screw through the batten and felt into the rafter. Use No 8 countersunk screws 25mm long, spacing them at 300–380mm (12–15in) intervals. Don't use nails as the vibration from hammering could dislodge and break the roof tiles. Stretch the roof felt across to the next rafter and fix the other edge onto the edge of that rafter, again screwing through a batten. Leave a space between the roof and the felt to allow air to circulate, otherwise you may find rot will form on the rafters.

An alternative to roofing felt is tempered hardboard: butt-joint each panel of hardboard to the next by screwing it to the centre of each rafter with No 8 countersunk screws 25mm long. You may have to trim your cut panels so they fit neatly in the middle of each rafter.

All this work can be done in easy stages; when you have finished, the roof space will certainly remain warmer in winter and will also be much cleaner – an important consideration if you are using the loft for storage.

Cutting sheets to size

Boards are available in 2440 × 1830mm (8 × 6ft) and 1830 × 1220mm (6 × 4ft) sheets. You need 25mm (1in) thick flooring grade chipboard or 6mm (¼in) thick hardboard. Cut the larger sheet into six convenient 1830 × 407mm (6ft × 1ft 4in) panels, or the smaller one into three panels of the same size. If the loft opening space allows, cut the larger sheet into three 1830 × 813mm (6ft × 2ft 8in) panels, or the smaller sheet into one similar size panel and one 1830 × 407mm (6ft × 1ft 4in) panel.

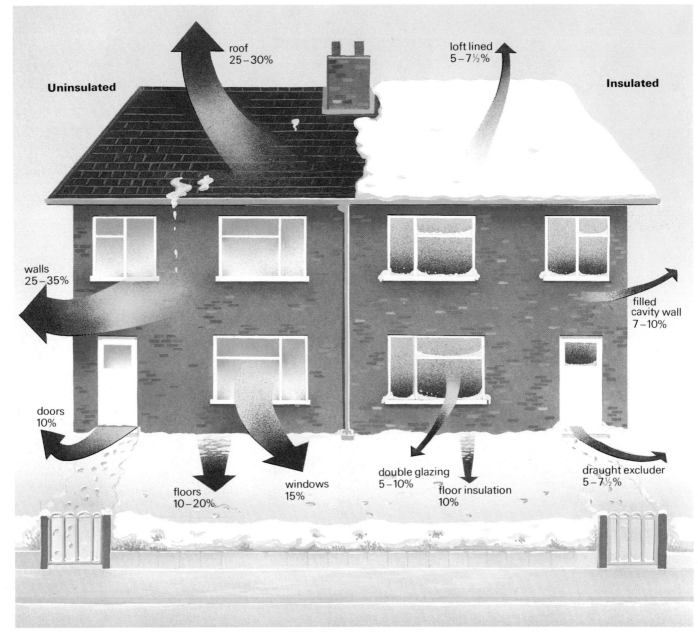

Uninsulated

roof
25–30%

loft lined
5–7½%

Insulated

walls
25–35%

filled
cavity wall
7–10%

doors
10%

floors
10–20%

windows
15%

double glazing
5–10%

floor insulation
10%

draught excluder
5–7½%

Reducing heat loss in the home

Many houses fall well below the minimum thermal insulation standards set under building regulations. Although some forms of insulation should be carried out by a professional, there is still much that can be done by the home handyman. Before you begin the process of keeping heat inside where it belongs, it is useful to understand the ways in which heat is lost from a house. The amount of heat lost does depend on the nature of

the building, its aspect and exposure to winds – and figures vary from house to house.
In a typical uninsulated house approximately one-quarter is lost through the roof, one-third through the walls, one-tenth through the doors, one-fifth through the windows and one-sixth through the floors. After insulation these losses can be cut down to approximately one-twentieth, one-tenth, one-twentieth, one-ninth and

one-tenth respectively. So although insulation does not prevent all the heat escaping, it substantially reduces the amount of loss and correspondingly diminishes the size of your heating bills. It shortens the time it takes to heat a room and enables you to keep down the number and size of radiators and the size of the boiler – or to install a less powerful and therefore less expensive central heating

system around the home. Forms of insulation vary from the simple rubber strip draught excluder on your door to insulating boards lining the walls. What you decide to do will depend on the amount of time and money you have available; but the more thoroughly you carry out the job, the greater the rewards will be in terms of comfort and eventual savings, which will well repay the initial expense and effort.

Working with electricity

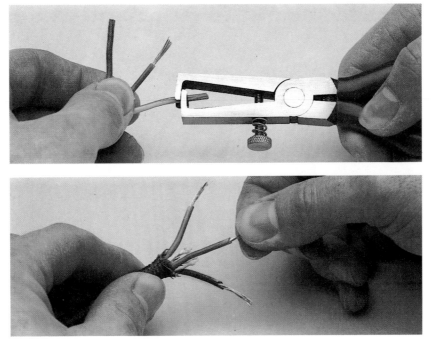

Simple electrical jobs in the home can be tackled
safely and will save hours of inconvenience while you
wait for the electrician to call. This section shows you
the correct way to strip cable and flex and the safe
way to join it. When you buy a new electrical fitting
or appliance, you can have it working in minutes by
fitting the plug on yourself. And when you are
plunged into darkness because of a blown fuse, you
can replace it immediately – and save your candles
for the next power failure. Follow carefully the
instructions and safety warnings and you should have
no fear of getting it wrong.

Stripping cable & flex

There are certain basic rules you must remember before you start to strip flex or cable for connecting to a plug or appliance or for wiring power or lighting circuits.

● Remove only sufficient insulation to enable the cores to be connected to the terminals; none of the bared wires should be exposed.

● Don't stretch the insulation when stripping or you will weaken the portion remaining on the conductor.

● Take care not to cut through the insulation of conductors, or through a conductor itself, or you will have to shorten the flex or cable and start again. If you damage a conductor the effective current capacity will be lowered and this could cause overheating. Current capacity will also be reduced if you sever any of the fine strands in a length of flex.

Stripping flex
The two most commonly used flexible cords are circular sheathed and braided circular flex. A third, now largely replaced by circular sheathed flex, is twisted twin non-sheath flex.

Circular sheathed Measure the length of sheathing to be removed and carefully run a knife round the sheath, making sure not to damage the core insulation. From this point, make a cut along the length of the flex to the end, cutting through to the inner insulation. Remove the sheathing with pliers, leaving the insulated cores exposed. Measure the length of insulation to be removed from each core and carefully take it off with wire strippers. Always twist the bared ends of each core together to ensure there will be no stray whiskers to cause a short circuit when the conductors are inserted in their terminals.

Circular braided Measure the length of braiding to be removed and cut it off with a sharp knife. Trim off the frayed edges and any textile fillers inside the braid and slip a rubber sleeve over the end to prevent further fraying. Strip the required length of insulation from each core and twist the wires together as before.

Twisted twin Since this type has no sheathing, you only need to strip insulation and twist the cores together.

Stripping cable
The method for stripping cable is basically the same as for stripping flex, but you must take extra care not to damage the conductors since cable is expensive to replace.

Sheathed Measure and strip off the required amount of sheathing using a knife and pliers as previously described. Strip off the insulation from each wire and slip a length of green (or green/yellow) PVC sleeving over the end of the earth wire. With the smallest cables (1.0 and 1.5sq mm), double the bared ends to provide greater contact area in the terminals. Cables of 4sq mm and above have stranded conductors and the ends must be twisted together with pliers.

Non-sheathed single core An example of this is the green/yellow PVC insulated earth cable; simply remove the insulation with wire strippers as described above.

1 Cut carefully along the length of the flex with a sharp knife
2 Use wire strippers to remove the sheathing and expose the insulated cores
3 Twist the wires together with your fingers
4 After stripping the insulation from cable, slip a length of PVC sleeving over the earth wire
5 On heavy cable, twist the conductors together with pliers

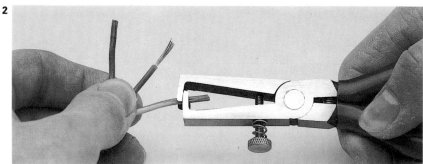

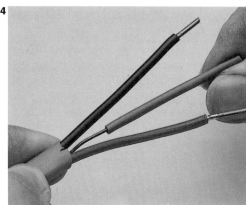

Joining flex

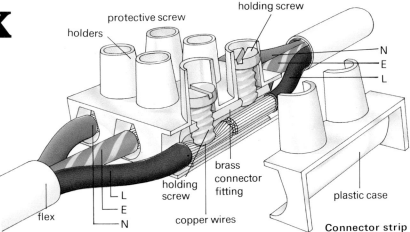

protective screw

holding screw

holders

N
E
L

brass
connector
fitting

holding
screw

plastic case

flex

L
E
N

copper wires

Connector strip

One of the real dangers involving electricity is the joining up of flex, which can be a fire hazard. If you really have to do this job, always use a proper connector and check you have wired it up in the correct way.

Whenever possible avoid joining flex. If you have to, always use a proper connector and never try to join two pieces of flex by twisting the bare wires together and covering them with insulating tape. No matter how careful you are there is always a danger the join may work loose or come apart because it is suddenly stretched. If a join does work loose it can create sparks that may in turn lead to a fire. Among the other hazards, the earth safety lead may become detached in a three core flex join or the essential separation between the live and neutral wires break down, causing a short circuit.

Flex connectors are useful for portable appliances like irons and hairdryers, if you want to use them some distance from a socket. But never use more than one connector on a length of flex and don't trail it under carpets, up the stairs or across a passageway. Apart from the electrical dangers, there is always the risk someone might trip over it. When you require temporary lighting for a Christmas tree, for example, the flex and connector should be tucked against a skirting board and secured with adhesive tape, never by staples.

Before you decide you need to make a connection, consider whether it is easier, possibly cheaper, and certainly safer to buy a longer length of flex and fit it permanently to the lamp or appliance. Alternatively it could be preferable, though more expensive, to have a new power socket fitted, especially if it is for a semi-permanent appliance like a fridge, television or room heater.

Fitting connectors
Proper flex connectors do not only keep the cores separate but the screw terminals keep them securely fixed. Always use the same kind of flexes when making a join; although they need not be the same exterior colour, the amps and number of cores must match – three core must be matched with three core and two core with two core.

Only trim sufficient outer insulating sheath and inner insulation to leave the minimum bare wire to enter the connector terminals. Make sure there are no bare strands of wire exposed by twisting together the strands in each core before connecting. Always connect the brown core with brown, the blue with blue and the green/yellow earth with earth and check the plug at the end of the extension flex is correctly wired and fused.

Types of connectors
Three kinds of connectors are available for use in the home. But check which one is most suitable for the type of appliance involved and where it is to be used.

Connector strips Sometimes called block connectors, they are made of plastic and pairs of screws hold the flex ends. The plastic section can be cut to suit single, two or three core flex, but since the

screw heads are not insulated they are only suitable where they can be protected and insulated, such as inside a table lamp or appliance, or in a plastic box with a screw-down cover.

Insulated flex connectors These consist of a screw-down plastic cover with screw terminals inside. You buy them to suit the flex and the appliance: 5amp for small lamps and 13amp for most other uses. They are generally designed to accommodate the live, neutral and earth of three core flex but can be used with two core flex.

Insulated detachable flex connectors Made of rubber or a tough plastic, these are like a self-contained plug and socket and strong enough for outdoor use. They are available in 5 and 13amp sizes. You must always fix the 'male' or plug part of the connector on the flex leading to the appliance and the 'female' or socket half should be connected with the flex end that will be joined to the plug connecting with the mains. If you join them the other way round and they become detached, the part with the pins would be live to the touch – and therefore very dangerous.

Above Plastic connector strip can be cut to suit single, two or three core flex
Below Insulated flex connector suitable for extending portable appliances such as hair dryers
Bottom Insulated detachable flex connector. Plug half must be connected to flex from appliance

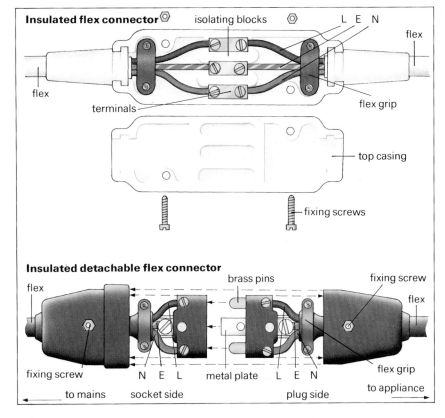

Insulated flex connector   isolating blocks   L E N

flex

flex

terminals

flex grip

top casing

fixing screws

Insulated detachable flex connector

flex   brass pins   fixing screw

flex

fixing screw   N E L   metal plate   L E N   flex grip

to mains   socket side   plug side   to appliance

How to wire up a plug

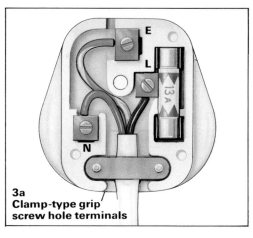

Houses that have been wired or rewired in Britain since 1947 will be fitted with ring main circuits. These are continuous loops of cable linking all wall sockets. The sockets are uniform 13amp outlets with rectangular holes to take the three flat pins of 13amp plugs.

This type of plug is supplied with a 3 or 13amp cartridge fuse (colour coded red and brown respectively). Always fit the fuse recommended by the manufacturer; as a general guide 3amp fuses are used with appliances rated up to 720 watts (for example table lamps) and 13amp fuses are used with larger appliances rated above 720 watts and up to 3000 watts (including kettles, irons and heaters). Some appliances (such as colour televisions, vacuum cleaners and spin dryers) although rated at less than 720 watts require a high starting current and should be used with 13amp fuses. In every case check first with maker's instructions.

Older houses will have radial wiring where separate cables radiate from the fuse board to each socket. These sockets are usually round pin in three sizes. The largest takes a 15amp plug used with larger appliances (such as heaters) while the other sizes take 5 and 2amp plugs used with smaller appliances (drills and table lamps respectively). The outlets may have two or three holes. The two pin sockets are not earthed and should only be used for light fixings with no exposed metal parts or for small double insulated appliances designed to operate without an earth connection and which are supplied only with two core flex.

Where possible it is safer to have radial wiring replaced (by your Electricity Board or a registered electrical contractor) with the properly earthed – and safer – ring main circuit.

Most plugs are made of tough, hard plastic but special rubberized types are available for equipment likely to be subjected to rough treatment, such as electric drills. Always buy a reputable make of plug because on poorer quality types the pins may move and cause a bad connection.

To fit a plug

First familiarize yourself with the colour code of the flex as it is most important the right core goes with the right terminal. With the new code blue is neutral, brown live and yellow/green earth. On older flex black is neutral, red live and green earth.

Remove the cover of the plug by undoing the large screw between the pins. When you look at the plug, with the largest pin (the earth) at the top and the flex outlet at the bottom, the live terminal is on the right (marked L) and the neutral terminal is on the left (marked N).

Prepare the flex by removing about 38mm (1½in) of the outer covering with a knife and fit the flex through the flex grip. This will be either a clamp type secured with two small screws (in which case loosen the screws, thread the flex through the grip and tighten the screws) or a V-shaped grip which

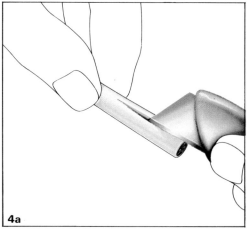

1 Types of plug: 13amp square pin; 15, 5 and 2amp round pin
2 Always check flex colour coding as right core must go to right plug terminal

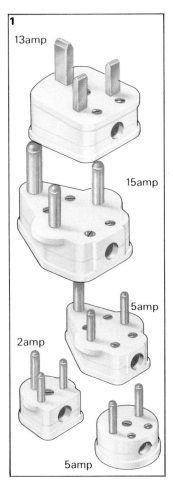

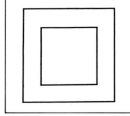
3a Clamp-type grip screw hole terminals

4a

5a

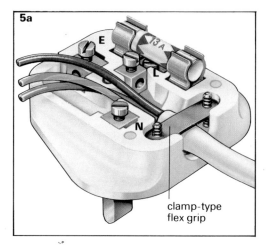
clamp-type flex grip

Earthing

When rewiring a plug make absolutely sure the earth wire (yellow/green or green) is properly connected. If it is not you run the risk of an electric shock should the metal casing of an appliance become accidentally live.

The only appliances which do not need earthing are double insulated ones supplied with two core flex and mains operated shavers which are intended for use with special shaver sockets.

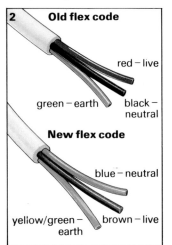

Left symbol for double insulation

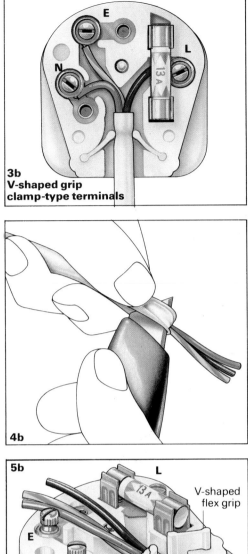

3b
V-shaped grip
clamp-type terminals

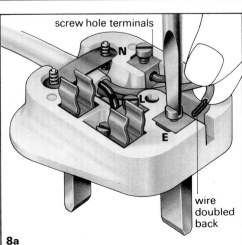

4b

5b

L

V-shaped
flex grip

E

N

holds about 6mm (¼in) of the flex covering inside the plug. Make sure each core of the flex will reach its terminal, then cut 12mm (½in) beyond this for joining to the terminals. With wire strippers carefully remove about 12mm (½in) of the insulation at the end of each core and twist the loose strands neatly together.

Check which type of terminals the plug has. If it has screw holes double back the wires, insert them into the terminal holes and tighten the terminal screws with a small screwdriver to secure the wires. If the terminals are of the clamp type remove the screws, wrap the wires around the terminal posts in a clockwise direction, replace the screws and tighten them. On some plugs the live terminal is under the fuse housing, in which case you will have to remove the fuse before wiring that terminal. Make sure the plug is neatly wired: the insulation must go right up to the terminals and there must not be any straggling wires.

If a fuse is required simply snap the cartridge into the holding clips. Finally double check wires are connected to correct terminals before refitting cover. **Warning** If a plug gets hot the terminal screws may have worked loose and need to be tightened. Always replace a cracked plug immediately; never repair it, even temporarily, with insulating tape since there is a considerable risk the casing will come apart as the plug is put into or removed from the socket and you could get an electric shock.

It is important to check the flex regularly since the point where it joins the plug is particularly susceptible to breaking and fraying (especially on irons and vacuum cleaners). At first sign of wear cut frayed piece to make new end and rewire plug.

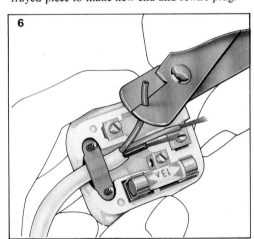

6

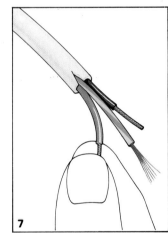

7

3a Screw hole terminals and clamp-type flex grip
3b Clamp-type terminals and V-shaped flex grip
4a Remove outer insulation by cutting along its length with sharp knife
4b Bend insulation away from flex and cut through fold
5a To insert flex in clamp-style grip, undo retaining screws, thread flex through grip and tighten screws
5b With V-shaped grip, simply push flex between two plastic strips
6 Check flex cores will reach terminals, allow 12mm (½in) extra for joining and cut off excess. Carefully remove insulation with wire strippers or sharp knife
7 Twist strands of each core neatly together

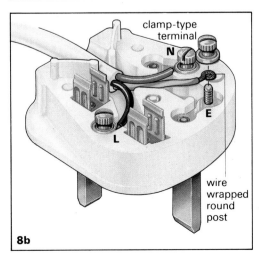

screw hole terminals

N

L

E

8a

wire
doubled
back

clamp-type
terminal

N

E

L

8b

wire
wrapped
round
post

8a With screw hole terminals, double back wires, loosen terminal screws and insert wires in terminals. Gently tighten screws, taking care not to sever wires
8b With clamp terminals, remove screws and wrap bare wires round terminal posts in clockwise direction. Replace screws and tighten

Consumer unit and fuse types

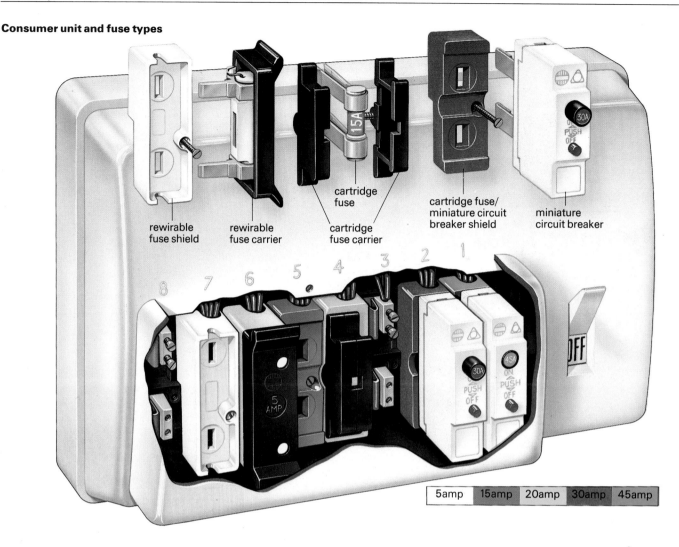

rewirable
fuse shield

rewirable
fuse carrier

cartridge
fuse

cartridge
fuse carrier

cartridge fuse/
miniature circuit
breaker shield

miniature
circuit breaker

| 5amp | 15amp | 20amp | 30amp | 45amp |

Repairing fuses

When electric current passes through a wire it causes heating: the thinner the wire the greater the heat. Even the thick wire used in domestic wiring will overheat if too much current passes through it – and may easily set the house on fire. To prevent this, a fuse is built into every circuit. This is a particularly thin piece of wire which will heat up quickly and melt if a more than safe quantity of current passes through it.

Types of fuses
All master fuses – one for each circuit – are mounted on fuse carriers in a fuse box close to the Electricity Board's supply meter. There are two main types, rewirable and cartridge, although miniature circuit breakers are sometimes fitted instead of fuses.

Rewirable This type has fuse wire stretched between two retaining screws on the porcelain or plastic fuse carrier. The wire is available in three ratings – 5, 15 and 30amp – and you can usually buy a card of wire carrying a supply of all three.

Cartridge This type cannot be rewired since the fuse is sealed inside a tube; once it blows the fuse must be replaced. The advantage of the master cartridge fuse is it is impossible to fit the wrong one

because each rating has a different size cartridge (as compared to plug fuses that are uniform in size). The fuses are also colour coded so they can be easily recognized: 5amp is white, 15amp blue, 20amp yellow, 30amp red and 45amp green.

Miniature circuit breakers Used in domestic fuse boxes instead of fuses, these automatically switch themselves off if a circuit is overloaded. When the fault has been corrected the circuit can be reconnected just by resetting the on/off switch.

Why fuses blow
A master fuse will blow if the circuit is overloaded, if the fuse wire is of too low a rating or if a faulty appliance is used with an unfused plug or socket. Before repairing the fuse check you are not using too many appliances on one circuit and make sure you are using the right size fuse for the circuit. If you suspect a faulty appliance, even though it seems to be working adequately, stop using it and call an electrician or contact the manufacturer.

Sometimes a fuse blows simply because it is old; all you need to do is replace it with a new one of the correct rating. If a fuse still blows after being replaced, call an electrician.

Labelled fuse box cover

Above Repairing rewirable fuse. **Left** Turn off mains supply and remove blown fuse.
Centre Loosen retaining screws, remove old wire and thread in new wire. **Right** Wind wires round screws in clockwise direction and tighten screws
Below Use metal-cased torch to check if cartridge fuse has blown. Remove base of torch; place one end of fuse on torch casing and other end on bottom of battery. If bulb does not light when torch is on, fuse has blown

Below right Never replace a correct fuse with a larger one, which will carry more current than is safe before blowing.
For lighting circuit (up to 1kW) – 5amp
For immersion heater (3–4.8kW) – 15/20amp
For ring main circuit (up to 7.2kW) – 30amp
For cooker (up to 10.8kW) – 45amp

Cartridge fuses

Warning Don't try to stop a fuse blowing by putting in a higher rated one.

Tracing faults
If one of your lights goes out see first whether those nearby are still working; if they are it is likely only the lamp bulb has blown. If all your lights are out check whether the street or your neighbours are in darkness too; if they are there is nothing wrong with your fuses – there is a general power failure and you will just have to wait for the power to be restored. If everyone else's lights are working you have an internal power failure, so turn off the relevant switch before investigating.

You will save time and trouble by keeping a small electrical screwdriver, a torch and replacement fuses or fuse wire handy by the fuse box. A supply of candles in the house is also good sense.

Rewiring fuses
Always turn off the mains supply switch before attempting any repairs. If you are really efficient you will have made a numbered plan of the carriers in your fuse box, labelling each one according to the circuit it controls (cooker, downstairs sockets,

upstairs lights etc.). This plan should be taped on the inside of the fuse box door so, when investigating a blown fuse, you can pick out the relevant carrier first time.

If you have not labelled them you must pull out each carrier in turn to find the blown fuse – look for one which has a broken or melted fuse wire. Undo the screws which clamp the fuse wire in place and remove the remains of the old wire. Stretch a new wire of the correct rating loosely between the screws and wind the ends in a clockwise direction round the screws, which must be carefully tightened until the wire is firmly held. Replace the fuse holder and close the fuse box before reconnecting the supply.

Replacing cartridge fuses
The only way of telling which cartridge fuse has blown is to remove one carrier at a time. Turn off the mains switch, remove a carrier, close the fuse box cover and switch on the mains supply. If everything else continues to work you have found the failed fuse. Take out the cartridge and replace it with a new one of the correct rating, refit the fuse carrier, close the box cover and turn on the main switch.

Protecting the home

No home should be left unprotected or invitations left for the prowling burglar. This section looks at the various ways you can guard against intruders and gives detailed instructions on how to fit locks securely to all types of doors and windows. Advice is given on what to do when you leave the house, whether for a short period or for a long holiday. Having spent time and money on improving the home, it is important all that effort is not wasted through a moment of carelessness. The intruder will often make quite a mess and it is heart-breaking to return and find your home in a shambles.

Introduction

Whenever you leave the house
- Lock all doors and windows and remove keys.
- Lock garages and sheds and lock away ladders and tools.
- Never leave visible notes for trades people.
- Don't leave keys under mats or in obvious positions.
- Never leave a key on a string behind the letter box; this habit will not go unnoticed.
- In the daytime open the curtains; at night close them and leave a light on – other than that in the hall; better still, fit a time switch to one or two lights so they come on as dusk falls.
- Never leave cars or bicycles unlocked, even if in a garage.
- Never leave a window open for the cat to get in and out; provide a cat door.
- When leaving your car always lock valuables in the boot, again even when in a garage. Better still, take them with you.
- When shopping never leave a purse where it can be stolen such as in a basket, on a counter or in a pram. Use a small holdall rather than a basket.

Before going on holiday
- Tell your neighbours and the police so they can watch the house for you.
- Cancel all household deliveries, such as milk and newspapers.
- Ask a friend or neighbour to draw the curtains each night (and open them in the morning) and leave one or two lights on to give the house a lived-in appearance. Again it would be a good idea to fit a time switch so the lights will not be on all night and attract attention. Also ask someone to remove any circulars from your letter box.
- If you intend to be away for a long time, make arrangements for your lawn to be mown – overgrown grass can be an obvious giveaway.

At home
- Always leave the security chain fixed so, when you open the door, no one can burst in.
- Always check the credentials of callers such as meter readers; all public employees carry official identification – ask to see it.
- Teach children not to open the door to strangers.
- Ensure the whereabouts of exit door keys is known to family and guests in the event of fire breaking out.
- Keep all documents, such as bank and credit cards, cheque books, insurance policies and passports in a safe place; but always keep cheque books separate from bank and credit cards which can be used to verify cheques.
- Keep duplicates of all keys in a secure place such as a safe; the loss of any could seriously affect security.

Insurance
Every home and its contents should be properly insured; but this is not sufficient security on its own. Insurance can never recover the real value you place on your possessions or compensate for the mental distress caused by intrusion.

Left Always cancel newspapers (and any other household deliveries) before you go away; ask a neighbour to remove circulars from your letter box
Below Windows near flat roofs can provide an easy means of entry for an intruder; have the windows fitted with security locks
Bottom Never leave keys under a doormat or hanging on a string behind the letter box

Locks for doors

The average home contains at least ten doors, most of which have various functions and require different locking devices. You should fit both interior and exterior doors with good quality locks which offer proper security and do not hinder everyday life for members of the household.

When considering home security it is a good idea to start by making a floor plan of your home; take exact measurements of door thickness and door stile widths and note the condition of locks already fitted. This plan will help you to examine the cost of overall security requirements and to order the devices and fittings you will need.

Types of door

Outside doors should be at least 45mm (1¾in) thick and made of stout hardwood. There is little point in fitting expensive security devices to doors which are weak and likely to be broken down easily.

Front door This is usually the most vulnerable door since it is the one you use to leave the house and therefore cannot be bolted from the inside. Approximately 28 percent of all break-ins occur from the front of private houses. Many front doors are fitted with old fashioned rim locks (a cylinder mounted inside and through the door); you can secure the door by adding a one bolt, five or six lever mortise deadlock (a box mounted inside the door) or replace it with a rim lock and a lockable handle which has the deadlocking function. If the stile is under 75mm (3in) wide, you will have to fit the former or a special narrow rim deadlock. The door must have a minimum thickness of 38mm (1½in) for both types.

If you decide to replace the rim lock, buy one of similar dimensions so only slight modification will be needed to fit it. The standard mortise lock has two keyholes and is fitted into a mortise in the edge of the door; it is suitable for double doors if one door is locked with flush bolts. Double doors with a rebate require a rebated forend and a rebated locking plate, which must be stipulated when the lock is ordered; you should quote the hand of the lock, whether the door opens inwards or outwards and the depth of the rebate. To determine the hand of a lock, view the door from the outside; the edge on which the lock will fit is the hand. If the lock is for the edge of the door on your right, a right-hand lock is required.

Two security or mortise bolts fitted top and bottom of a front door will give additional security. A security chain will guard against unexpected intrusion if you remember to secure it before opening the door to strangers. Fit a door viewer to allow visitors to be identified before the door is opened.

Back door and side door Approximately 62 percent of break-ins take place at the back of houses. Low security locks should be replaced with a standard or two bolt mortise deadlock of at least five levers and two bolts can be added as additional security. If the door is glazed, it is better to use mortise bolts; if trades people and callers are expected you should fit a chain and door viewer.

French windows An intruder can easily open these

If you are in any doubt about a security problem, go to your local police station and seek the advice of the crime prevention officer. CPOs can be found in virtually every area of Britain and their experience and knowledge of security devices, including details of how to fit them, will prove invaluable. The service is free.

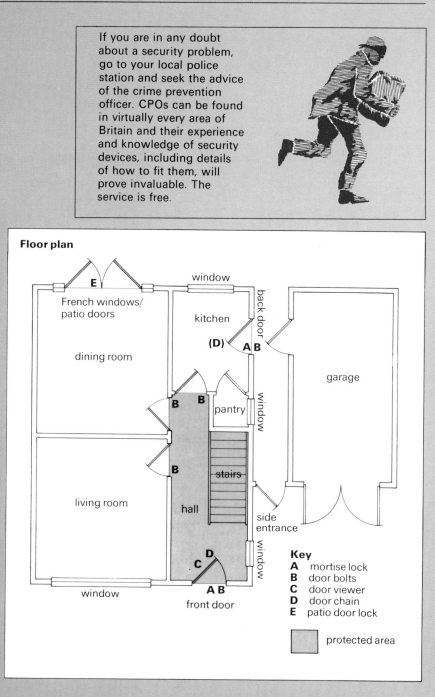

Floor plan

French windows/patio doors

dining room

window

kitchen

(D)

back door

garage

window

pantry

B   B

B

stairs

living room

hall

window

side entrance

window

D

C

Key
A mortise lock
B door bolts
C door viewer
D door chain
E patio door lock

protected area

window

A B

front door

types of door. Fit a mortise lock and mortise bolts, one shooting upwards into the top of the frame on one door and the other to the second door (which overlaps the first), shooting down into the floor.

Metal doors These are normally made of galvanized steel or aluminium and are supplied with good locks. Aluminium replacement doors for domestic use are usually supplied with narrow stile widths which require rim fitting mortice deadlocks or other types of special lock. A locksmith will advise on suitable locks for metal doors and may also be able to fit them for you. A surface-fitting, key-operated bolt can be added to metal doors.

Sliding patio doors Some sliding patio doors are supplied with a lock fitted to the centre stile, which prevents the door being slid open. However, many do not have this facility and rely solely on the locks at the edge of the door, which can be easily overcome if force is used. In this case it is best to fit an additional lock to the top or bottom rail. You can do this yourself, but great care must be taken; if

Fitting mortise lock to timber door
1a Mark out mortise
1b Drill line of holes and chisel out waste
1c With lock inside mortise, mark round forend; chisel out marked area to form recess for forend
1d With face of forend flush with door edge, mark through keyhole to give drilling point; chisel out drilled hole to form keyhole shape
1e With lock fitted, hold escutcheon in place and mark position for fixing screws
1f Throw bolt and mark top and bottom of bolt on jamb; continue lines round to inner jamb and retract bolt

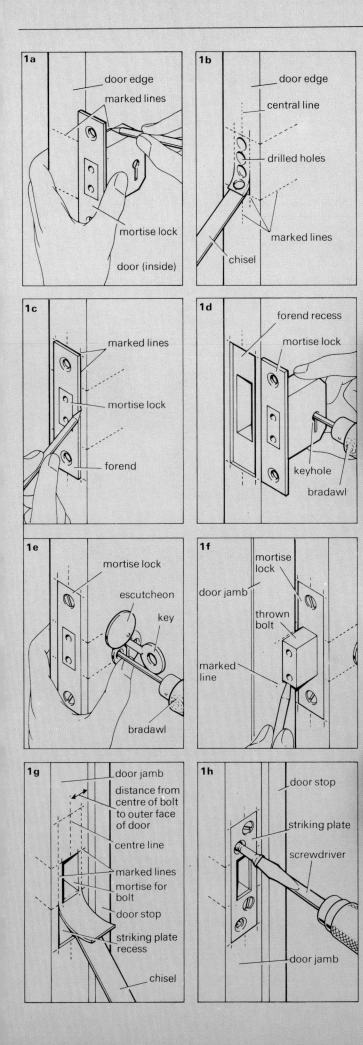

1a
door edge
marked lines
mortise lock
door (inside)

1b
door edge
central line
drilled holes
marked lines
chisel

1c
marked lines
mortise lock
forend

1d
forend recess
mortise lock
keyhole
bradawl

1e
mortise lock
escutcheon
key
bradawl

1f
mortise lock
door jamb
thrown bolt
marked line

1g
door jamb
distance from centre of bolt to outer face of door
centre line
marked lines
mortise for bolt
door stop
striking plate recess
chisel

1h
door stop
striking plate
screwdriver
door jamb

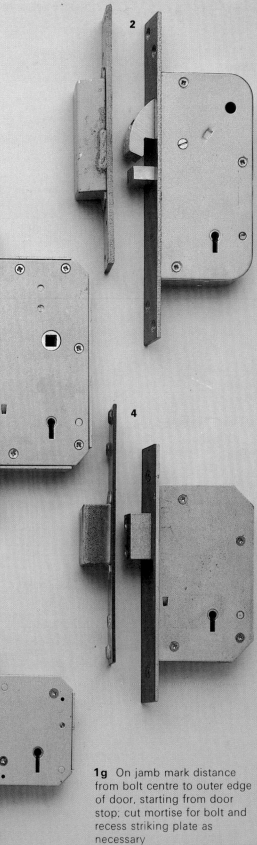

1g On jamb mark distance from bolt centre to outer edge of door, starting from door stop; cut mortise for bolt and recess striking plate as necessary
1h Screw striking plate in position
2 Hook bolt mortise lock
3 Upright two bolt mortise lock
4 High security mortise deadlock
5 Mortise deadlock

you are in any doubt, it is best to have the lock fitted by a professional.

Timber sliding doors There are several types of lock suitable, but these doors are best secured with hook bolt mortise locks which have a deadlocking action. You can use a lock with a claw bolt action which grips a recess in the striking plate, but these are not usually available with deadlocking function.

Interior doors Doors inside the house offer a valuable second line of defence against the would-be intruder, provided the layout is not open plan. In isolated areas or in situations where the house may be left empty for long periods, an intruder could cause considerable damage by smashing down locked interior doors. But since some insurance companies may insist interiors doors are left locked in this kind of situation, it is probably the best course to take. In any case, check your insurance policy before making a decision.

The floor plan shows how locking interior doors can prevent easy access to the hallway and rooms on the ground and first floors. In most cases, the original locks fitted by the housebuilder will offer poor security. Here you can fit mortise bolts at the top and bottom of the door (to operate sideways on single doors), installing them with the keyholes facing the hallway.

Fitting locks
Until the recent advent of magnetic and electronic locking devices, lock mechanisms had involved only two principal methods: a fixed obstruction (or 'ward'), which prevents any but the correct key operating the lock, and a more effective method involving detainers or levers, which are brought together in pre-selected positions by a key. The latter is the principle of the modern range of mortise deadlocks; when properly fitted they are designed to be stronger than a timber door. This means, in the event of a break-in, the wood itself would fail before the lock. The locking bolt is enclosed inside a steel box to prevent the lock being picked; some have up to three anti-picking devices as well. The bolt itself is often enclosed and reinforced with steel rollers which rotate to prevent a thief cutting through the bolt. Once the bolt is locked, it is secured automatically.

When more than one lock is fitted, you can obtain a key which will open all the locks, but you must ask for this when you order the locks. Some manufacturers offer a registration service which ensures replacement keys are only given to the registered lock owners. You should complete the registration document and return it to the manufacturer.

Fitting a mortise lock should offer no problems to the experienced DIY person as long as the manufacturer's instructions are carefully followed. If in any doubt, you should contact a professional since a poorly fitted lock will be inefficient and may reduce overall security. There is a wide range of mortise locks available and many reasonably priced devices provide good security. The British Standard BS 3621 is worth looking for when choosing locks because those with this stamp are resistant to drilling and manipulation from outside, have a minimum of 1000 key variations and comply with a number of other exacting requirements.

Fitting a mortise lock Different manufacturers will suggest different methods of fitting; but as a rule the lock is placed along the central rail (slightly lower than halfway down the door) on a panelled door, or along the outer stile on a hardboard door.

6 Standard rim lock. **7** Rim automatic deadlock; handle can be locked from outside. **8** Rim automatic deadlock; handle can be locked from both sides of door. **9** Door pull. Fitting rim lock: **10a** Hold supplied template on door and mark key cylinder position; drill small holes first then large hole. **10b** Chisel out recess for forend. **10c** Remove fixing plate from deadlock and position plate on door so screw holes coincide with four holes in door. **10d** Fit key cylinder and mark length of protruding bar (should be at least one notch longer than door thickness); remove cylinder, cut bar to required length and fix cylinder with screws (don't overtighten). **10e** Throw bolt on deadlock

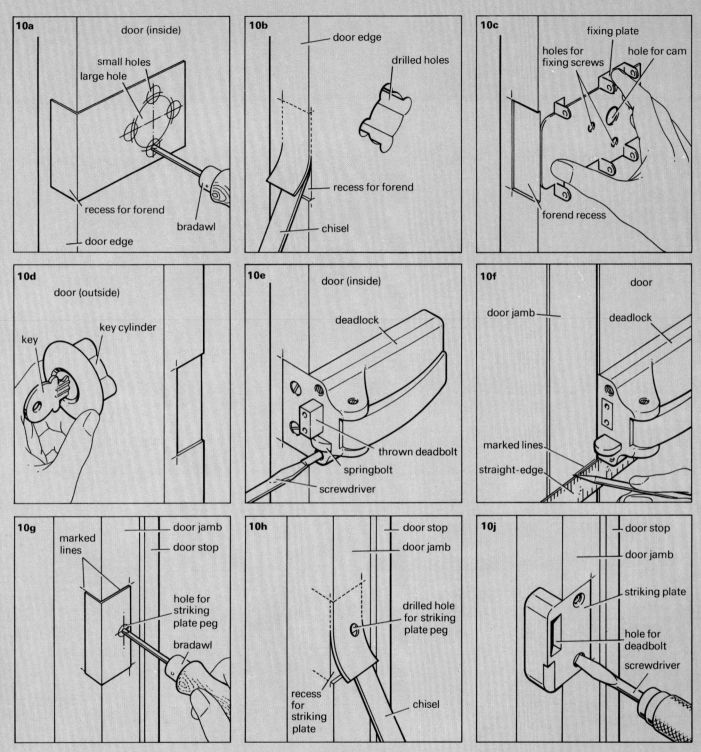

10a door (inside); small holes; large hole; recess for forend; door edge; bradawl

10b door edge; drilled holes; recess for forend; chisel

10c fixing plate; holes for fixing screws; hole for cam; forend recess

10d door (outside); key cylinder; key

10e door (inside); deadlock; thrown deadbolt; springbolt; screwdriver

10f door; door jamb; deadlock; marked lines; straight-edge

10g marked lines; door jamb; door stop; hole for striking plate peg; bradawl

10h door stop; door jamb; drilled hole for striking plate peg; recess for striking plate; chisel

10j door stop; door jamb; striking plate; hole for deadbolt; screwdriver

and position deadlock over fixing plate so connecting bar is engaged in cam. **10f** Turn key to retract bolt and, with door closed, mark position of striking plate on jamb. **10g** Put supplied template on jamb, mark position of striking plate and drill peg hole to required depth (peg is on striking plate). **10h** Chisel out recess for striking plate. **10j** Place striking plate in position with peg in hole; secure plate with screws

Position the lock on the inside of the door and draw round it; drill a series of small holes in the area marked and chisel out the mortise. Fit the lock into the mortise so it is flush with the edge of the door; drill out key holes on both sides as recommended by the manufacturer and chisel to key-hole shape. Check you have drilled the key holes correctly and the lock is aligned before fitting the lock and escutcheons. The striking plate is secured to the door frame after you have marked out its correct position in relation to the bolt of the lock. Drill and chisel out a mortise for the striking plate and roughly fit the plate to the frame; any adjustments should be made to the plate and not to the lock position.

Fitting a rim lock This mortise deadlock is not mortised into the edge of the door, but secured

through the door. The deadlocking action varies depending upon construction; most deadlock automatically when the door is closed and some require the key to be turned before they deadlock. The lock is supplied in three parts – a key cylinder, deadlocking portion and striking plate or staple. Again, manufacturers will supply detailed fitting instructions relevant to their particular model; in general terms you will have to drill through the door and some manufacturers will supply a template for this. Insert the key cylinder from the outside of the door and cut the connecting bar to length, according to fitting instructions. Fit the deadlock to the inside of the door and screw the striking plate into the door frame after alignment. You can buy a pull which fits beneath the key cylinder flange.

Additional security devices

A mortise lock fitted to an interior or exterior door will often be all that is needed to upgrade your home security; however there are certain weak areas which may need additional devices to deter the intruder. For example, the porch door is your first line of defence and should be fitted with a good two bolt, five lever mortise lock.

Two bolt mortise lock This is similar to the standard mortise lock but has an extra latch bolt with the deadlocking function. The lock is suitable for exterior doors. The two bolt version is fitted in the same manner as the standard mortise lock.

Hook bolt mortise lock This is widely used to secure timber sliding doors, either flush or single ones, provided there is sufficient space to accommodate the box striking plate in the rim of the door. Installation is similar to the standard mortise lock and the deadlocking function can be triggered either by closing the door or turning the key.

Security mortise bolt This type can be used to secure exterior or interior doors and French windows. They are usually fitted in pairs (to top and bottom of the door) and a standard key opens all the bolts. All that is required for installation is a hole of recommended size drilled into the edge of the door and frame, two shallow rebates cut to accommodate the locking plate and the flange and enable the bolt to be fitted flush into the edge of the door and a hole in the face of the door to take the key. A circular bolt is thrown back by the key, which operates from only one side of the door.

Surface fitting bolts These are the traditional bolts which are usually fitted at the top and bottom of a door. Ensure you use the correct size bolt – for

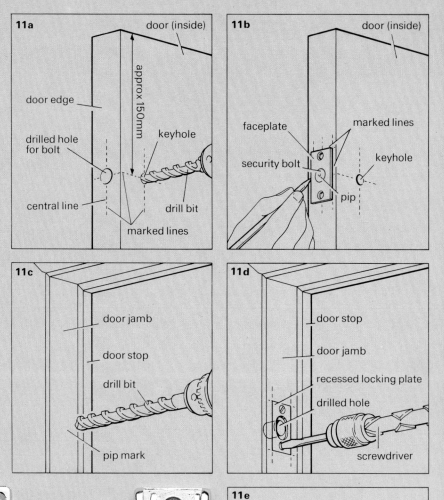

Fitting security bolt: **11a** Mark out and drill bolt hole and keyhole; stop keyhole at bolt hole. **11b** With bolt in hole and faceplate on edge of door, mark and recess faceplate; secure with screws. **11c** With door closed, turn key so pip marks centre point for locking plate on jamb; drill hole to take bolt. **11d** Cut recess and screw locking plate in place. **11e** Fix key plate in position with screws

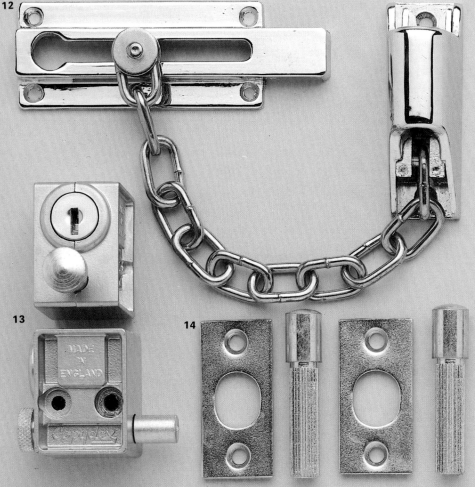

12 Lockable security chain
13 Lock for sliding doors
14 Hinge bolts
15 Security mortise bolt
16 Surface fitting bolt
17 Door viewer

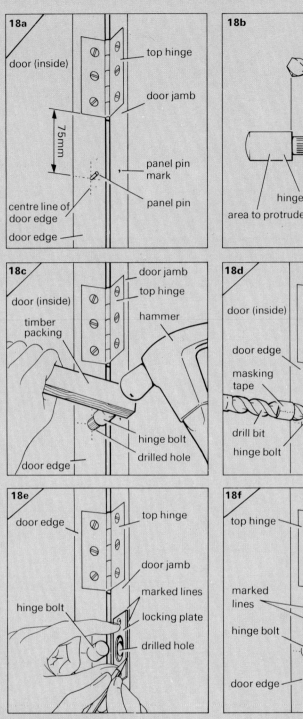

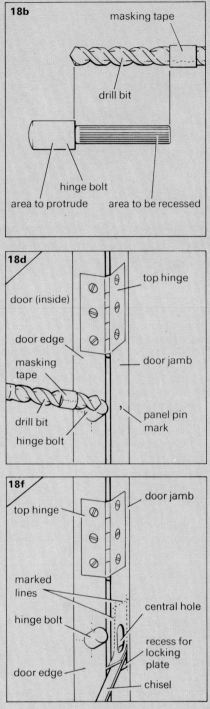

18a
door (inside)
top hinge
door jamb
75mm
panel pin mark
panel pin
centre line of door edge
door edge

18b
masking tape
drill bit
hinge bolt
area to protrude
area to be recessed

18c
door (inside)
timber packing
hammer
door jamb
top hinge
hinge bolt
drilled hole
door edge

18d
door (inside)
door edge
masking tape
drill bit
hinge bolt
top hinge
door jamb
panel pin mark

18e
door edge
hinge bolt
top hinge
door jamb
marked lines
locking plate
drilled hole

18f
top hinge
marked lines
hinge bolt
door edge
door jamb
central hole
recess for locking plate
chisel

exterior doors the minimum bolt length should be 200mm (8in) – and the correct size screw; undersized bolts and screws could be forced.

Hinge bolts These are particularly important for outward opening doors where the hinges are exposed. The bolts fit inside the frame, close to the hinges. The keep is rebated into the door frame and the bolt is fitted into the door by drilling a hole for it. Hinge bolts will provide solid protection for a door and frame even if the hinge pin is removed.

Door chains These should be fitted to front and rear exterior doors as a precaution against casual visitors; they allow you to examine visitors' credentials and prevent violent intrusion into the home. Always keep them fixed when the house is occupied. They are easily fitted with screws. Some types incorporate an unlockable plunger which enables the chain to be secured when leaving the house and also prevents a successful intruder locking you out of the house.

Door viewer This is essential when outward vision is hampered by solid door construction or frosted glass; fit a porch light as well for night use. The door viewer comes in two parts, one part screwing into the other through the door. Drill a hole of the required size through the door to fit a door viewer; place a block of wood behind the door when drilling to prevent the drill bit bursting through and damaging the finish of the door.

Anti-jemmy plates These are used where there is a perceptible gap between the edge of the door and the door frame. They are mounted to reduce this gap and to prevent the use of jemmies and other devices of the housebreaker, which might open a non-deadlocking rim lock for example.

Fitting hinge bolt: **18a** Mark position of bolt with pin; close door so pin marks position on jamb. **18b** Use masking tape round drill bit to mark drilling depth; remove pin and drill bolt hole. **18c** Drive in bolt. **18d** Drill hole for bolt in jamb to required depth. **18e** With locking plate over hole, mark round edge and central hole. **18f** Chisel central hole to shape, form recess and fix plate with screws

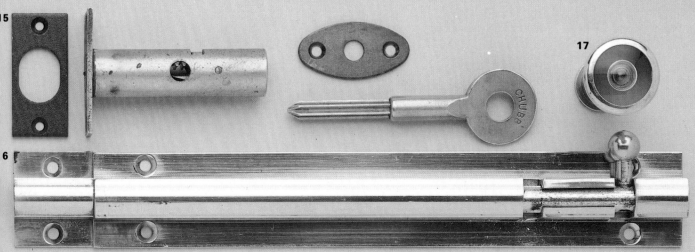

Locks for windows

Over 60 percent of household break-ins occur through windows; intruders choose this route because an unsecured window can be quickly opened from outside. For example, it could take an experienced burglar less than 15 seconds to enter a house through a casement window by breaking or removing a pane.

There is a wide range of window security devices (WSDs) available to secure windows properly, preventing easy access and causing as much obstruction as possible to an intruder. It is worth fitting these to all the windows in your house, even to those which are above the ground floor, since an agile intruder could scale a drainpipe or building projection or climb scaffolding or a ladder which has been carelessly left out. Fanlights should also be protected, as should small permanently shut windows, since once the glass has been removed these can provide access for a slim intruder.

Fitting most WSDs is within the capability of the home handyman; usually, you will find any experience you have gained in installing mortise locks or bolts on doors will be valuable since fitting WSDs often requires similar tools and expertise. Remember too that although an intruder may gain access through a window, he may be unable to retreat through the same opening since the stolen goods may be too large; you should make sure all exterior doors are secured as well.

Preparing for installation

Start by making a plan of window locations and note the size and type of each window and its existing fittings. Check how frequently windows are usually opened since this is a feature you should consider when choosing the WSD you will fit. Examine windows for loose joints and panes and look for rotten sections in timber frames; complete any repair work before fitting security devices.

Window security devices fit to and secure existing fittings or are fitted between moving and fixed window sections. The costs of individual WSDs can vary considerably, but as a general rule those which are fitted to existing fittings semi-permanently are cheaper than key-operated types which are fitted permanently to fixed and moving frames and allow windows to be opened quickly. When selecting WSDs it is best to avoid choosing cheaper semi-permanent types for windows which are regularly opened since they will need to be frequently removed from and replaced on the fitting and may be lost or not used as a result.

Anti-child locks Care should be taken in selecting WSDs for households with young children; in this case the devices will be used to prevent windows being opened easily from inside as well as outside. Devices which lock directly onto handles and stays are suitable since these are difficult to remove.

Warning Where screw heads securing WSDs are visible from outside, it is worth using clutch head screws since these cannot be unscrewed. Alternatively you can file the heads of slot head screws and drill out the heads of cross head screws so they cannot be undone with a screwdriver.

If you are in any doubt about a security problem, go to your local police station and seek the advice of the crime prevention officer. CPOs can be found in virtually every area of Britain and their experience and knowledge of security devices, including details of how to fit them, will prove invaluable. The service is free.

WSDs for timber casements

Timber casement windows are usually fitted with cockspur handles and window stays; securing them can involve replacement of these fittings with more secure types or installing devices which give extra security in addition to the existing fittings.

Replacement units Replacement handles and stays are available in matching sets of various designs and may involve the use of conventional or special keys. With one make, the handle is secured with a conventional key and the lockable window stay can be secured in up to nine positions; so while ventilation is provided, opening the window from outside is extremely difficult. Both the handle and stay are fixed in position using the screws provided.

Window locks There is a variety of window locks available. One type fits flush to the edge of the window and you move a catch to lock a bolt section fitted to the opening frame into a keep recessed into the fixed frame when the window is closed; when you want to open the window undo the lock with the key supplied. There is a version of the same lock for use with metal frame windows and the same key can be used for both versions. Another type of device locks automatically when

1 Casement and fanlight lock
2 Lockable window stay
3 Security bolt for timber casement window
4 Automatic self-lock for timber window (hinged or pivot)
5 Lockable window latch for timber window
6 Fixing of casement lock on timber frame window
7 Fixing of automatic self-lock on timber frame window

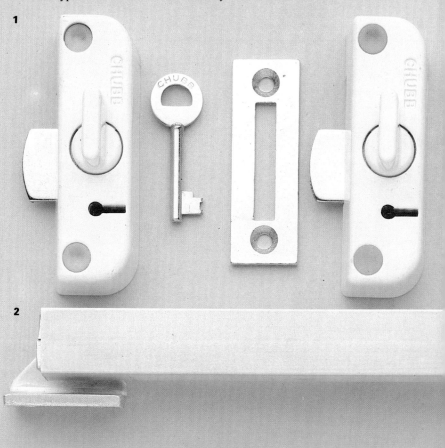

1

2

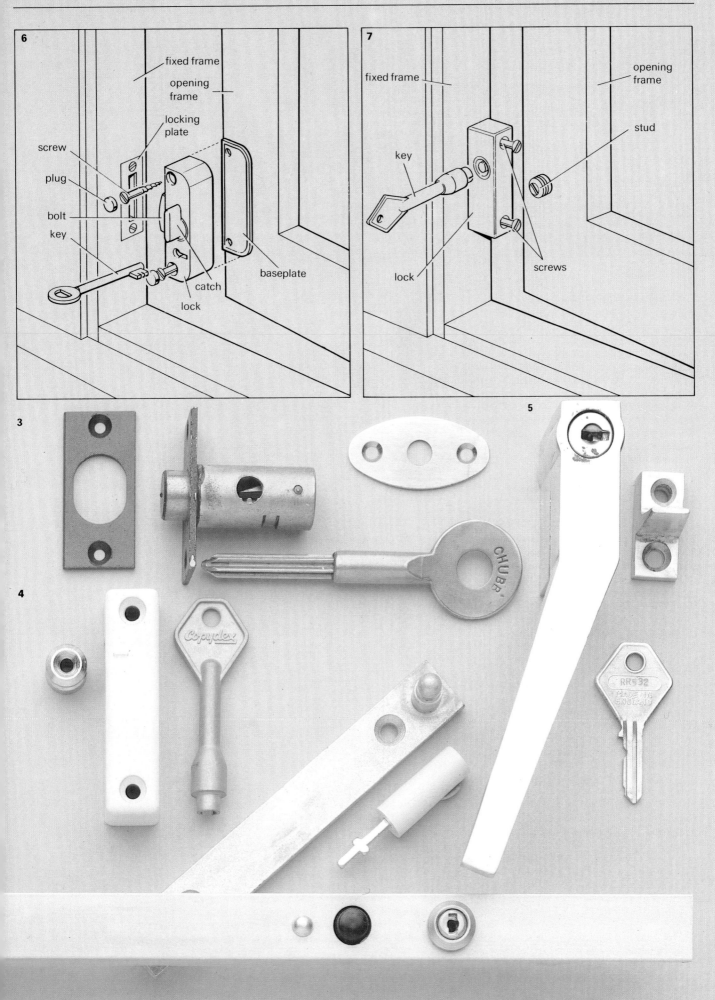

6

fixed frame

opening frame

locking plate

screw

plug

bolt

key

catch

lock

baseplate

7

fixed frame

opening frame

stud

key

lock

screws

3

4

5

the window is closed, in case you forget to lock up. You use a key to open the window.

Warning If you have young children in the house, make sure the keys to locks are not in an easily accessible position since children can quickly learn how they are used.

Window security bolts These are slightly smaller than the security bolts which are used to fit on doors; fitting them involves basically the same process. The bolt section and its casing are mortised into the edge of the opening frame in a central position and, when operated by a splined key, the bolt locks into a plate recessed into the fixed frame; the width of the frame should be 38mm (1½in) minimum. Security bolts have the advantage of being virtually invisible from outside. On larger casement windows, if the window frame depth will accommodate them, you can use larger door security bolts to give extra bolt depth.

Warning Window security bolts usually require a depth of at least 38mm (or 1½in), plus suitable glazing clearance; so measure your window frame carefully to make sure its depth is sufficient before buying this type of device.

Stay locks These are inexpensive, easily fitted, threaded units which replace the existing stay pins. (If they are in good condition, you can use the screws which secured the old stay pin to secure the new threaded pin; but remember the screws will be accessible when the window is secured in some open positions and treat as described above.) The thread passes through the existing hole in the window stay and is secured from above by a special nut, which is tightened with the key supplied. You can secure a window in a partially open position by fixing through the hole further down the stay; however, since this means removing the locking nut, stay locks are best used on windows which are infrequently opened.

One type of stay lock is available for securing window stays without holes; it is fitted using two screws and is secured with a special locking key.

Other locking devices A number of small locking devices, usually operated with special keys which lock the moving and fixed parts of timber frame windows together, are also available.

WSDs for metal casements

As with timber casement windows, metal ones are usually secured with cockspur handles and window stays and, again, there is a variety of devices you can fit to provide a proper level of security.

Window locks With one typical variety the lock is fixed to the opening part of the window frame and the bolt locks into the fixed frame to secure the window. Special fixing screws are supplied to ensure strong fixing to metal window frames. The keys of this type of lock are interchangeable with those for a version designed for timber windows.

Securing handles There are several other WSDs for securing existing fittings. For example, cockspur handles on metal frame windows can be secured by a device which fits on the fixed frame beneath the handle. When the window is closed, a bolt is locked in an upright position to prevent the cockspur portion of the handle passing; if you want to open

8 Window stay lock
9 Stay lock for timber frame window
10 Stay lock for metal frame window
11 Window latch lock
12 Wedge lock for metal casement window
13 Lock for metal casement window
14 Transom lock
15a Fixing of lock for latch on metal casement window
15b Fixing of lock for latch on metal casement window where window is rarely opened
16 Fixing of wedge lock on metal casement window
17 Dual screw with key
18 Lock for timber sash window
19 Disc tumbler window lock
20 Snap-on lock for sliding windows and doors
21 Lock for sliding windows and doors

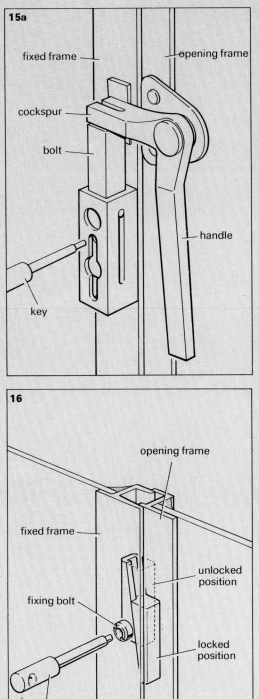

15a

fixed frame — opening frame

cockspur

bolt

handle

key

15b

fixed frame — opening frame

cockspur

locking screw

key

handle

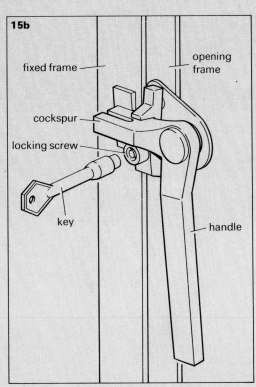

16

opening frame

fixed frame

unlocked position

fixing bolt

locked position

key

17

18

19

20

21

the window, you can release the bolt with a special key. This device is fitted with the self-tapping screws provided; you should drill holes for these according to the manufacturer's instructions. When fitting, make sure the swing of the cockspur misses the bolt body. To secure the handle in the 'shut' position on a window which is infrequently opened, you can fit a device which locks directly onto the cockspur using the special key provided – no tools or screws are necessary.

Securing window stays These fittings can be secured to a metal frame in several ways. They include a device which you can fit to the existing stay without screws or fixing tools; it locks the stay to its

retainer to prevent stay movement and the window being opened.

Wedge lock This is fitted in the edge of the casement; when locked with an oval-shaped key, it secures the casement to the frame. It is fitted by drilling one hole (using the template provided) through the casement and securing the lock with an escutcheon screw.

WSDs for other types

For securing other types of window, you can sometimes use the devices available for casement windows; but there are devices which are manufactured specifically for use in these situations.

Transom windows Otherwise known as vents and usually situated above larger casement windows, these are normally fitted with window stays; you can use stay locks to secure them if there is a suitable timber sub-frame. There is a D-shaped clamping device available which is specially designed to prevent stay movement in metal frame transom windows; it is easily fitted with screws.

Timber sash windows These can often be opened from the outside since the centre latch can be undone by a knife or similar tool. If the windows are opened infrequently, you can secure them with strong screws. Otherwise, you can fit a device operated with a special key; a protruding bolt prevents the two sliding panes passing. There are several types available. With one type the bolt is fitted to the upper sash about 100mm (4in) above the striking plate which is fitted to the top of the lower sash. When the key is turned until the bolt is fully extended, the window may be opened a small distance to provide ventilation, but any attempt to force it will be thwarted when the bolt hits the striking plate. Other types have the bolt fixed to the top of the lower sash; the bolt locates in one or more locking plates on the upper sash to coincide with the fully closed and slightly open positions. Again, the bolts are released with a key.

Metal sliding windows These are generally fitted

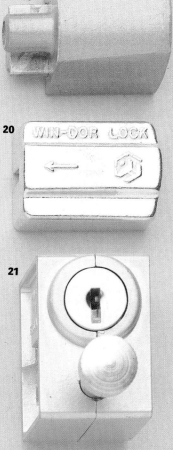

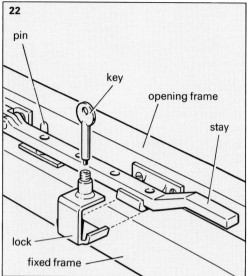

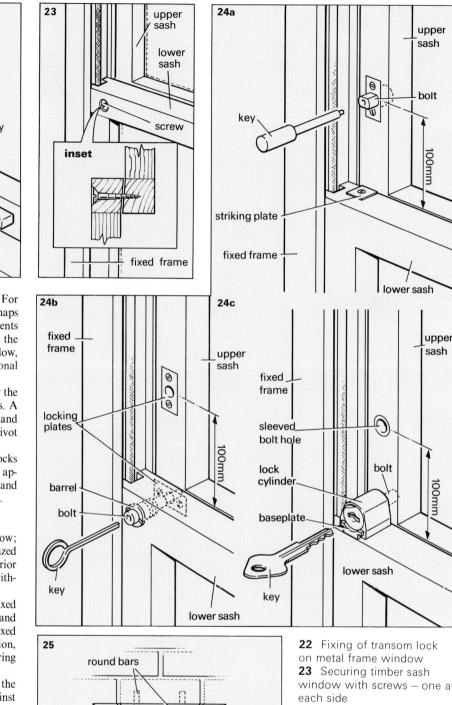

with special locks which provide good security. For
extra protection, you can fit a device which snaps
onto the sliding window runner and prevents
window movement; another device locks onto the
frame. For many types of metal sliding window,
you can fit a patio door lock to provide additional
security.

Centre pivot windows These are best secured by the
window locks available for casement windows. A
window lock with versions for both metal and
timber frame windows will adequately secure pivot
windows with frames of either material.

Fanlight windows For these, the window locks
available for casement windows are usually appropriate. Many fanlights have narrow frames and
this is a point to consider when buying locks.

Securing fixed pane windows

Most homes have at least one small fixed window;
to provide adequate security, this should be glazed
with 6mm ($\frac{1}{4}$in) thick wired glass. Check the interior
beading is strong and securely fitted so it will withstand any attempts at forcing it.

Where you have a window with a large fixed
pane, make sure the frame is in good condition and
the pane is properly secured. Where a large fixed
window is in a particularly vulnerable position,
such as a basement area, it is worth considering
the installation of a security grille or iron bars.

Security grilles In some situations, these are the
only effective means of providing protection against
intrusion. They are supplied in designs to match
the existing decor and character of the house.
Installation of a grille is best left to the specialist.

Iron bars These should be round iron of not less
than 19mm ($\frac{3}{4}$in) diameter or square iron of not less
than 19mm ($\frac{3}{4}$in) section. They should be fixed
vertically to the inside of the window at 125mm
(5in) intervals; grout them into the brickwork at the
top and bottom of the window to a depth of at least
50mm (2in) and recessed at least 50mm (2in) from
the wall surface. The bars should pass through flat
horizontal iron tie bars, the distance between which
should not exceed 450mm (18in), and kept in
position by welding or flattening the bars above and
below the tie bars. The ends of the tie bars should be
cut, splayed and grouted into the brickwork.

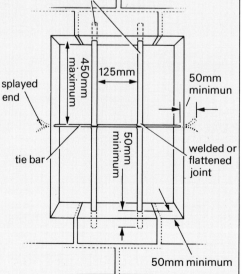

22 Fixing of transom lock
on metal frame window
23 Securing timber sash
window with screws – one at
each side
24a Fixing of locking
window stop on timber sash
this lock allows window
to be locked in slightly
open position to provide
ventilation
24b Fixing of dual screw on
timber sash window; second
locking plate fitted to
upper sash allows window
to be locked in slightly
open position
24c Fixing of lock on
timber sash window; again
upper bolt hole allows
window to be locked in
slightly open position
25 How to secure fixed pane
windows with iron bars

Appendix

1

2

Basic tool kit

When you start to stock up your workshop with a selection of basic tools, don't rush into buying the first ones you see. The real craftsman never blames the tools – and that surely is a good enough reason for buying the best you can afford

Most of the jobs tackled by the DIY novice involve simple techniques such as screwing fitments to walls, making shelves, laying floor coverings and so on. And you do not need a vast range of tools to take care of these everyday tasks.

The tools shown here and on the following pages are all useful but you do not have to buy all of them at once. So if you already have an electric drill you can get by without a hand one. A cross pein hammer and veneer tenon saw are not essential, while a vice will keep you going until you invest in a proper workbench. And you can always hire specialist tools (or if you are lucky borrow them from friends) as and when the need arises.

As your experience grows you will learn how to get the best out of your existing tools, when to make do with substitutes and when to acquire new ones. Top quality tools are expensive and it is a temptation to balance your budget by going for cheaper ones. But this policy usually proves more expensive in the long run and our advice is to buy the very best tools you can afford and to maintain them well.

1 Electric drill Go for a two-speed model which has a 12mm ($\frac{1}{2}$in) capacity chuck and also incorporates a hammer action. When drilling into different materials – wood, metal and so on – speeds from slow to fast are needed and variable speed facility allows for this. The 12mm ($\frac{1}{2}$in) chuck will enable you to bore large diameter holes and the hammer action to drill into really hard materials, such as the concrete lintel above a window to fix a curtain rail. (Black & Decker D720H 12mm/$\frac{1}{2}$in two-speed drill plus hammer action)

2 Hand drill (wheel brace) and countersink bit You can drill holes with it in a variety of materials using wood or masonry twist drills. It is usually supplied with a removable handle so you can work in tight corners often inaccessible to a power drill. Countersink bits make a neat, perfectly round recess for countersunk screws. (Stanley double pinion open gear hand drill 803, three-jaw chuck, chuck capacity 0–8mm/0–$\frac{5}{16}$in, countersink bit 137, 12mm/$\frac{1}{2}$in)

3 Steel measuring tape A 3m (10ft) length will be enough to cover all normal measuring jobs. Dual markings enable you to work in metric or Imperial units. Plastic window at top of case gives instant, accurate measures of internal recesses, drawer interiors. (Stanley Top Sight rule, 3m/10ft)

4 Combination square Version illustrated incorporates inside/outside try square (for measuring angles), straight-edge/marking edge, depth gauge, mitre square, small spirit level, scriber, protractor and screw gauge for screws Nos 4–12. The stock slides along a 305mm (12in) steel rule and can be locked in anywhere along it. (Stanley DIY combination square 46–150)

5 Try square Simpler alternative to combination, 229mm (9in) blade. (Stanley try square 19)

6 Cutting knife Multi-blade 127mm (5$\frac{1}{4}$in) long tool with range of blades to tackle cutting of materials from laminate to vinyl. (Stanley trimming knife 199A including five blades, blade guard, plus 5194 laminate blade)

7 Steel (cabinet) scraper This type gives a fine finish to hardwood surfaces, veneers and laminate edgings, shaving rather than scraping the surface.

3

15

16

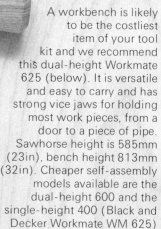

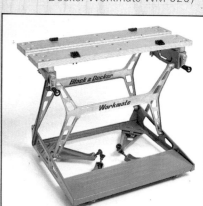

You can make your own by cutting up an old piece of saw steel into a square; file each edge square and you will have four working edges on each side. (Sandvik 474 scraper)

8 Block plane For a range of trimming jobs a model such as the one illustrated is most useful. The depth of cut is adjustable for coarse or fine work, including plastics. If you progress to more sophisticated woodwork you can buy a smoothing plane later. (Stanley 60½ low angle, adjustable block plane, 152mm/6in length)

9 Bradawl Essential for marking timber and other soft materials prior to drilling. It is pressed into the surface to provide an accurate guide for the drill bit. You can use a small worn screwdriver instead; file the blade to a chisel edge.

17   **18**   **19**

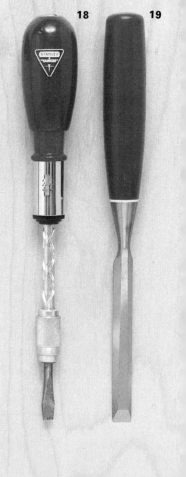

10 Nail punch For sinking pin and nail heads below the surface of timber without the hammer head bruising the work. You could start off with a 152mm (6in) nail with the point blunted.

11 Plumb bob Essential for establishing true verticals. You can make one yourself by tying a weight to a length of string.

12 Hacksaw A smaller type such as the one illustrated is useful for cutting through metal, sawing through rusty nuts, bolts, screws and nails. (Eclipse Junior 675)

13 Veneer tenon saw A fine tooth saw for small jobs where the larger panel saw with its coarser tooth setting would be impractical. Ideal for laminates, mitring and dowelling, it does not have the hard spine (back) common to most traditional tenon saws and offers greater cutting scope. (Sandvik hard point 324)

14 Panel saw Although there is a vast range of saws, each designed to do different work, the panel saw will cope with most straightforward sawing jobs. It is worth buying a hardpoint version as it will last longer than a conventional saw before the teeth blunt. 550mm (22in) long with seven teeth (eight points) per 25mm (1in). (Sandvik 2000 Supercut hardpoint handsaw)

15 Claw hammer Dual purpose type, one side of the head for normal banging, the other shaped like

a claw for extracting nails. 680g (24oz). (Stanley Jobmaster 90)

16 Warrington cross pein hammer For driving home small nails and pins, either side of the head can be used. The cross pein (narrow rectangular side) is useful when working in confined spaces or where the size of nail head restricts normal holding. 225g (8oz). (Stanley WO)

17 General purpose flat file Select a file that is coarse cut on one side for rough filing and fine cut on the other for smoothing and finishing metal. Apart from keeping your scraper sharp, this file will help in a variety of smoothing jobs. (Stubs FB246T dual-cut handyman's file)

18 Yankee screwdriver Range of interchangeable bits makes this several screwdrivers in one, coping with various screws from electrical equipment sizes right up to large No 12s, including Pozidriv screws with cross slot heads. Its pump action makes work easier. You can also make pilot holes with it. (Stanley Yankee Handyman 133H 245mm/9⅝in spiral ratchet screwdriver, 6mm/¼in slotted bit)

19 Bevel edge chisel Basically intended for light work, this sloping-side chisel can reach into tight corners. With a plastic-handled type you can use a hammer without fear of the handle breaking. Start with a 12mm (½in) size, adding 6mm (¼in) and 25mm (1in) sizes as you need them. (Stanley 5002 series)

Care of basic tools

DON'T leave steel measuring tape extended, especially with blade on edge, on workbench or floor in case something falls onto it; damaged tape will be virtually useless

DO hang up saws by handle or frame when not in use and put blade guard over cutting edge; if left lying about teeth may get damaged. Lightly oil blade to prevent rust. Sharpen teeth, or replace blade, regularly.

DO tie chuck key of electric drill to lead with string, but allow enough length to turn key without having to untie it. Service drill regularly as worn parts will impair efficiency.

DO keep hammer heads clean and free of any traces of adhesive; rub hammer face squarely with fine glasspaper round block of wood. Bang loose heads back into place and/or use wedging pins.

DON'T use hammer on wood-handled chisels; side of hammer head can be used on plastic handles. Ideally use mallet to prevent damaging handle. Never use chisel as screwdriver or you will ruin edge. Maintain good cutting edge by regular sharpening.

DON'T use screwdrivers as levering devices or for raking, chipping or digging holes. If shafts are bent or blade ends not squarely cut they will not turn screws efficiently.

DO check plane blades are correctly adjusted. Hold bottom of plane squarely up to light; blade should be parallel to bottom so it cuts evenly across its full width

DO rest planes on their side to avoid damaging blade or bottom and keep regularly sharpened. After use, store in dry place to avoid rusting.

Steel measuring tape

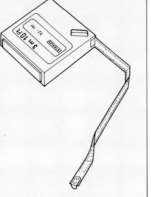

Saw

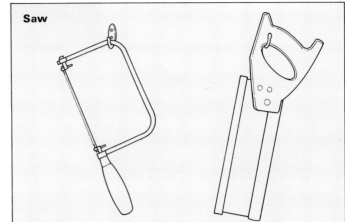

Electric drill

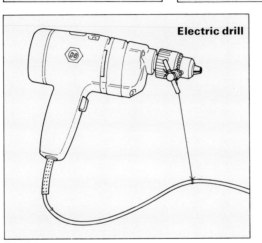

Hammer

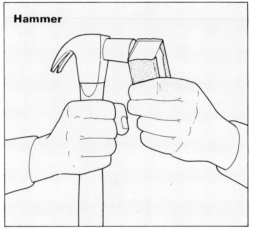

Chisel

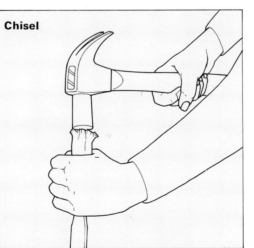

Screwdriver

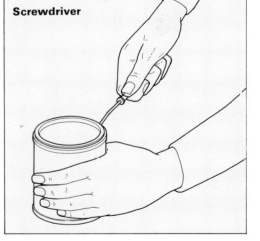

Plane

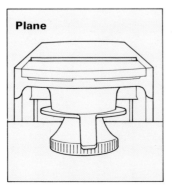

Plane

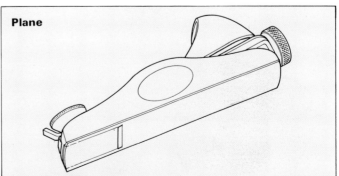

Fix it up to stay up

When you fix something up, you want to make sure it's not going to fall down as soon as your back is turned. So it's important you use the right type of fixing for the material on which you plan to put your fitments.

The correct fixing method depends not only on the construction of the wall but also on the weight and nature of the object to be supported.

There are two basic types of wall – solid (brick or block built) or hollow partition. From the point of view of wall fixings cavity construction can be regarded as solid brickwork. If you tap the surface of your wall you will get either a solid or hollow response depending on the construction. Remember where a thick plaster coating is applied to brickwork it is important to get your fixing securely into the brickwork for maximum support. Hollow types consist of sheets of plasterboard or laths and plaster fixed to a timber framework and are mainly used for partitioning.

Decide exactly where you want to place the fitment on the wall and then mark the fixing holes accordingly. Drill holes in the fitment first, if not already made. Don't attempt to fix heavy items on partition walls unless you can drill into the framework of the partition.

Drilling into a wall

For this job you will need a tungsten carbide-tipped masonry drill bit fitted into the chuck of an electric or hand drill. The tough carbide tip ensures a long life for the drill bit even with the rapid wear and tear involved in drilling masonry. If your drill has more than one speed, operate it as slowly as possible.

If you find a section is extremely hard, such as a concrete lintel above a door or window, you may need a hammer action electric drill or a drill fitted with a hammer attachment. The hammer drill bit is driven into the wall by turning and hammering simultaneously.

If a power or hand drill is not available then a hole can be made with a jumping bit (such as the Rawldrill or Stardrill) and a club hammer (a heavy duty hammer with a large striking face).

Rawldrill Used for punching holes in all types of masonry. This bit is made from a high quality steel for toughness and durability. The bit is fitted into a special holder through its tapered shank; it is fluted so that debris from the hole is cleared out as work progresses.

Fit a bit of the correct diameter into the tool holder. Mark clearly with a pencil where the hole is to be made, place the bit on the mark and gently tap the holder with a hammer. Turn the holder slightly between blows and continue until you reach the required depth. Use the special ejector tool to remove the bit from the holder.

1 Nylon wall plugs with helical wings (Fischer type GB)
2 Nylon collapsible anchors (Fischer type NA)
3,4 Spring toggles with hook or washer (Fischer types KDH3 and KD3)
5,6 Spring toggles (Rawlplug)
7,8 Gravity toggles (Rawlplug)
9 Fibre wall plugs (Rawlplug)

1

2

3   4   5   6   7   8

9   10   11

10,11 Nylon wall plugs with
ribbed barrels, plain necks
(Fischer type S, Rawlplug)
12 Plastic wall plugs
(Rawlplug)
13 Rubber sleeved anchors
(Rawlnuts)
14 Nylon anchors (Fischer
type A)
15 Nylon toggle plug
(Fischer type K)
16 Stardrills
17 Masonry drill
18 Rawldrill holder and
Rawldrills
19 Expansion bolts – loose
(left) and bolt-projecting
(Rawlbolts)

Stardrill Suitable for all types of masonry including
the toughest concrete. This specially toughened tool
has four fluted edges to ensure quick penetration
and efficient dispersal of debris from the hole.

Hold the drill where the hole is to be made and
strike with a hammer, turning slightly between
blows until you reach required depth. When using
either of these tools wear protective spectacles or
insert a fine metal mesh screen over the bit to
protect you from flying particles.

Choosing the drill bit
Remember the bit to make the hole must be the
same diameter as the fixing device and the screw
being used (for example you would use a No 8 wall
plug and a No 8 screw). But many plastic devices
take more than one size of screw.

The depth of the hole made in the wall should
usually be about the same as the length of screw to
be embedded in it. That depth also dictates the
length of the plug. To make sure you drill to the
correct depth wrap a piece of adhesive tape, or fix a
special rubber collar, around drill bit. Stop drilling
when edge of tape or collar meets the surface.

Types of wall fixings and how to use them

Situation	Type of fixing	How to use
Masonry, brickwork and concrete 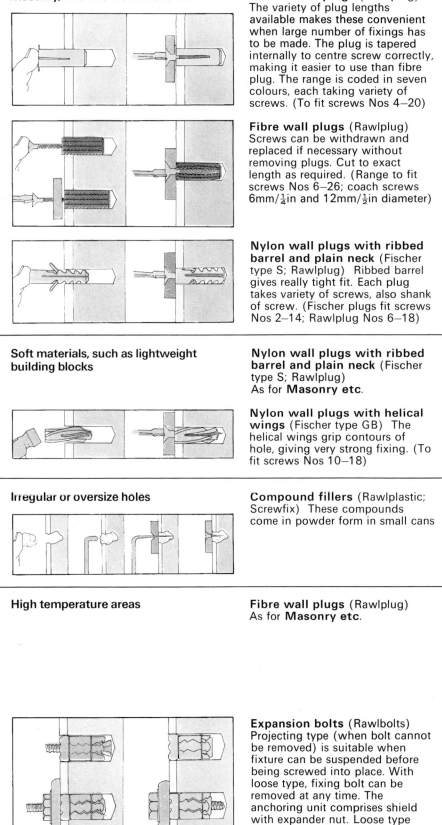	**Plastic wall plugs** (Rawlplug) The variety of plug lengths available makes these convenient when large number of fixings has to be made. The plug is tapered internally to centre screw correctly, making it easier to use than fibre plug. The range is coded in seven colours, each taking variety of screws. (To fit screws Nos 4–20)	Drill hole to same depth as wall plug. Push plug into hole, slip screw through fitment into plug and tighten.
	Fibre wall plugs (Rawlplug) Screws can be withdrawn and replaced if necessary without removing plugs. Cut to exact length as required. (Range to fit screws Nos 6–26; coach screws 6mm/¼in and 12mm/½in diameter)	Drill hole and insert plug to just below wall surface. Turn screw into plug up to shank and then withdraw it. The plug expands to fit hole tightly making it easier to find centre of plug when fixing fitment into place and to drive screw home firmly. Note that plug should be as long as threaded part of screw.
	Nylon wall plugs with ribbed barrel and plain neck (Fischer type S; Rawlplug) Ribbed barrel gives really tight fit. Each plug takes variety of screws, also shank of screw. (Fischer plugs fit screws Nos 2–14; Rawlplug Nos 6–18)	Drill hole slightly deeper than wall plug being used. Push plug into hole, slip screw through fitment into plug and tighten.
Soft materials, such as lightweight building blocks	**Nylon wall plugs with ribbed barrel and plain neck** (Fischer type S; Rawlplug) As for **Masonry etc**.	Drill hole slightly deeper than wall plug being used. Push plug into hole, slip screw through fitment into plug and tighten.
	Nylon wall plugs with helical wings (Fischer type GB) The helical wings grip contours of hole, giving very strong fixing. (To fit screws Nos 10–18)	Drill hole of same diameter as plug body. Overall diameter of plug will be twice drill hole, so you must hammer plug into wall. Slip screw through fitment into plug and tighten.
Irregular or oversize holes	**Compound fillers** (Rawlplastic; Screwfix) These compounds come in powder form in small cans	Moisten sufficient amount of powder with water and ram into hole either with special tool (often provided with filler) or any flat piece of metal about same size as hole. When filler is still moist make indentation with sharp tool where screw is to go.
High temperature areas	**Fibre wall plugs** (Rawlplug) As for **Masonry etc**.	Drill hole and insert plug to just below wall surface. Turn screw into plug up to shank and then withdraw it. The plug expands to fit hole tightly making it easier to find centre of plug when fixing fitment into place and to drive screw home firmly. The plug should be as long as threaded part of screw.
	Expansion bolts (Rawlbolts) Projecting type (when bolt cannot be removed) is suitable when fixture can be suspended before being screwed into place. With loose type, fixing bolt can be removed at any time. The anchoring unit comprises shield with expander nut. Loose type allows bolt to be inserted after shield is in place	Drill required hole. If using projecting type insert it, position fitment on bolt end and tighten nut. With loose type, insert shield and position fitment over it; pass bolt or stud through fitment into shield and tighten.

Types of wall fixings and how to use them

Situation	Type of fixing	How to use

Extra hard walls

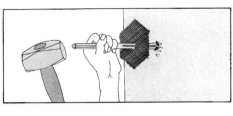

Nylon wall plugs with ribbed barrel and plain neck (Fischer type S; Rawlplug)
As for **Masonry etc**.

Drill hole slightly deeper than wall plug being used. Push plug into hole, slip screw through fitment into plug and tighten. You cannot make hole with a standard hand drill when surface is very hard. Use jumping bit (Rawldrill; Stardrill) or hammer drill to make hole. You must wear protective spectacles or insert fine metal mesh screen over drill bit to protect you from flying particles.

Plasterboard, hardboard, lath and plaster

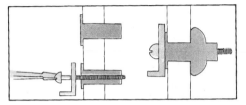

Rubber-sleeved anchors (Rawlnut) Used in thin, cavity walls and especially useful in thin sheets of metal or plastic because fixing is vibration-proof. When screw is tightened, rubber sleeve is compressed against reverse side of wall. The anchor will remain in place if retaining screw removed. (Variety of sizes available; screws supplied with anchors)

Drill hole of same diameter as rubber sleeve and insert anchor until flange touches wall surface. Slip screw through fitment into anchor and tighten.

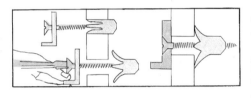

Nylon anchors (Fischer type A) Very useful when cavity in hollow wall is particularly small. If screw is removed anchor is lost. The screw should be at least equal in length to thickness of fitment plus thickness of wallboard and length of anchor. (Three anchor sizes to fit screws Nos 6, 8 and 10)

Drill required hole. Insert screw through fitment into anchor, with two or three turns only, before pushing it through hole into wall cavity. Pull fitment towards you to compress anchor tongue against wall and tighten screw at same time.

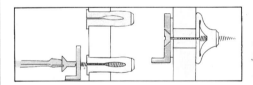

Nylon collapsible anchors (Fischer Rivet Anchor type NA) As screw is tightened, body expands; device remains in place if screw is removed. (Four sizes to fit screws Nos 6, 8 and 10)

Drill required hole and push anchor through until flange touches wall surface. Slip screw through fitment into anchor and tighten.

Spring toggles (Fischer types KD3 and KDH3; Rawlplug) Metal thread screw and two spring-loaded metal arms which spread load over wide area on reverse side of wall cavity. Toggle is lost if screw removed. (One size of each Fischer type and either metal thread screw or hook supplied. Three sizes of Rawlplug type, with or without screws)

Drill hole just big enough to allow toggle to be passed through with its spring-loaded arms squeezed together. Pass fixing screw through fitment into toggle. Push toggle through hole until arms spring apart, pull fitment towards you and tighten screw.

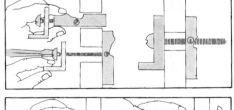

Gravity toggles (Rawlplug) When toggle is passed through hole, bar drops down at right-angles to fixing screw. The toggle is lost if screw is removed. These can only be used when fixing to vertical surfaces. (Three sizes, with or without screws)

Drill hole just big enough to allow toggle to be passed through when bar is parallel to fixing screw. Pass fixing screw through fitment into toggle and push toggle through hole until bar drops. Pull fitment towards you and tighten screw until fitment is firm.

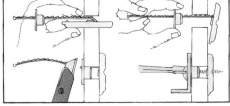

Nylon toggle plugs (Fischer type K and KH) The notched nylon strip makes it possible to use device on any thickness of wall or board as plugs are easily adjusted. The toggle remains in place if screw is removed. (Toggle 32mm/1¼in or 57mm/2¼in long, both take No 8 screw)

Drill required hole so toggle collar fits neatly into it with flange touching surface of wall. Push toggle through hole, fit collar in place and pull notched nylon strip towards you until device is tightly in place. Cut off any surplus from strip. Slip screw through fitment and collar into toggle and tighten.

Index